Creating the Cape Colony

Creating the Cape Colony

The Political Economy of Settler Colonization

Erik Green

BLOOMSBURY ACADEMIC
LONDON • NEW YORK • OXFORD • NEW DELHI • SYDNEY

BLOOMSBURY ACADEMIC
Bloomsbury Publishing Plc
50 Bedford Square, London, WC1B 3DP, UK
1385 Broadway, New York, NY 10018, USA
29 Earlsfort Terrace, Dublin 2, Ireland

BLOOMSBURY, BLOOMSBURY ACADEMIC and the Diana logo
are trademarks of Bloomsbury Publishing Plc

First published in Great Britain 2022

Cover image: *Ox-Span for Covered Wagon and Plow*, by Jan Brandes, 1806. Dutch Colonial
painting of a Dutch settler's farm in Lochner, South Africa. Courtesy of Rijksmuseum.

A catalogue record for this book is available from the British Library.

A catalog record for this book is available from the Library of Congress.

ISBN: HB: 978-1-3502-5823-5
        ePDF: 978-1-3502-5824-2
       eBook: 978-1-3502-5825-9

Typeset by Integra Software Services Pvt. Ltd.

To find out more about our authors and books visit www.bloomsbury.com
and sign up for our newsletters.

Contents

List of maps   vi
List of figures   vii
List of tables   viii
Acknowledgements   x

1   Understanding the creation and expansion of settler colonies   1
2   Indigenous agency, the cost of trade and initial steps towards
     a settler colony   23
3   Factor endowments, institutions and the expansion of the frontier   41
4   Was the Cape Colony a slave economy?   75
5   Unequal we stand   103
6   Elites, coalitions and settler resistance   129

Concluding remarks   151
References   155
Index   167

List of maps

2.1 Sketch map of the Cape, showing approximate positions of Khoesan
groupings in the seventeenth and eighteenth centuries   26
3.1 Map of the Cape Colony, comparing 1682, 1705, 1731 and 1795
boundaries with modern-day boundaries   42
3.2 Settler expansion at the Cape through 1750   48
3.3 Boundaries of freehold farms at Cape Colony, 1717 (Cape Peninsula
excluded)   55

List of figures

3.1 GDP per capita (1990 international Geary–Khamis dollars) for the
   Cape Colony, 1701–93   45
3.2 Comparison of GDP per capita estimates, 1701–73   46
3.3 European population in the Cape Colony, 1703–93   49
3.4 European and slave population in the Cape Colony, 1703–93   50
4.1 Estimated number of Khoesan, 1701–95   90
5.1 Wealth inequality among settler-farmers in Cape Colony, 1663–1757   111
6.1 Graph of settler privilege and incorporation into governance 132

List of tables

2.1   The Company's distribution and losses of stock, 1652–69   29

2.2   Sources of livestock obtained by the Dutch settlers, 1662–1713   32

3.1   Freehold land grants, 1657–1717   53

3.2   Mean settler livestock holdings at the Cape Colony, 1663–1773 (selected years)   56

3.3   Mean settler production of wine, wheat, rye and barley in the Cape Colony, 1663–1773 (selected years)   57

3.4   Revised estimates of total land allocated for farming, 1657–1717   58

3.5   Net value of arable and pastoral farms (in guilders) at the Cape Colony, 1731–80   61

4.1   Mean holding of adult male slaves by district and farming types, 1705–99/1800 (selected years)   81

4.2   Percentage distribution of holdings of adult male slaves by district, 1705–99/1800 (selected years)   83

4.3   Percentage distribution and median price of adult male slaves sold at rural auctions in rixdollars, 1682–1795   85

4.4   Average price of agrarian produce at public auctions and Official Company price (in rixdollars), 1716–1800 (selected years)   87

4.5   Estimated number of Khoesan and slaves by region, 1663–1773 (selected years)   91

4.6   Estimates of population in various districts in Cape Colony, 1790   92

4.7   Estimated slave productivity with and without Khoesan labour on wheat farms in various districts   93

4.8   Estimated slave productivity with and without Khoesan labour on wine farms in various districts   94

4.9   Estimated slave productivity with and without Khoesan labour on mixed farms   94

4.10 Slave productivity with and without Khoesan labour, all arable farmers split by the number of slaves   95

4.11 Number of slave men, women and children in Cape Colony, 1687–1793 (selected years)   98

5.1   European settler-farmers, 1705: capital and income   109

5.2 European settler-farmers, 1731: capital and income 110

5.3 Income inequality (Gini) among European settler farming
population in Cape Colony, selected years 112

5.4 Percentage change of real incomes at various percentiles
among the European settler farming population in the Cape
Colony, 1700–57 113

5.5 Wealth and inequality of settlers and Khoesan population in
Swellendam, 1825 114

6.1 Revenues, expenditures and deficits (in guilders) as
percentages of GDP 134

6.2 Accumulated debt of Stellenbosch and Swellendam districts in
selected years, 1702–93 135

6.3 VOC income from *pacht* as proportion of total revenues
(selected years) 137

6.4 Average price of wheat (per muid) and wine (per leaguer) in
rixdollars paid by VOC and at the auction floors 138

Acknowledgements

The idea behind this book came to me in 2017, but it wasn't until 2019 that the work began. This was made possible through the Riksbankens Jubileumsfond sabbatical grant, 'The establishment and expansion of a settler colony: The case of the Cape Colony 1657–1840 (SAB18-1070:1)'. The grant allowed me to spend a year at the department of economics at Stellenbosch University, and I will be forever grateful for the hospitality I received from my colleagues at the department, especially from Ina Kruger, Ursula Wanza and Prof G. A. Schoombee. The final manuscript was finished in Sweden and in part financed by Riksbankens Jubileumsfond's generous programme grant, 'The legacy of a settler colony: Quantitative panel studies of the political economy of the Cape Colony' (M20-0041). The text would not be readable if it was not for the editing of Susan Hatch from Oxford Editing Services. Thank you Susan for making the book come true. In the final stages of the book's production I had the pleasure of working with Dawn Cunneen, Abigail Lane, Joanne Rippin, Maddie Holder and Faye Robinson at Bloomsbury Publishing. I am grateful for all their feedback and constructive collaboration.

A chief source of inspiration for this book has been the recurrent conversations I have had with colleagues and friends, especially with participants of the Cape of Good Hope panel project. Professor Johan Fourie, who I met for the first time in Stellenbosch in 2010, and who I have collaborated with since 2015 has been a major facilitator and a source of inspiration. Johan and I often agree to disagree and I have been forced to sharpen my arguments during many of our constructive academic exchanges. Johan; I am forever grateful for your inputs. Jeanne Cilliers, Calumet Links, Igor Martins, Auke Rijpma and Dieter von Fintel have also played a major role in the creation of this book. They have opened my eyes to alternative explanations of historical events, forced me to question some of my assumptions, and broadened my understanding of how to interpret quantitative data. I would like to thank you all from my heart, and I look forward to years of continued collaboration. I have had the opportunity to work with Professor Robert Ross – a leading Cape historian – and I have learned a great deal from his knowledge of all aspects of Cape society. He has taught me how minor details in historical sources can significantly affect how we understand long-term patterns and drivers of long-term socio-economic change. Robert, I appreciate your generosity, curiosity and sharpness.

Three other people have been central to the writing of the book. My two young sons, Elliot and Oliver, who were brave enough to leave Sweden to spend a year in an English speaking school in South Africa. You left Sweden on a cold winter day with very limited knowledge of English, and returned a year later speaking English fluently and with many new South African friends. Your courage and openness to new cultures make you both role models in my life. I love you very much. Lastly, my wife Jeannette Green, who accepted the role of part-time housewife in South Africa – a role that many Swedish women would find both discouraging and challenging. Your energy and patience made our stay in South Africa worthwhile. Without you, I am incomplete. I may not believe in an interventionist God, but I know that I love you.

Erik Green, Lund 11 March 2022

Understanding the creation and expansion of settler colonies

Introduction

From the sixteenth century onwards, European powers managed to take control of vast territories around the globe. Numerous Europeans then migrated into those colonies. Between the sixteenth and eighteenth centuries, roughly 1,410,000 Europeans settled overseas (Altman and Horn 1991). While considerable, this migrating European population was not evenly distributed among the newly established colonies. Some areas attracted more settlers than others. The largest number went to the Americas, but a sizable group also went to the Cape of Good Hope at the southernmost tip of Africa (Lloyd and Metzer 2013). The question of why Europeans settled in greater numbers in certain locations and how this settlement may have impacted long-term economic and social development has received a great deal of scholarly attention in recent years. Less attention, however, to how these colonial societies and their specific institutional orders came about and affected the lives of ordinary people among both the settling intruders and of the indigenous societies. The more recent literature tends to describe the establishment of European settler colonies as an exogenous event driven by the interests of the colonizing metropole and/or the settlers. This confuses processes with their outcomes. Certainly, colonizers eventually took control over vast areas of the Global South and subjugated the indigenous inhabitants to their rule. This did not, however, happen overnight – nor was it inevitable. The settler economies and their institutional fabric evolved gradually and were an outcome of both collaboration and conflicts between the colonizers and the colonized. It is these processes of gradual, uncertain, fractured change that form the focal point of this book.

The book uses the Cape Colony as a case study to analyse the factors that led to the creation and expansion of European settler colonies more generally.

In 1652, the Dutch East Indian Company (hereinafter VOC, *Vereenigde Oostindische Compagnie*) established a trading post at the Cape of Good Hope. One hundred and fifty years later, the VOC was in control of an area the size of Italy. This book is an attempt to identify and analyse the factors that led to the creation of the colony and drove its continued geographical expansion. This expansion was neither intended nor planned. How did it come about? This book will show that the founding and growth of the Cape Colony can only be understood as a combined effect of settler and the indigenous Khoesan agency, leading to an institutional order that reinforced the enlargement of the colony's borders. Focusing on the gradual and uncertain processes that characterized the creation of the Cape Colony helps us to understand the evolution of a colonial institutional order. Without a proper understanding of these processes, moreover, we cannot accurately analyse the long-term legacies of colonialism.

The book is based on the rich literature examining the social, political and economic history of the Cape Colony. Scholars like Robert Ross, Nigel Worden, Leonard Guelke, Hermann Giliomee, Wayne Dooling, Susan Newton-King and Shula Marks, to name a few, have greatly contributed to our understanding of the history of the Cape Colony and have provided invaluable sources of information and inspiration in the writing of this book. In recent years we have seen a revised interest in the economic history of the Cape, with important publications from a new generation of scholars like Johan Fourie, Dieter von Fintel, Jeanne Cilliers, Kate Ekma, Calumet Links and Igor Martins. Combining history with statistical methods and economic theory, this group of scholars have provided new insights into the Cape Colony's long-run development trajectory. This book has greatly benefitted from their work.

The reader may react to the fact that the book does not cite any of the high quality scholarly work that has been published in Afrikaans. That is indeed a limitation of the book and stems from the fact that I do not read Afrikaans. It would not feel right to mention and/or cite literature that I am only able to understand on a superficial level. Readers will also notice that no primary sources are cited in the book. Having said that, the book does to a significant extent rely on my own use of primary sources in papers that have already been published. Of special importance for this book has been my joint work with Johan Fourie, Dieter von Fintel, Jeanne Cilliers, Calumet Links, Auke Rijpma Igor Martins and Robert Ross in constructing the Cape of Good Hope Panel database, the longest-running and most detailed such dataset in existence for the Global South. The panel dataset will contain longitudinal, demographic and economic information at the individual level over a period of 180 years (1660–1840). The construction of the dataset is still in progress but has already provided us with the ability to analyse and revise arguments made in the larger literature on settler economies around the globe.

Below, I offer a brief review of the literature on settler colonialism with a focus on scholarly work that uses the frontier as a conceptual tool to understand the processes by which European settler societies were established. This is followed by an outline of the theoretical point of departure of this book. Rather than presenting a fixed model, the section identifies the key factors that influence the expansion of settler societies. First, however, I provide a very brief description of the seventeenth- and eighteenth-century Cape in order to give the reader a rough sense of the context before moving on to the previous literature on settler economies and the analytical and conceptual guidelines that are used in this book.

To understand how settler colonies expanded, one needs, as a point of departure, an analytical framework that takes into account the uncertain and fragile processes that characterize the evolution of a new social order, one initiated by intruders in regions where very different social orders were already present. These uncertainties and fractal developments affected the institutional fabric in a way that laid the groundwork for the institutions that we can identify in the nineteenth-century Cape and in twentieth-century South Africa, including racial segregation, unequal land distribution and extreme wealth existing side by side with deep poverty.

To capture these gradual developments, I return to a concept that a few decades ago inspired the historians and geographers who studied settler colonies but has in recent years played a marginal role in the field: the concept of the frontier (Lamar and Thompson 1981; Elphick and Giliomee 1989a; Penn 2005; Willebald 2016). I define the frontier in economic/sociological terms and distinguish between an open and a closed frontier. In simple terms, an open frontier represents a situation in which no clear institutional order has yet been established and no group has gained power and judicial control over a territory. A closed frontier represents the opposite, that is, a clear and hierarchical political and economic order based on institutions that are firmly embedded in the society, both in de jure and de facto terms. From this perspective, the book understands the first 150 years of the Cape Colony's history as a process of frontier closure in which certain 'European' institutions did develop naturally as a consequence of economic and political struggles over economic resources. The approach taken here differs from the rational-choice political economy literature in a meaningful way. While that scholarship focuses on the role of institutions, technology, human capital, inequality and growth in a closed frontier, this book centres on the process that led to the closing of the frontier.

A very brief history of the Cape Colony, 1652–1796

Europeans first settled at the Cape of Good Hope in 1652 under the auspices of the Dutch East India Company with the goal of administering a refreshment station for passing ships. Due to their failure to procure sufficient provisions from the indigenous Khoesan population, the VOC eventually decided to allow Europeans to establish farms near the fort. In 1657, the first handful of company servants freed from their contracts were granted lands along the Liesbeek River, behind Table Mountain. This sparked a geographical expansion of the European settler community into the interior, which first moved north and then east along the coast. Twenty-five years after the establishment of the trading post, the area of the VOC's territorial control was still small, encompassing roughly 650 km². By the end of the eighteenth century, it had expanded to roughly 250,000 km². Throughout the period, the European population at the Cape was doubling approximately every generation (Ross 1993). By 1793, there were twenty-five thousand European settlers at the Cape, twenty thousand slaves and about twenty-five thousand indigenous Khoesan (Guelke 1985; Fourie and Green 2015; Dye and La Croix 2020).

Settler agriculture formed the basis of the colonial economy. European farmers in the south-western Cape invested mainly in wheat farming and viticulture. Farther into the interior, pastoralism dominated. The farms were smaller than plantations in the Americas, with an average size of 50 hectares. The settlers operated their farms with the help of imported slaves and indigenous Khoesan labourers. Slaveholding was widespread. In 1773, 75 per cent of all settlers owned slaves (Worden 1985). In contrast to the plantations of Latin and North America, the average farm at the Cape had a low number of slaves. By the mid-eighteenth century, more than 50 per cent of farmers held fewer than five slaves, compared with the 'median sugar estate' in Jamaica, which held an average of 204 slaves (Fourie 2013a; Green 2014). Previous estimates indicate high levels of economic inequality at the Cape, both among settlers and for the entire population (Guelke and Shell 1983; Fourie and von Fintel 2010a; Cilliers and Green 2018). A few settlers became very affluent, while others hardly made ends meet.

The establishment and geographical expansion of the Cape Colony was met with resistance from the Khoesan. Several wars and conflicts broke out as settlers moved eastward (Marks 1972; Links, Green and Fourie 2020). Between wars, resistance continued by other means. The Khoesan recurrently stole cattle from the Europeans, which occasionally forced settlers to abandon their farms (Penn 2005). Meanwhile, settlers treated their indigenous labourers with brutality, which spurred further resistance from the Khoesan (Newton-King 1999).

Settler economies and rational-choice political economy

Views of settler colonialism have strikingly shifted back and forth since the early twentieth century. Early on, liberals and socialists alike saw the diffusion of European powers across the globe as necessary to unleash the productive forces of non-European regions (Lenin 1917; see also Mamdani 2015 for a critical review of the early literature on 'American exceptionalism'). By the middle of the twentieth century, with the rise of independence movements in Africa, this positive view of settler colonialism shifted dramatically. It was by that point often described as a type of 'diehard colonialism' characterized by aggressiveness and exploitation (Veracini 2013: 313).

In the 1980s, this view partly changed as scholars became increasingly interested in understanding why certain parts of former European colonies had performed distinctively better in economic terms than did others. The latter colonies were found in tropical Asia, Africa and Latin America and the former in the temperate zones in the southern and northern hemispheres. In his prominent comparative work, Denoon (1983) explained this difference by distinguishing between the number of Europeans who settled in each region. These developed into settler capitalist economies, driven by a continued expansion of the land frontier.

The diversity of economic development paths among former colonies has more recently been picked up by the literature that Austin (2008) describes as *rational-choice political economy* (RPE). The RPE literature, in line with Denoon, argues that regions where Europeans settled in greater numbers (so-called neo-Europes; see Crosby 1986) have performed better economically and socially than former colonies where the Europeans were relatively few (Engerman and Sokoloff 2000, 2002, 2005; Acemoglu, Johnson and Robinson 2002; Acemoglu and Robinson 2012; Easterly and Levine 2012). The explanation for this, according to the RPE literature, is to be found in the institutional order established by the colonizers. In regions where Europeans settled in greater numbers, they brought with them institutions – such as private property rights and the rule of law – that facilitated economic growth. In colonies with few settlers, an institutional order was established that enabled these settlers to extract natural and human resources but also created high levels of inequality and hindered long-term economic growth. The current income gap between Latin and North America is commonly used to epitomize the divergent legacies of colonialism. Latin America is poorer today, it is argued, because it attracted fewer settlers, leading to an extractive institutional order that prevented long-term economic development. In contrast, the larger number of Europeans that settled in North America formed a critical mass that ensured the establishment of growth-enhancing institutions. A number of scholars – while they identify different transmission channels, such as technology and human capital formation – have lent support to the idea of a positive relationship between the number of settlers and European population densities in the colonies across the globe (e.g. Angeles 2007; Baker, Brunnschweiler and Bulte 2008; Bruhn and Gallego 2008; Putterman and Weil 2010; Easterly and Levine 2012). It seems that we are back in the early twentieth century, with a range of viewpoints seeing the diffusion of European institutions and knowledge as having facilitated long-term economic development.

The RPE literature has been exposed to critique. The common ground for the critique can best be summarized by the words of Gonzales and Montero, who claim that the RPE literature is 'a basically anti-empirical way of reasoning' (2010: 255). It does not offer an empirical investigation of how institutions, inequality or economic growth evolved over time in different colonies. Instead, it assumes that European settlers established specific institutional orders that persisted over time. A number of scholars argue that these assumptions lack empirical support (Coatsworth 2008; Frankema 2009; Williamson 2015). Latin America was neither poorer nor more unequal than the United States during the colonial period. It was only at the end of the nineteenth century, about three hundred years after being colonized, that the two regions diverged. Coatsworth (2008: 553) concludes that 'what little quantitative evidence there is does not suggest that ownership of land, or other assets for that matter, was more concentrated in Latin America than in the United States'.

The RPE literature not only lacks an empirical understanding of the divergent institutional orders once they had been established, but also sees its establishment as an exogenous event plainly driven by European interests (Lloyd and Metzer 2013; Frankema, Green and Hillbom 2016). Writing of the establishment of the institutional order in Latin America, Acemoglu, Johnson and Robinson (2002: 1375) state: 'Soon after the conquest, the Spanish crown granted rights to land and labour (the *encomienda*) and set up a complex mercantilist system of monopolies and trade regulations to extract resources from the colonies.'

Similarly, Engerman and Sokoloff conclude that Latin America 'early on' developed an institutional order based on high levels of inequality and the extraction of economic rents, as compared to North America, which began 'with relative equality and homogeneity', leading to the development of growth-facilitating institutions (2013: 67). In neither of the two cases are we provided with any detailed accounts of how these institutional structures emerged. Historians have convincingly shown that the process of establishing overseas settler societies was complex and can hardly be understood as exogenous (Lamar and Thompson 1981; Elphick and Giliomee 1989a; Weaver 2003). What we imagine today to be intended outcomes were gradual processes that neither happened overnight nor were inevitable. Settler economies and their institutional fabrics evolved gradually and constituted endogenous processes rather than exogenous events (Frankema, Green and Hillbom 2016).

Critics have also acknowledged that twentieth-century colonialism in Africa differed from the broad patterns described in RPE scholarship. First, the relationship between European population densities and the degree of extractive activities seems to be positive, rather than negative (Arrighi 1970; Austin 2008; Fibaek and Green 2019). Instead of lobbying for growth-enhancing institutions, settlers pushed for a coercive and segregationist institutional order. South Africa and colonial Zimbabwe (Southern Rhodesia) are often cited as an example of how settlers successfully managed to persuade the colonial authorities to establish an extractive institutional order. In colonies with small settler populations, in contrast, coercive policies were less common and levels of inequality lower. Second, the relationship between European population densities and relative economic prosperity within Africa is far from clear-cut (Hillbom and Green 2019). According to the African Development Bank, South Africa and Kenya, both former settler colonies, were in 2019 on the list of the ten richest countries on the continent in terms of income per capita (South Africa was number two and Kenya number nine). Meanwhile, the former *non*-settler colonies Nigeria and Ethiopia made it onto the list at number one and number eight, respectively. The question that needs to be asked in light of the inconclusive evidence for Latin and North America is whether Africa may be the continent that proves the RPE literature wrong. What is needed is a more systematic study of how specific colonial institutional orders gradually evolve. The so-called frontier literature provides a useful starting point for such an exercise.

The early frontier literature and the people without history

Few publications had an impact on the scholarship on European settler colonialism in the first half of the twentieth century as Turner's 'The significance of the frontier in American history' (originally given as a paper at the American Historical Association meeting in Chicago in 1893 and reprinted in 1921). The article does not deal with the establishment of a settler society per se, but with the continued enlargement of a settler society's borders. The expansion of the frontier was to Turner a process in which the 'disintegrating forces of civilization entered the wilderness' (1921: 21). It was a gradual process, often beginning with individual traders moving farther west, later to be followed by groups of settlers looking for economic opportunities. In Turner's words, 'Each expedition was an epitome of the previous factors of western advance' (24).

Turner's work focused solely on the European settlers who managed to make productive use of what Turner regarded as empty virgin land on the western frontier. In some cases, the expansion was halted by resistance from native Americans, but that was temporary and successfully struck down by the superior weapons and more sophisticated organization of the settlers (23). This expansion created its own unique institutions and cultures. Free from the feudal chains still felt in Europe, the expansion and establishment of family farms promoted individualism, mobility, equal opportunities and political freedom. According to Turner, 'The existence of an area of free land, its continuous recession and the advance of American settlement westward, explain American development' (1).

Although not always explicitly mentioned, Turner's frontier thesis inspired much of the scholarship in the first half of the twentieth century on European settlement expansion overseas (e.g. Bowman 1928; Price 1950). It is also notable how Turner's idea of the spread of individual 'pioneering' family farmers forms the foundation of the understanding of the history of North America in the more recent RPE work on settler economies. The divergence between North and Latin America is primarily explained by an institutional order that in the former case formed around independent settler family farms that could operate at arm's length of the government. Similar arguments developed in the early twentieth century regarding the establishment of the Cape Colony. As early as 1909, Leo Fouché gave a lecture on 'Die Evolutie van die Trekboer' in which he described the emergence of a class of wandering pastoral farmers – the *Trekboers* – in the first fifty years of the Cape Colony. According to Fouché, these became the 'spiritual fathers' of the settlers who, a century later, would migrate north-east in what was known as the Great Trek, the historical experience thought to have laid the foundation for South Africa as a nation.

The old frontier literature can be criticized on several accounts. With today's eyes, it is easy to see how it presents a romantic view of the frontiersmen and the whole process of frontier 'opening'. Conflicts and brutal violence are either neglected or mentioned only in passing. One early exception to this is the liberal historian Eric Walker who, already in 1930, argued that the roots of racism in South Africa lay in a specific frontier culture. In general, however, the Europeans are described as the agents of civilization, while the indigenous peoples are either neglected or regarded as passive agents. One can also question, as Furniss (2006) does, whether Turner's agrarian populist account – which sees the main economic and political conflicts as those between government and big business on the one hand and the ordinary people on the other – accurately capture the dynamics of a frontier society. Turner ignored other factors that presumably affected the sociopolitical structure of the frontier societies, including class conflict, urbanization and slavery. The idea that it was a relatively isolated frontier that shaped the sociopolitical institutions in the colony has also been questioned. The early literature ultimately treated the frontier in a rather static way.

The opening and closing of frontiers: A dynamic account

After being neglected for decades, the frontier concept re-emerged in the 1960s and 1970s. The emerging frontier literature criticized the earlier works for neglecting the role of indigenous people and social and economic conflicts. Turner's thesis was especially attacked, accused of being not only simplistic, but to some extent even racist (Berkhofer 1981). In his work on US history, Forbes (1968: 207) critiqued Turner's frontier hypothesis as one-sided in its focus on Europeans. Instead, he argued the frontier must be understood as 'an inter-group situation' (without discussing in any great detail the interplay between the groups). Slotkin (1992) went further when he described the American frontier as areas marked by conflicts, domination, repression and marginalization. The earlier literature was also criticized for treating the frontier as isolated from the political and economic centre of the economy. Looking at the Cape Colony, Legassick (1980) claimed that the frontier should not be seen in isolation from the centre of the colonial economy, but as an extension of it. According to Legassick the racism that liberal historians described as a frontier phenomenon was instead brought from the centre to the frontier.

The focal point in the later literature is on frontier closure. Lamar and Thompson (1981) define the frontier as a territory where two or more distinct societies meet. The social and economic order is fluid and uncertain. According to these authors, the frontier remains open until a single political authority has established hegemony over the area. This authority can either represent one of the groups or constitute a hybrid of them. Taking our point of departure as frontier closure leads us to conclude that it is the interaction and conflicts between various groups and societies in the opening frontier that determine the institutional order that will dominate once the frontier is closed.

The distinction between an open and a closed frontier has been applied to the case of South Africa as well, most explicitly by Giliomee (1989), who argued that the frontier has two dimensions: social and geographical. The latter remains open as long as there is still a possibility for the intruders to move spatially. The social dimension is about political and social control. In an open frontier, the social order is fluid. Various groups are fighting to gain political power. No political authority is recognized as legitimate by all parties, which makes the use of coercion common. A closed frontier is characterized by the establishment of a political authority and a social order that can be more or less egalitarian. In his work, Giliomee focused mainly on the expansion of the eastern frontier at the Cape. Writing merely two decades later, Penn (2005) used a similar framework to analyse the expansion of European settlers into the northern frontier of the Cape.

The outcome of frontier closure is uncertain. It may be political and economic victory of the European settler population, but it may also be a defeat. The uncertainty shapes how people behave and hence the evolution of institutions. This is partly neglected in the RPE literature as it deals with frontiers that have already been closed – that is, areas where the European settlers managed to establish political authority and where the indigenous populations have become marginalized or – even worse – eliminated. Neglecting the process of frontier closure means that the RPE literature misses out crucial factors that determined how the socio-economic institutions evolved over time and why certain institutions developed, persisted or vanished. As Denoon (1983: 27) observes, 'it is the qualities of the indigenous society which profoundly influenced the kind of settler society which could be superimposed upon it, or which might entirely replace it'.

Although the frontier literature provides useful insights into understanding the establishment and expansion of a settler colony, it is not without problems. A major limitation, Lamar and Thompson (1981) pointed out, is the lack of a coherent and analytically stringent way of defining the frontier or the key variables shaping the frontier process. Does the expansion imply a diffusion of capitalism, markets and commercialization of production as well as relations of production? Or, as the earlier literature argued, does the expansion of a frontier entail the creation of a unique set of institutions based on family businesses that are only partially integrated into the capitalist economy? How should we understand conflicts at the frontier and the groups involved in these conflicts? Should one simply classify the latter into two groups, the arriving settlers and the already present indigenous populations? Or is the process more complex, with various interest groups and/or social classes that do not necessarily align with their ethnicities? And how exactly should one define a frontier? When is a frontier 'opened' and when is it 'closed'?

Let us start with the question of defining the opening and closing of a frontier. As I mentioned, Lamar and Thompson (1981) suggest that the opening of a frontier occurs when the first 'representative' of an intrusive society arrives in a specific region. It closes when the intruders have gained political authority over that region. This definition neglects the possibility of the frontier being closed if the intruders are chased away or when the political authority contains a hybrid between new and old interest groups among the intruders and the already present populations. Reducing the opening of a frontier to a clash and/or interaction between two distinct societies both simplifies the process and confuses it with the process of closing the frontier (Berkhofer 1981). To avoid this pitfall, I define the opening and closing of a frontier from an economic perspective. A frontier is opened when a new group of people arrive in a specific location and use the resources available there in a way that changes the extraction of resources and the economic relations between groups. It is not necessarily or only closed when a certain group has gained political control over the territory, but rather when a new way of extracting resources has been established and has become necessary for reproducing the population of the region. This definition allows us to see the opening of a frontier not only as a conflict between two or more groups over political control, but as conflicts (and cooperation) among various economic interests that gradually (or, in exceptional cases, dramatically) lead to a transformation of the economy in that area. This way of using the concept of opening a frontier incorporates the fact that there are already people present at the frontier who are engaged in various economic activities. These activities may not immediately be threatened by the arrival of a new group, as long as there is an abundance of resources that can be put into productive use. This is the view taken by Giliomee (1989) and to some extent Ross (1993) when they discuss frontier expansion at the eighteenth-century Cape. They argue that initially, although conflicts did occur between the European settlers and the indigenous Khoesan people, they were sporadic. Over time, as the frontier was closing, clashes between Europeans and Khoesan became more prevalent, eventually leading to the subjugation of that indigenous group. Not everyone agrees with this interpretation. Newton-King (1999) argues that conflict and coercion were common characteristics in the very early years of the opening of the frontier. One could explain such divergent views in relation to their focus on different factors of production. Elphick and Giliomee (1989b) take the abundance of land as their point of departure, while Newton-King mainly discusses the scarcity of labour. As I argue in this book, however, land and labour cannot be treated separately. More specifically, the way the settlers managed to take control over land influenced the extent to which they could access and control Khoesan labourers. From this perspective, conflicts, coercion and violence may not end as the frontier is closed, but they change character. At an open frontier two economic systems collide. In a closed frontier, different social classes are fighting over access and control of productive resources within a given economic system.

Institutions, factor endowments and forces of expansion

Which factors can explain the expansion of an agrarian settler frontier? The most obvious starting point would be shifts in factor endowments – the totality of factors of production available for use. In line with Legassick (1980), I argue that developments at the frontier should not be viewed in isolation from developments at the economic centre. The opening of a new frontier is a consequence of previous frontiers being closed. In this way, the expansion of a frontier will only occur when resources at the old frontier have become scarce, leaving settlers, in this case, with no opportunity other than to move farther into the interior. As Carter and Sutch (2013) have shown, the economic growth of settler colonies was significantly facilitated by continued immigration from Europe. Continued immigration requires more land to be cleared for cultivation and hence stimulates an expansion of the frontier. It spurs extensive growth by increasing the number of people ready to work without diminishing the share of capital. For the Europeans, it was a win-win situation. The reduction of capital–labour ratios in the longer run created increased demand for investments, which facilitated increased savings and/or capital imports. Capital formation was further facilitated by the fact that the typical immigrant was a young male who tended to save heavily. As Ross (1983) observed, however, the eighteenth-century Cape Colony does *not* represent a case of continued immigration from Europe (see the more detailed discussion of this in Chapter 3). He argues that rather than being an effect of the arrival of European migrants, the expansion of the frontier was a consequence of high population growth among the European settlers residing in the colony.

Independently of the source of population growth, this path is conditioned by two factors. First, fertile land must be available. If not, population growth will lead to an increased share of marginal land being taken under cultivation, which will lead to a reduction in production and/or increased demand for capital and/or labour investments. Second, the immigrants and/or indigenous people must be willing to work on the established settler farms. This is less likely as long as land is in abundance, creating what is known as a *Nieboer-Domar condition*, in which labour scarcity forces farmers to pay a market wage that eats up their profits (Nieboer 1900; Domar 1970). One solution to this is to coerce labour and/or prevent potential labourers from accessing land. It is the latter that makes it difficult to distinguish between institutions that govern access to land from those regulating access to labour.

Relative access to land should not be narrowly analysed as an effect of population growth. The way the use of factors of production are informally and/or formally regulated may also create 'artificial scarcity', a situation in which producers restrict the availability of land beyond what is strictly necessary (Austin 2014; Frankema, Green and Hillbom 2016). Scholars have pointed out that the observed tendency of large European landowners in Latin America and Africa to take control of more land than they had the resources to utilize efficiently actually made economic sense (e.g. Griffin, Rahman and Ickowitz 2002; Gibbon 2011; Green 2013). Low population densities characterized both regions. Under such conditions, landowners would take control of more land than they needed in order to create land scarcity with the aim of increasing the supply of labour, a process that in Marxist terms is labelled 'primitive accumulation'. In a frontier context it would also be a strategy of avoiding competition from late arrivals, who would find it difficult to establish farms because land had become a scarce resource.

A system of landed property rights may further induce an expansion of the colonial frontier. There is a vast literature in economics and economic history arguing that secure property rights enhance investment in land and thus foster agricultural growth (e.g. North and Thomas 1973; de Soto 2000; Acemoglu, Autor and Lyle 2004). Secure property rights are also identified as a key institution promoting long-term economic development in colonies (Acemoglu, Johnson and Robinson 2002; Acemoglu and Robinson 2012). In a frontier context, this claim needs to be modified. As researchers have noted, the opening of a frontier was a process characterized by fluid social orders, conflicts and negotiations. The expansion of the frontier may also be disrupted from time to time. This, in turn, will shape how institutions evolve at the frontier. Before it is closed, the institutional set-up of the settler society has to be adaptable in order to be able to deal with various forms of resistance. In such a scenario, flexible rather than secured property rights may initially be the preferred choice. Recent research has shown that – in contrast to claims made by Acemoglu, Johnson and Robinson (2002) and Engerman and Sokoloff (2005), among others – in most settler colonies, landed property rights were weak – at least during the initial phase of frontier expansion (Alston, Libecap and Mueller 1998; Weaver 2003; Dye and La Croix 2020). I argue that this could be explained by the fluidity and recurrent conflicts that characterize an open frontier.

The reason such rights were weak is that secure property rights are associated with the high fixed investments that come with the proper surveying, demarcation, registration and additional measures, such as fencing, needed to strength the control of land boundaries. At the frontier, conflicts can be harsh, forcing either the intruders or the indigenous people to flee, leaving behind land and all the fixed investments made on it. Under the uncertain conditions that characterize an open frontier, settlers may prefer a landed property system that requires fewer fixed investments but that is also less secure and less well defined. Such a system would spur further expansion. Without clear boundaries between farms, arriving settlers will establish farms that are spaced farther apart from each other in order to avoid conflicts over land with settlers already present.

Systems of inheritance are also key in the expansion of colonial borders. Inheritance transfers are commonly divided into two principal systems: primogeniture and multigeniture. Primogeniture means that all wealth is passed on to the oldest child (most commonly a son), while in multigeniture, the wealth is passed on to all children (or at least to all sons). It has been argued that primogeniture systems lean towards land concentration and the establishment of large farms and plantations, while multigeniture transfers will lead to smaller, family-operated farms (Alston and Shapiro 1984). If this is correct, one would expect the force of expansion to be stronger under a primogeniture system of inheritance. Under such a system, in each generation, a large group will have to leave in search of new land. This tendency may be counteracted, however, by the demographic effect of the inheritance system. In a seminal paper, Habakkuk (1955) argued that the population will grow more slowly under a primogeniture inheritance system than in a multigeniture system. The reason is that in the former system, all children but the eldest son will feel pressured to postpone marriage until they have managed to establish their own farms. Forces of expansion would thus diminish over time, due to slower population growth.

The factors discussed above – factor endowments, artificial scarcity, property rights and inheritance systems – are to some extent interlinked and difficult to keep separated. They could reinforce or counteract one another. For example, a primogeniture inheritance system could lead to increased land concentration, a process that may be speeded up by settlers who see an opportunity to increase their wealth by creating 'artificial' scarcity. One could also imagine a new settler society in which land is in abundance, but where the first to arrive manage to impose artificial scarcity, while multigeniture transfers of wealth simultaneously lead to smaller farms over time. Under such a scenario, expansion will gradually slow down.

The factors mentioned above present only half of the story. They help us understand whether settlers have incentives and/or a need to migrate into the interior. They do not tell us whether this will actually happen, as it all depends on the settlers' capacity to move and the cost of doing so. The indigenous people already present at the frontier play a crucial role in this regard, a fact integrated into much of the frontier literature since the 1970s. This scholarship has shown that the economic, political and military strength of the indigenous populations mattered. Fundamentally, their strength depends on the resilience of their economy as well as its capacity to produce a surplus. The size of the indigenous population obviously has an impact on the capacity of the settlers to expand the frontier. The larger the size of the indigenous societies, the more difficult and costly it will be for the intruders to enlarge their colony (Engerman and Sokoloff 2013; Lützelschwab 2013). The better organized they are, the more difficult it will be for the Europeans to defeat them.

In the literature on states in precolonial Africa, scholars often point out that, in general, the level of indigenous political centralization was low as a result of a combination of factors such as low population densities, absences of inheritable land tenure and limited fiscal capacity (Goody 1971; Bates 1983; Herbst 2000). It may seem logical to ascribe the failure of resistance against the European intruders as partly an outcome of this limited political centralization. A centralized political system would make it easier to assemble and coordinate forces of resistance. The claim needs to be modified, however. While resistance may be weaker among politically fragmented systems, one can also hypothesize that it may have been more difficult for settlers to gain control over politically decentralized areas. Contemporary experience of modern warfare between states and loosely organized military groups of various kinds shows that the former face great difficulties in putting an end to recurrent waves of resistance and conflicts.

What this brief summary shows is that one should be careful in assuming a mono-causal relationships between factor endowments, institutions and the expansion of colonial borders. Frontier expansion was a complex process, in which the role of different factors and how they interacted must be understood from a proper historical context rather than being assumed a priori.

The closing of the frontier

What we have outlined so far are the factors that are crucial for understanding the establishment and expansion of a settler colony. I have so far only looked at the factors that affect the initial phase of frontier expansion. It is equally important to identify the variables that facilitate a process towards frontier closure. That entails going from a period characterized by a fluid social order with recurrent clashes between different groups to a stage where a new economic system has emerged and is guarded by a well-defined political authority. The institutional order of a closed frontier cannot be understood separately from the process of frontier closure. If defeating organized indigenous resistance is a necessary precondition for the expansion of a frontier, equally important is the question of how the once-independent indigenous peoples are incorporated into the colonial economy. Are they partially or fully integrated? Does a process of primitive accumulation transform the indigenous people into a class of wage workers? Or do they remain semi-independent, having only intermittent contact with the colonial economy in the form of causal labouring or trade? Elkins and Pedersen (2005) argue that a chief difference between settler colonialism in the pre-modern and modern ages was that the establishment of the former was characterized by the logic of elimination of indigenous populations, while nineteenth- and twentieth-century European settler societies to a large degree became dependent on the local populations to ensure sufficient supplies of labour.

Elimination is too strong of a word, however, in regard to pre-industrial settler colonies. It is true that the size of indigenous populations declined with the establishment of settlements in the sixteenth and seventeenth centuries as a result of violence and exposure to new diseases. However, it would be more accurate to describe this as a gradual process of marginalization. All settler colonies initially depend on the indigenous inhabitants in various ways (Ross 1983). This means that groups of indigenous people always have some room for manoeuvre in shaping the path of frontier closure. Highlighting the role of indigenous agency by no means implies that the establishment and expansion of a European settler society was a process which equally benefited the intruders and those being colonized. As Veracini (2011: 1) has pointed out, (settler) colonialism 'has two fundamental and necessary components: an original displacement and unequal relations'. Within these overall unequal relations, however, there are always pockets of opportunities that the indigenous people may utilize for their own purposes. The role and destiny of the indigenous people present us with a paradox. If indigenous societies are successfully defeated as independent political units and their population declines in either relative or absolute terms as a consequence of violence, disease and/or migration, the more difficult it would be for the Europeans to extract human resources from those still present within the borders of the colony.

While acknowledging the importance of the role played by the indigenous people, I would suggest that to understand the process by which societies moved towards frontier closure, one should focus on the role and relationship of the elites – in this case, settler elites. This is in line with the RPE literature, but unlike it, we do not assume that the settlers constituted a homogenous group or that their interests were in line with those of the colonial authorities.

A recent attempt to theorize the role of elites and economic and political transformation comes from the work of North, Wallis and Weingast (2009) on states and social orders. Their focus is on the transition from one type of state to another, mainly from what they call a *natural* state, characterized by a *limited-access social order*, to an *open-access order* state. While the descriptions of 'open' states and transitions between states have been criticized, the theories of 'natural' states have seen support (Bates 2010). They argue that most states in the past can be described as a natural state. In a natural state, social relationships are organized though personal bonds and an institutional order that enforces inequality and insecure property rights. This is because the state represents a coalition of elites held together by the common goal of denying the population at large open access to politics and markets. These elites rely on securing economic rents and, to do that efficiently, they have an interest in preventing violence from breaking out. This requires balancing the various divergent elite interests within the coalition, which makes the natural state inherently fragile and vulnerable to exogenous shocks. These shocks can easily lead to violence or to major shifts in the composition of the elites that make up the governing coalition.

In this book, I regard frontier closure as a process leading towards the establishment of a natural state based on a limited-access social order. My point of departure is that the expansion of the colonial frontier is not driven by the authorities. It is largely a process initiated by the settlers. Once the settlers have established themselves at the frontier, the authorities try to gain control over the territory. This process can be characterized as a natural state that extends its territorial control. The extent to which this will be manageable depends on the balance of power of the existing coalition and how it is affected by the establishment of new settler farms and the potential rise of a new elite. In that regard, the closure of the frontier involves the formation of a new 'frontier' elite, which is something that needs to be dealt with by the existing coalition of elites. This implies that the economic and political developments at the frontier cannot be understood in isolation of the developments at the economic centre.

Given that we are dealing with a settler colony governed by a chartered company (the VOC), the connection between the local elites (a specific group of settlers) and the local authorities may be blurry because the authorities, at least initially, represent the interests of their shareholders. Does the coalition consist of elites in the metropole and the authorities in the colony, or is it made up of local elites? In a study of the (British) East Indian Company, Bogart (2015) analyses its actions through the lens of changes in the elite coalitions in Great Britain, instead of its interaction with the elites in India. This book focuses on the relationship between the local elites and the colonial authorities. The chief reason is that the Cape Colony was never a prioritized area of interest for the VOC. The Company did not have any major investments in the colony that it needed to protect. It was up to the local authorities to finance their recurrent expenditures and the VOC would not intervene as long as the local authorities continued to ensure a steady supply of provisions for passing ships.

A problem with North, Wallis and Weingast (2009) is that they do not offer conceptual tools to help identify the glue that held the elites together. To identify how elite coalitions are formed and kept intact under such complex circumstances, one could use the concept of social contracts, more specifically Nugent's (2010) classification of productive, permissive and coercive social contracts. In a coercive contract, the right to govern is linked to the capacity of the rulers to impose their will through violence or the threat of violence. Ultimately, subjects give up their political influence in exchange for being spared from harassment. The political authority gains full de facto power, where de jure elements are negligible. The permissive contract implies some sort of negotiation between rulers and subjects as to how the latter can have its integrity preserved through the rule of the former. If the de jure power can be agreed upon, the de facto power can just be a function of it. In a productive contract, de jure and de facto power coexist in a specific balance. While the ruler claims de jure power, it does not fully exercise it de facto, creating a sort of grey area where social norms determine what is permitted and what is not. The power of the ruler, however, rests on the fact that this balance is a deliberate choice; in other words, the ruler can exercise de facto power any time its power is threatened.

In this book, I take Nugent's three types of social contract as a point of departure but extend and modify them. As an extension, I employ the contracts to understand the relationship not only between authorities and the population at large but also between different classes of the population. I modify them by not only allowing for the existence of multiple contracts in a society at any given point in time, but also by arguing that the existence of one contract can be predicted based on the presence of another. For example, the relationship between the authorities and certain, presumably wealthy, groups in the society may be productive, but only so long as those groups are allowed to use coercive measures against other groups in the society. The different mix of contracts ultimately depends on negotiations among the elite groups and the political and economic strength of those groups. At the same time, changes in one contract may affect all contracts and hence – in the longer run – change the balance of power among the elite coalitions in a way that also affects the institutional order as the frontier is closed.

The structure of the book

Taking inspiration from the frontier literature and the literature on institutions, factor endowments and social contracts this book now begins its journey, which starts in the seventeenth century and ends in the late eighteenth century, when the VOC loses control over the territory.

The book is structured as follows. Chapter 2 provides background context on the VOC's presence at the Cape. It will reveal a dialectic process. The VOC never intended to establish a settler colony. Instead, it founded a trading post as a way of lowering the monitoring and enforcement costs of trading with the indigenous Khoesan. The effect was largely the opposite, leading the VOC to allow a few settlers to establish their own farms to ensure supply of provisions to VOC ships. This unintentionally sparked a process of expanding settlement over which the VOC had little control.

Chapter 3 focuses on the expansion of the colonial borders. While shifting factor endowments was part of the story, the institutions that governed landed property rights were equally important. Border expansion continued even when the land–labour ratio was low, mainly because weak property rights led to a dispersion of the European settler population. The weak property rights system was largely an effect of Khoesan resistance, which caused settlers to want to minimize fixed investments in landed property. The sad irony is that Khoesan resistance gave settlers incentives to expand, which then weakened the Khoesan further.

In Chapter 4, I analyse the extent to which the Cape Colony was a slave economy, that is, the degree to which slavery as an economic institution was necessary for the growth of the settler farming economy. It concludes that the Cape was indeed a slave economy, but not for the reasons given by previous scholars. While slave labour played an important role for settler-farmers, especially arable farmers, I argue that prior research has exaggerated both the role and efficiency of slave labour. Directly related to this is the tendency to neglect the role of Khoesan labour. By including the Khoesan, I show that the returns of slave labour were well below those of the slave economies of Latin America and the United States. The reason slavery was important for the Cape economy, I argue, is that it gave slaveholders access to both labour and capital. Slaves were not only an agricultural input. They could also be used as collateral and leased out to other farmers. This generated much-needed capital for the settler-farmers.

Chapter 5 deals with inequality, especially inequality levels and trends among the settler farming population. It relates to Chapter 4 by again highlighting the role Khoesan labour played in the evolution of inequality at the Cape. In this chapter, I show that the increased inequality seen from the 1740s onwards was largely driven by a concentration of wealth and income in the upper tail of the distribution. While previous research has implicitly or explicitly discussed inequality at length, less time has been devoted to identifying the drivers of inequality. Human capital, access to land and slaves, and immigration policies have been mentioned as possible causes. I argue that in order to understand the evolution of inequality at the Cape we need to look at the capacity to initially accumulate wealth and income. In the early years, this could be done by taking control of domestic trade channels, investing in urban services and/or investing in farming. A small group, with political connections, generated substantial amounts of wealth through trade and investments in urban services. However, a larger share of settlers, who would become the Cape gentry, initially took on an accumulation path based on farming. Key to this strategy was not possession of slaves, which at the time were too expensive, but rather the ability to attract a sufficient number of Khoesan labourers to their farms. The first to establish farms in the south-western Cape took advantage of a lack of clear land policies, by gaining control of as much land as they possibly could. They then used this land to attract weakened Khoesan to settle on their farms, allowing them to restock their cattle in exchange for labour. The few who had the capacity to attract a sufficient number of Khoesan could make productive investments in land that generated the wealth needed to initiate a more slave-based agricultural system.

Finally, the chapter discusses the persistence of wealth. It concludes that there was a significant degree of elite persistence. This is somewhat surprising given the system of partible inheritance, but it can be explained by marriage strategies that kept wealth within families, even though ownership of landed property recurrently changed hands. Focusing on the relationship between the VOC and the settlers, I argue that the VOC authorities were weak and that their very existence depended on continuous cooperation with the settler elites. This was achieved by giving a small group of settlers control over the highly lucrative trade in wine, grain and livestock. While this provided a fairly stable elite collation, it occasionally came under threat, mainly because of opposition from rising new elites. On one occasion, the settler elites even managed to get the governor of the VOC replaced. A potential threat to the elite came from the majority of the settlers who were not allowed to engage in the trade. To ensure that this group accepted the status quo, the VOC allowed them a large measure of freedom in their treatment of and obligations towards the Khoesan labourers. On a district level, this freedom was ensured through the Cape gentry's influence over district authorities. In short, the chapter refutes the notion that the settlers were a homogenous group whose interests aligned with the VOC. On the contrary, their interests diverged, which rendered the VOC presence at the Cape inherently fragile.

The last chapter provides a brief summary of the lessons that can be drawn from the local economic history of the Dutch Cape Colony for the global study of settler colonialism. I argue that the establishment of a settler colony is best understood as a gradual and complex process, with important roles played by the actions of a range of groups with divergent economic interests – including the indigenous populations.

2

Indigenous agency, the cost of trade and initial steps towards a settler colony

Introduction

The establishment of the Cape Colony was not part of a grand plan. It was a gradual and unintended consequence of the VOC's determination to increase its control of the lucrative trade with the East Indies by providing a refreshment station at the Cape. The chief problem was how to secure supplies of meat for ships passing on their way to and from Asia. To understand why this eventually led to the establishment of a settler colony, we need to put the agency of the indigenous Khoesan at the forefront of the analysis. It was the increased difficulties the VOC experienced coordinating the trade with the Khoesan that eventually led it to establish a trading post. But this did not solve the VOC's problems. If anything, the cost of trade with the Khoesan increased, eventually leading the governor to allow Europeans to settle as farmers in the south-western Cape. This marked the beginning of the expansion. This expansion continued throughout the era of Dutch rule, and the VOC had little control over it, as subsequent chapters will show.

The indigenous people at the Cape

When VOC employees first settled on the shores of Table Bay in the mid-seventeenth century, they encountered people whom they called 'Bushmen' (the San) and 'Hottentots' (the Khoe). The terms 'San' and 'Khoe' are still in use, but anthropological and historical research has shown that these are not discrete ethnic categories. It used to be commonly believed that the San were smaller in stature than the Khoe, but scholars like Shula Marks (1972) say the evidence is inconclusive. Historians therefore commonly refer to the Khoe and the San as one group, the 'Khoesan'. An alternative is to follow Elphick (1977) and Penn (2005) and distinguish between the Khoe and hunter-gatherers, categorizing the indigenous people on the basis of their economic activities rather than along ethnic lines. Penn argues that this distinction is necessary as the hunter-gatherers and the pastoral Khoe reacted differently to the expansion of the colonial frontier. The Dutch themselves did not distinguish between Khoe and San by physical appearance but classified them according to their socio-economic systems: Khoe owned cattle, San did not. Khoe could be reclassified if they lost their livestock and became hunter-gatherers, and hunter-gatherers could be reclassified if they obtained livestock (Marks 1972). To avoid confusion, I follow current historiographical convention by using the term 'Khoesan' in this book, distinguishing where necessary between pastoral Khoesan and hunter-gatherer Khoesan.

Hunter-gatherers had been present at the southern tip of Africa for about twelve thousand years. They lived in small, family-based foraging bands of usually ten to fifty people, sometimes coming together in hunting groups that could contain several hundred people. These large bands were seldom fixed but could form and dissolve seasonally. The bands often moved within a defined area and lived in makeshift shelters or caves (Adhikari 2010). The Khoesan were a nomadic pastoral people descended from migratory groups who arrived in the Western Cape around 1000 CE, originating from northern Botswana. They were originally hunter-gatherers, but sometime around the first millennium BCE they underwent a pastoral 'revolution'. The need to keep moving to new pastures to support their growing herds eventually led them to the Cape. Evidence of how they migrated is scarce. According to Elphick and Malherbe (1989), they first moved into the grassland of the western part of what is now Zimbabwe and then south into what is now Gauteng, in South Africa. They then split into two groups, one going south-west to eventually reach the Cape of Good Hope and the other, known as the Nama, going westward along the Orange River until they reached the Atlantic. The group that went to the Cape were pastoralists who herded cattle and sheep. They grew no crops except *dagga* (cannabis).

The hunter-gatherers, already present in what was to become the Cape Colony, came into contact with the Khoesan in various ways: through armed conflict, trade and economic cooperation, or by being incorporated into a Khoesan group as subordinates or through intermarriage (Elphick 1977). Conflicts mainly arose over access to resources. The pastoral Khoesan needed grazing for their livestock; the hunter-gatherers wanted the land preserved for game. Trade consisted of goods like honey, meat, skins and bows and arrows. The trade could lead to the hunter-gatherers becoming integrated as part of Khoesan society, although probably living under their own chief in an encampment close to the Khoesan. By the time the Europeans arrived, the hunter-gatherers and the Khoesan had intermixed for centuries, making it impossible to distinguish between them among ethnic lines; hence the term 'Khoesan'.

The Khoesan societies at the Cape were constantly on the move, dispersing into vast areas in search of fresh pastures. As long as population densities were low, there was no need to regulate access to land and the societies were organized according to kinship and possession of cattle, rather than land. Kinship groups were related to each other through the male line. It was quite common that these patrilineal clans were loosely grouped as 'tribes', each with a chief at its head. In general, however, the chiefs had little power over the clans, who could simply move on with their cattle, which happened often (Elphick and Malherbe 1989).

The pastoral economies were fragile. Wealth took the form of livestock (cattle and sheep), which were vulnerable to theft by other Khoesan, attack by wild animals and loss from disease and drought. As the livestock were owned by families rather than clans, a wealthy family could be impoverished overnight. The family was then faced with a choice of either stealing livestock from neighbours or hiring themselves out as herders to wealthy Khoesan who would pay them primarily in cattle. A third option was to fall back on hunting and gathering. The hunter-gatherers the Dutch called 'Bushmen' may thus have been Khoesan who had lost their livestock (Elphick 1979).

At the time the VOC trading post was set up, many Khoesan groups were living in the Cape Peninsula or close by (see Map 2.1). In the peninsula itself, the Goringhaiqua, the Gorachouqua, the Goringhaicona and other scattered groups were all living under a single chief. North of the bay there were the Cochoqua and, farther north, the Guriqua. West of the Bay there were the Chainouqua and farther west the Hessequa. Hunter-gatherer groups were scattered around the region. There are no reliable estimates of the size of the indigenous populations in the south-western Cape at the time of European arrival. Guelke (1974) estimates that there were approximately two hundred thousand in the mid-seventeenth century, which is also the number later used by Fourie and Green (2015). Elphick (1977) suggests a more modest estimate of one hundred thousand, while Elphick and Malherbe (1989) and Guelke and Shell (1992) suggest that in 1652 there were about fifty thousand. The first commander of the Cape, Jan van Riebeeck, estimated in 1660 that there were about thirty-four thousand indigenous people living in the peninsula (i.e. most likely only including the Chainouqua and the Cochoqua). In his recent review of previous estimates, La Croix (2018) finds

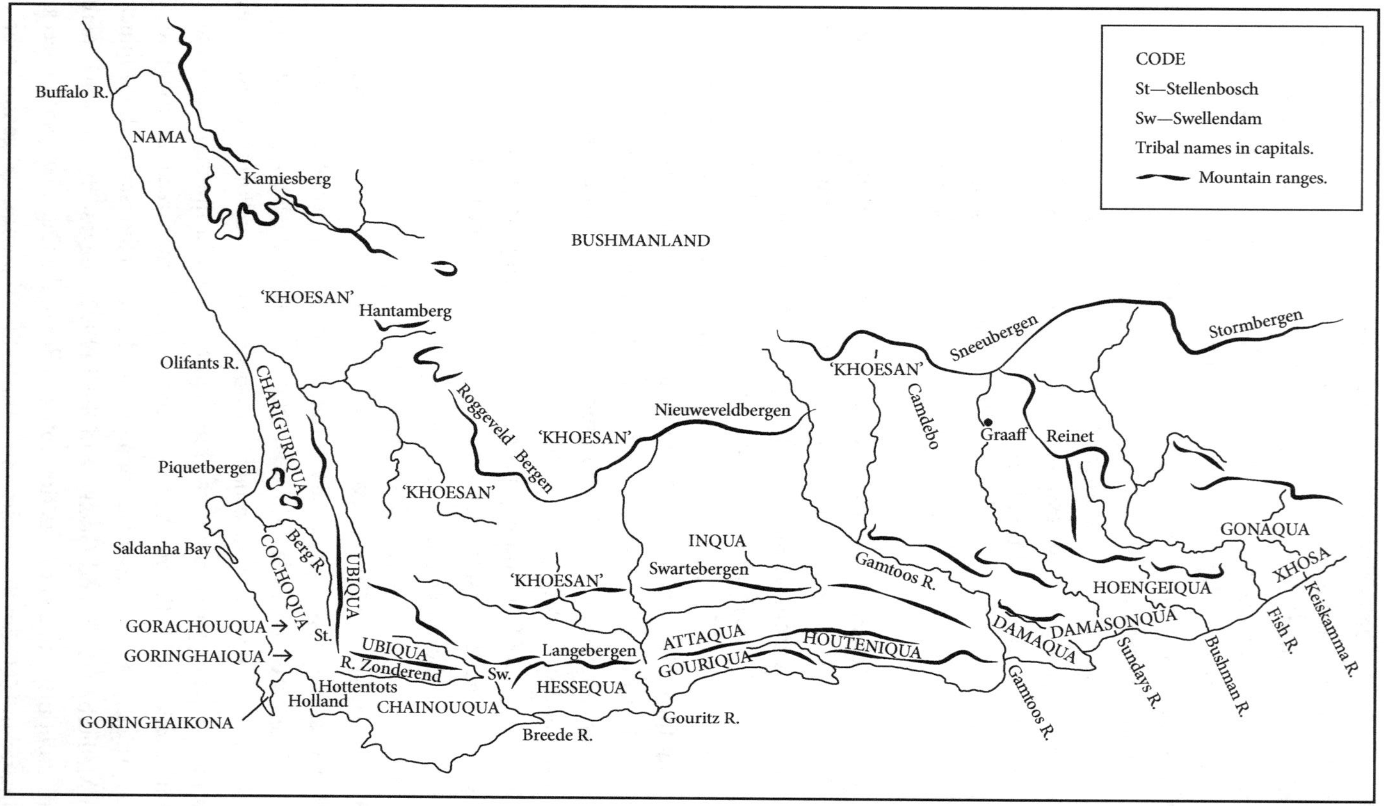

Map 2.1 Sketch map of the Cape, showing approximate positions of Khoesan groupings in the seventeenth and eighteenth centuries.

that fifty thousand is the most accurate estimate of the size of the Khoesan population, although he admits that this is probably a slight underestimation. The large differences in the estimates are due to different methods being used (such as backward projections or assumptions about the carrying capacity of the soil) and variations in the size of the region that is included.

An estimated fifty thousand people in the south-western Cape, an area of approximately 130,000 km², gives us a population density of 0.38 per km², while an estimate of two hundred thousand gives us 0.65 per km². In either case, the Cape was, by 1650, a typical open frontier, not empty but sparsely populated by scattered groups.

Coordination costs and the establishment of the refreshment station

By the end of the sixteenth century, the Portuguese commercial empire was facing intensified competition from England and the United Provinces of the Netherlands. Both the English and the Dutch stopped at the Cape for provisions on their outward and homeward voyages. The Portuguese had around fifty trading posts or forts on Africa's east and west coast but, by using the Cape, the English and the Dutch could avoid the east coast of Africa and cut directly across the Indian Ocean. The Dutch East Indian Company (VOC) had been established in 1602 by uniting a number of commercial undertakings, each governed by shareholding directors (*bewindhebber*). Seventeen of these directors, the 'Heren XVII' or in English the 'Lords XVII', formed the executive council. Abroad, the Company's affairs were managed by the governor-general and Council of India (located in Batavia) (Shutte 1989).

Initially, the relationship between the VOC and the Khoesan was relatively peaceful. Both sides wanted to avoid conflict – the Khoesan because they wanted European goods and the Europeans because they needed meat to supply their ships. But harmonious relationships did not last long. After a decade of exchanging cattle for iron and copper, in 1610 the Khoesan began demanding payment in copper only (Elphick 1977). To make matters worse, they especially wanted copper beaten into sheets, not in lumps, so that it could be turned into jewellery. Once the Europeans had adjusted to the new demand, the Khoesan started asking for brass.

These changes made it difficult for the VOC to coordinate their trading activities. Ships arrived from Holland loaded with iron, only to find that the Khoesan were no longer willing to trade with them. To deal with these uncertainties, Dutch salesmen began to stay at the Cape for longer periods in an attempt to build more trusting relations with the Khoesan. As they arrived, they would build minor redoubts and other fortifications. These attempts to reduce the coordination costs met with little reward and by the end of the seventeenth century the Cape 'was no longer regarded as a paradise for meat-eating seamen' (Elphick 1977: 82). Although the indigenous people in general distrusted the Europeans, they still believed that they had no intention of settling, let alone moving farther into the interior. That was about to change, with terrible consequences for the Khoesan.

In March 1647, the VOC ship the *Nieuwe Haarlem* was wrecked in Table Bay. The crew, all of whom survived, built a temporary fort where they could wait for passing vessels that would take them back to Holland. In a few months, fifty-eight of the crew had left, but sixty-two stayed to salvage the cargo from the wrecked ship. Among these was a junior merchant, Leendert Janszen. Janszen's view of the Khoesan was in general positive, and he was convinced that it would be profitable for the VOC to establish a permanent settlement in the Cape Peninsula. This would enable them to control the trade with the Khoesan and thereby not only ensure a more reliable supply of meat but also allow the VOC to extract monopoly rents. In 1650, the Lords XVII approved Janszen's recommendation to build a fort and establish a permanent trading post (Elphick 1977). In 1652, the trading post was formally established.

Indigenous agency and increased cost of trade

The Lords XVII of the VOC had no intention whatsoever of establishing a settler colony at the Cape. The VOC had given van Riebeeck – the man who would become the first governor of the Cape Colony – clear instructions not to *colonize* the Cape – that is, not to allow agricultural settlement. As Shutte (1989) points out, a large portion of the profits were invested in the company itself to keep shareholders' capital investments as low as possible. Investing in territorial control overseas was by no means an objective. As a commercial enterprise, the VOC remained pragmatic in its strategies in order to secure profits.

Though they accepted the establishment of a trading post at the Cape, the Lords XVII were not willing to invest in it. Instead, its costs were financed through trade with passing ships. To ensure that the ships would stop at the Cape – which was far from guaranteed, as the VOC paid a premium for ships that arrived early in Batavia – there had to be a sufficient supply of meat of decent quality. This depended on building up trust and a sustainable relationship with the Khoesan elites, which meant that VOC officials had to strike a balance between sticks and carrots. VOC authorities at the trading post had to ensure that their policies for building the relationship were implemented by Europeans employed at the trading post and crew members from the ships – not an easy task.

Somewhat ironically, the establishment of the fort made the Europeans even more vulnerable to Khoesan agency. A growing number of passing ships increased the demand for meat, and the employees at the fort also had to be fed and oxen were needed to maintain the fort. Data on what was actually bought and how it was distributed is scarce, but Elphick provides an illustrative example (see Table 2.1). Although the estimates do not reveal changes over time, they do usefully allow us to see how the livestock were distributed. Most of it, by far, went to VOC ships. However, taking the losses into account, it is clear that about 34 per cent of the cattle and over 40 per cent of the sheep went to the Company's trading post (and after 1657 to the small number of European settler-farmers), which makes it clear that the establishment of the trading post obliged the VOC to depend even more heavily on trade with the Khoesan.

Very little detailed information is available about the early relationship between the trading post and the Khoesan communities. In early historical work, the indigenous Khoesan are merely mentioned in passing. C. W. de Kiewiet, in his book *A History of South Africa, Social and Economic* (1957), summarized the development of the Khoesan societies as the Europeans arrived thus: 'The

Table 2.1 The Company's distribution and losses of stock, 1652–69.

	Cattle	Sheep
Disbursed to freemen	390	383
Company establishment	511	2,684
Ships	2,997	10,120
Hospital	111	3020
Losses (robberies/deaths)	536	1,660
Other (including sales to company servants and to foreign ships)	111	636
Total	4,656	18,683

Source: Elphick (1977: 153).

Hottentots broke down undramatically and simply. Their end had little of the tragedy which lies in the last struggles of a dying race' (20). They were passive victims who had no alternative than to adjust to the demands of the European intruders. Similarly, J. S. Marais, in his *Cape Coloured People*, published the same year, observes that 'the Hottentots put up a remarkably feeble resistance to the weak white community' (1957: 6–7).

Thanks to later and far more detailed research by historians and geographers, we now know that the Khoesan were not passive victims. Groundbreaking work by Marks (1972), Elphick (1977), Elphick and Malherbe (1989) and Penn (2005), to mention but a few, have helped make the 'missing' indigenous people visible. They show that the agency of indigenous populations played an important role in the early years of the trading post and the move towards the expansion of the colony's borders. Unfortunately, although their actions made sense in the short term, the eventual result was that the Khoesan lost their independence.

In theory, there were three ways the VOC could ensure a supply of sufficient provisions for the fort and the passing ships. They could enslave the indigenous population, steal their cattle or move farther into the interior to establish contact with Khoesan societies that might be larger and own more cattle than the ones near the trading post (Elphick 1977). It is questionable whether the first option could have been realized without further financial and personnel assistance from the Lords XVII in the Netherlands. But in practice the enslavement of the Khoesan never came into question. The Lords XVII prohibited the local authorities from taking any action in that direction. According to Shutte (1989), the reluctance of the VOC to allow the indigenous people to be enslaved was mainly due to the commercial character of the Company. It made profits from trade deals (not always fair or achieved without a degree of coercion) and by keeping recurrent costs low. Enslaving the indigenous people was deemed too costly and, more importantly, too risky. It is likely that the VOC would have found the use of enslaved Khoesan a viable option if slavery as an institution had been present in the region from the start, as it was in west and east Africa. Its absence meant that the VOC was not prepared to take any steps that could threaten their commercial relationships with the Khoesan.

Turning to the VOC's second option – thieving – one needs to keep in mind that the Dutch settlement at the Cape was fragile. Contemporary literature described the VOC trading post in general and its fort in particular in impressive terms. In 1688, in a volume called *The Regions of Africa*, a Dr Dapper described the fort as 'so strong that an army of one hundred thousand Hottentots only could take it' (quoted in Trotter 1903: 26). While this may have been true, life within the fort was tough. In its early years, the Europeans were hit by disease and acute shortages of food. In the *Journal of Cape Governors*, one reads that in 1652 the VOC employees at the Cape said: 'Life is a growing misery' (quoted in Trotter 1903: 24). The first war between the Khoesan and the VOC, in 1659, serves as a case in point to illustrate the vulnerability of the Dutch settlement. European settlers had just then been allowed to take up farming close to the trading post. In May 1659, the Khoesan in the Cape Peninsula, led by a former interpreter by the name of Doman, directed a series of well-coordinated and successful raids on the European settlers' livestock. For a year, they stole plough-oxen and took up guerrilla warfare on rainy days when the muskets of the Dutch would not fire. The settlers responded by urging the VOC to retaliate. The Lords XVII mounted a punitive expedition and allowed the settlers to seize and shoot Khoesan on sight, but with little result. The small group of Dutch settlers were left with no alternative but to withdraw back to the fort. The Khoesan were very close to succeeding in their mission of getting rid of the Dutch. During the war, which lasted a year, almost half of the European settler-farmers and VOC servants tried to flee by boarding passing vessels (Marks 1972).

Rather than enslavement or theft, VOC operatives went for the third option: expanding their trade relations with Khoesan communities deeper in the interior. Van Riebeeck, the first commander of the fort, was initially hostile to the Khoesan. After arriving at the Cape, he wrote to the Lords XVII that the Khoesan were a 'dull, rude, lazy, stinking nation' (Elphick 1975: 96). He soon came to realize, however, that in order to sustain the trading post he had to be sensitive to Khoesan demands and build a trusting relationship with the wealthier Khoesan societies farther inland (van der Merwe [1938] 1995). Estimates provided by Elphick (see Table 2.2) show that these Khoesan societies supplied a large share of the colonists' livestock. These estimates do not capture changes over time; they provide only aggregates for a period that stretches up to 1713. It is likely that in the very early years, the proportion of the livestock supplied by the peninsular Khoesan was larger. As demand increased, however, the VOC were left with no option but to move farther into the interior to ensure sufficient livestock provisions.

Doing so meant that they became increasingly dependent on collaboration with the Khoesan in the peninsula and its immediate surroundings. They needed them as travel guides and interpreters. One of these was 'Herry', the leader of a small group of Khoesan who had lost their cattle and lived at the bay. Herry knew English, as he had been taken on a ship by the English East India Company and had later served as an interpreter for both Dutch and English visitors to the

Table 2.2 Sources of livestock obtained by the Dutch settlers, 1662–1713.

	Cattle	Sheep	Ratio of sheep to cattle
Peninsular	613	1,951	3.2 to 1
Cochoqua	2,310	9,328	4 to 1
Eastern peoples (chiefly Chainouqua and Hessequa)	6,634	10,475	1.6 to 1
Northern peoples (Guriqua and Namaqua)	99	372	3.8 to 1
Unknown or a combination of the above two	4,707	10,682	2.3 to 1
Total	**14,363**	**32,808**	

Source: Elphick (1977: 160).

Cape. He was soon accused of enriching himself and establishing a monopsony by preventing other Khoesan from trading directly with the VOC. In just a few years, he had progressed from owning no livestock at all to owning a herd of more than two thousand head of cattle (Marks 1972; Elphick 1979).

The strategy of moving farther into the interior was initially not as effective as the VOC had envisaged. The Khoesan in the interior feared that the VOC had come there not to trade but to raid. Sometimes they would even flee, leaving their cattle behind, when the VOC approached (Elphick 1975). The VOC had to spend much time and effort to convince the Khoesan that they were not on raiding missions. Van Riebeeck's description of what happened in December 1653, when he and a party of twenty VOC servants approached a group of Khoesan, can serve as an example of the difficulties of establishing trusting relationships.

> Every now and then as we came gradually nearer … some of them would get up and in great fear take their heels, afterwards returning again. When this had happened ten to twelve times we at last left another four of our men behind, and when the three of us alone advanced they waited for us, not daring, however, to trust us completely yet and trembling and shaking with fear. At long last eight or ten of them awaited us, the rest standing at a distance to see how matters would develop. When we reached them they immediately saw and recognized the Commander of the fort in person, and stepping towards him held out their hands in welcome and as a further sign of good feeling and friendship clasped us around the neck.
>
> (quoted in Elphick 1975: 95)

The Khoesan in the Cape Peninsula, whom the VOC needed for the interior trade, offered their services only reluctantly. They feared that if the VOC managed to make direct contact with the Khoesan in the interior they would lose their position as intermediaries. The interior trade therefore continued to depend on costly expeditions to build up trust and did not yield the returns expected. Meanwhile, the wealth the peninsular Khoesan received from trade created tensions with other Khoesan communities. Though originally less wealthy overall than their neighbours to the east and north of the Cape, their increasing wealth began to cause the groups in the interior to feel threatened, and conflicts ensued (Elphick 1975). The tensions further increased the cost of trade for the VOC.

What the VOC officials had difficulty in understanding was that a major reason for the reluctance of the Khoesan to engage the Dutch in extensive trade stemmed from the structural weaknesses of their pastoral economies, rather than from political concerns. These economies were fragile. Selling off too many cattle could lower one's social position in the community, and restocking could take years. If several households in one Khoesan society traded extensively with the VOC, the whole society could be weakened and made vulnerable to attacks from other Khoesan societies. The Khoesan therefore preferred to sell sheep or only cattle that were sick and old. Before the establishment of the trading post, this had not been a major problem. But when the VOC increasingly demanded young cattle for breeding purposes, the situation changed. The Dutch complained that the Khoesan herds were increasing even while sales were on the decline, and that most of the cattle sold to them were subpar (Elphick 1975).

At the same time, officials at the Cape were under pressure from the Lords XVII, who wanted to cut costs by making the Cape less dependent on grain imports from Asia. The Lords XVII even threatened to cut off its supply of grain (van der Merwe [1938] 1995). The trading post at the Cape was increasingly viewed as an unnecessary cost. Steps needed to be taken to make it profitable.

The failure of intensive farming

In an attempt to solve the problems of the limited supply of provisions, authorities at the Cape changed strategy in 1657 and decided to allow a small group of Europeans to settle along the Liesbeek River behind Table Mountain (Marks 1972). This group – known as the *Vrye Burghers*, or 'free burghers', but hereinafter referred to as 'settler-farmers' – were granted land in exchange for raising cattle on behalf of the VOC. Initially, the idea was to combine this with the promotion of intensive farming in a limited geographical area. Van Riebeeck was very optimistic about the potential. Shortly after his arrival at the Cape, he inspected the eastern side of Table Mountain. He concluded that

> even if there were thousands of Chinese or other tillers they could not take up or cultivate more than a tenth part of this land. It is moreover so fertile and rich that neither Formosa, which I have seen, nor New Netherlands, which I have heard of, can be compared with it.
>
> (Thom 1954: 35–6)

The plan was not to establish a farming settler society that could outcompete Asian agriculture; rather, VOC officials believed that the abundance of water and the fertile soil and favourable climate would enable a small number of Europeans to supply the VOC with sufficient meat and grain through intensive farming practices. Each farmer was granted a portion of land of only 28 acres. The Company would remain in control of the developments, as the grants depended on these farmers handing over 10 per cent of their annual produce. The rest could be sold, but only to the VOC at a fixed price (Guelke 1979).

The intensive farming plan failed. The south-easterly winds were often strong and long-lasting during the harvest season, causing recurrent, severe losses of wheat crops. More importantly, the labour needed for intensive farming was in short supply. Low population density made it difficult to attract sufficient numbers of Khoesan to work on the farms. Systematic use of coercion was, at least on paper, prohibited by the VOC. The alternative was to employ European company servants, import slaves, or both. As I argue in Chapter 4, neither option was viable as long as the profitability of European farming remained low. It was simply too expensive to employ Europeans or buy slaves. Instead, the farmers came to rely on intensive farming, in which cattle played an important part. In 1666, Wagenaer, the second Cape commander, stated that the policy of establishing European farms on the Cape Peninsula had been a failure and that some European farmers had 'abandoned all hopes, all inclination for farming' (quoted in Katzen 1969: 195). By the late 1670s, only about a third of settlers were engaged in crop farming (van der Merwe [1938] 1995).

Not only did the intensive farming plan prove to be a failure, but the subsequent decision to allow a small group of VOC employees to establish farms beyond Table Mountain made it even more difficult for the Company to satisfactorily control trade with the Khoesan. Two factors can explain this. The first is that the establishment of a few European settler farms near the fort increased tensions between the VOC and the Khoesan, especially because the Dutch farmers were beginning to move farther into the interior in search of grazing land for their livestock. This threatened Khoesan access to pastures and water, and hostilities almost immediately broke out. It was especially the Europeans – at this point relatively free of VOC control – who misbehaved. Thieving and harassment were common (Guelke 1979). This led to the aforementioned first war between the Khoesan and the Europeans, in 1659. The VOC eventually managed to negotiate a peace deal, but it did not reveal a clear winner. The Khoesan had to accept the presence of the settlers and allow them to graze their livestock. Meanwhile, and against the settlers' wishes, the Khoesan were allowed to stay in the area and use grazing land unoccupied by the white farmers (Elphick 1977). Mistrust increased, making VOC trade with the Khoesan increasingly difficult.

The second factor is that, in order to survive, the European settler-farmers also engaged in trade with the Khoesan. In 1652, the Company banned trade between Khoesan and Dutch settler-farmers. It feared that allowing this trade would push up prices and eventually strip the Khoesan of their livestock altogether and destroy the source of supply. They also feared that the trade would encourage the farmers to go on their own trading expeditions into the interior, beyond the control of the VOC, and potentially threaten the presence of the Company by acting in a hostile manner towards the Khoesan. The VOC authorities at the fort soon heard reports of farmers not only trading livestock directly with the Khoesan, but sometimes coercing them to sell (Penn 2005).

The tension between the settler-farmers and the local authorities was exacerbated by the Company's pricing policy. The farmers complained about both low purchasing prices and delayed information about the prices. In 1658, farmers urged the VOC, in the *Journal of Cape Governors*, to 'Set us a price soon, because we will farm no land as long as we do not know the price, for we do not wish to be Company slaves' (quoted in van der Merwe 1995: 2–3). An already fragile situation became worse, and the VOC had to face the reality and accept that they were losing control.

The first steps towards frontier expansion

Understanding that the plan to establish land-intensive wheat farming was a failure, and having managed to weaken the Khoesan living on the Cape Peninsula, the VOC focused once again on building up a more sustained trading relationship with the Khoesan living near the peninsula, especially with the Cochoqua, who lived just northwest (see Map 2.1). The presumably much-wealthier Cochoqua had remained neutral during the first Khoesan–Dutch war, which, according to both Marks (1972) and Elphick (1977), is one reason why the Dutch managed to survive the war and negotiate peace. No longer being dependent on the Khoesan in the peninsula to the same extent as before the war, the VOC decided to intensify expeditions into the interior to establish or improve contacts with other Khoesan groups. The Lords XVII approved the decision and gave a bounty to explorers. During the several expeditions that were made, the explorers were especially struck by the favourable conditions they found north-east of the peninsula, in a place that later came to be known as Hottentots Holland. As early as 1657, Governor van Riebeeck described the area in his journal:

> Three freemen had without our knowledge proceeded inland about fifteen hours' walk, mainly southwards ... In the vicinity of a very beautiful river, on both sides of which bitter almond trees grew in profusion and in such fine, fertile soil that, according to them, the Cape valleys bear no comparison therewith, they have found two native encampments, numbering about five to six hundred people ... who ... called this place their Fatherland or Holland, to give our men an idea of the abundance of food and excellent pasturage to be found there.
>
> (quoted in Heap 1993: 18)

Impressed by the surroundings, which they deemed far more suitable for intensive wheat farming, the VOC made a second attempt to establish a few settler farms. In 1672, a number of company servants were sent into the region to sow grain there. Others followed a few years later and set up farms in the Tijgerberg region (van der Merwe [1938] 1995). Just as with the previous attempt to establish intensive agriculture, however, the developments in the Hottentots Holland area were not as good as initially hoped. Three years after the initiative, the area where the VOC had envisaged a second settlement had merely become a cattle trading post. A major reason for the failure was that the attempt to establish a settlement in the area provoked a second, longer war (1673–7). Initially the conflict was not related to the expansion of settler agriculture but to a growing mistrust between the VOC and Gonnema, the influential chief of a sub-group of the Cochoqua. Unlike other Cochoqua chiefs, he generally avoided contacts with the colonists. In the early 1670s, the colonial authorities became convinced that Gonnema was planning a series of attacks on the Europeans. If this was true, it is difficult to tell. The Company had evidence of only one case of Gonnema being involved in attacks on European farmers. Their suspicions were mostly based on accusations made by Khoesan enemies of Gonnema. Nevertheless, for four years the VOC made four punitive expeditions against Gonnema, often with support from other Khoesan groups. Only once did Gonnema make a counterattack. Instead, he usually used a more efficient weapon: he told his people to disperse their livestock over vast areas, making it nearly impossible for the VOC to defeat him. In frustration, the colonists instead started to attack other Khoesan groups who had only loose connections with the recalcitrant chief. Eventually a peace agreement was reached, in 1677. The war, which had included several Khoesan groups east and north of the Cape Peninsula, created tensions between them and the European farmers and temporarily put an end to the idea of further expansion. In 1679, there were only about seventy European farmers in that area of the peninsula (Guelke 1979).

Against this background, the VOC again changed its policy, in 1679. After twenty years of controlled expansion, the Company decided to allow settlers to move freely beyond the Cape Peninsula. No legal limits were placed on the size of an individual's land claim, but the land had to be cultivated within three years or be forfeited (Guelke and Shell 1983). Farmers moved east to what were to become the Stellenbosch and Drakenstein districts and a few years later they also moved up north of Tijgerberg. Soon the VOC would lose control of the expansion.

Unintended consequences and indigenous agency

The plan to establish a settler colony at the Cape was not part of a grand long-term well-thought-out strategy. It arose out of a series of events that started a cumulative process leading to an initial expansion of the colony's effective borders. As I argue in the following chapter, once this process was on the move, it created its own logic of expansion. The decision to establish a trading post and its early development cannot be understood without acknowledging that Khoesan actions and reactions had a fundamental impact on how it developed. It was the way the VOC handled the unwillingness or inability of the Khoesan to trade their cattle that drove the process. Ironically, every step the VOC took – from establishing a trading post to allowing a small number of settlers to establish farms – increased the cost of trade and obliged the VOC to take additional steps to encourage the establishment of settler agriculture. It would thus be a mistake to treat the establishment of the Cape Colony in its early years as an exogenous event, solely imposed from the outside. It was rather a gradual process, driven by indigenous agency and unintended consequences.

I am hardly the first to acknowledge the importance of the indigenous populations. This is well in line with recent research in African economic history in general and among Cape historians in particular (see especially Austin 2008; Frankema, Green and Hillbom 2016). Yet, this fundamental fact has been surprisingly neglected in recent research on the economics of settler colonialism.

The process that led to the establishment of a settler colony at the southern tip of Africa was complex and entailed the encounter of a variety of groups with different interests and demands, giving rise to new forms of conflict and cooperation. The transition from a trading post to a few farms being established beyond Table Mountain was largely the consequence of a clash between two economic systems that could not derive mutual benefit through trade. On one side, we have a Company whose commercial interests were founded on the lucrative trade with Asia; on the other were nomadic pastoralists whose fragile livelihood depended on maintaining their herds intact. Given the vulnerability of the pastoral economy, the Khoesan were seldom willing to supply the VOC with as much meat as it required. From the Company's perspective, this problem could not be solved by exercising increased control over one or several Khoesan groups. In the short term, this could have helped to increase the provision of livestock, but it would eventually have led to the collapse of the Khoesan pastoral economy and put an end to the supply. What the VOC could and did do was to engage in trade with a larger number of Khoesan societies over time.

The problem then was that the cost of trade increased and made the VOC even more dependent on the various Khoesan groups with whom they sometimes lived in peace and other times in conflict. To make matters worse, the wealthier Khoesan societies tended to be located farther away from the Cape Peninsula, where the climate was more suitable for pastoralism. To access these sources of cattle, the VOC needed to collaborate with the Khoesan in the peninsula, whom they needed as guides and interpreters. All this meant that the trade with the Khoesan demanded the establishment of a trusting relationship, not only between the VOC and the peninsular Khoesan but also between the peninsular Khoesan and those in the interior.

Establishing a trading post was the VOC's attempt to create more sustained trading relations with the Khoesan. Instead, the effect was the reverse: it worsened the relationship. When the Khoesan realized that the Europeans had come to stay, they began to fight back – not all groups, and not at the same time, but a pattern of recurrent resistance made the situation uncertain for the VOC and the settlers. In the early years, it was far from clear who would come out as the winner in this struggle. In the end, the Khoesan lost because they could not prevent the VOC from encouraging European settlement. Once this decision had been taken to allow a small number of European settlers to establish farms, the logic of an expanding settler colony changed character. It came to be driven less by indigenous agency and more by the way European settlement affected factor endowments and institutions, as I argue in the next chapter.

3

Factor endowments, institutions and the expansion of the frontier

Introduction

The history of the Dutch Cape Colony is, to a large extent, a history of geographical expansion. Twenty-five years after the establishment of the trading post the area of the VOC's territorial control was still small, encompassing roughly 500–650 km². Expansion took off from 1680. By early 1700, the area controlled by the VOC totalled about 1,440 km² (see Map 3.1). By the end of the eighteenth century it was roughly 250,000 km², or about the same size as modern Italy – a truly remarkable expansion (Guelke 1985). This chapter deals primarily with this expansion and the factors that made it both necessary and possible. The literature commonly identifies four characteristics of a settler economy: initial low population densities, a continuous inflow of migrants, extensive economic growth through an expansion of borders, the latter being supported by secure landed property rights (as discussed in Chapter 1). Only two of these were true of the Cape Colony: initial low population densities and extensive economic growth through the expansion of the frontier. Immigration of Europeans was low and their property rights were weak.

Cape historians have argued that the expansion of the frontier was caused by the natural growth of the settler population. In this chapter, I modify this demographic account of the expansion. I argue that increased population pressure alone is not sufficient to explain the expansion of the colony's borders. Rather, it was population growth in combination with a set of institutions governing landed property rights that spurred migration into the interior. Contrary to what one might expect, the settlers' landed property rights were in general terms weak and fluid. Private property rights were only implemented in the south-western Cape, a part of the colony that was closed by the end of the

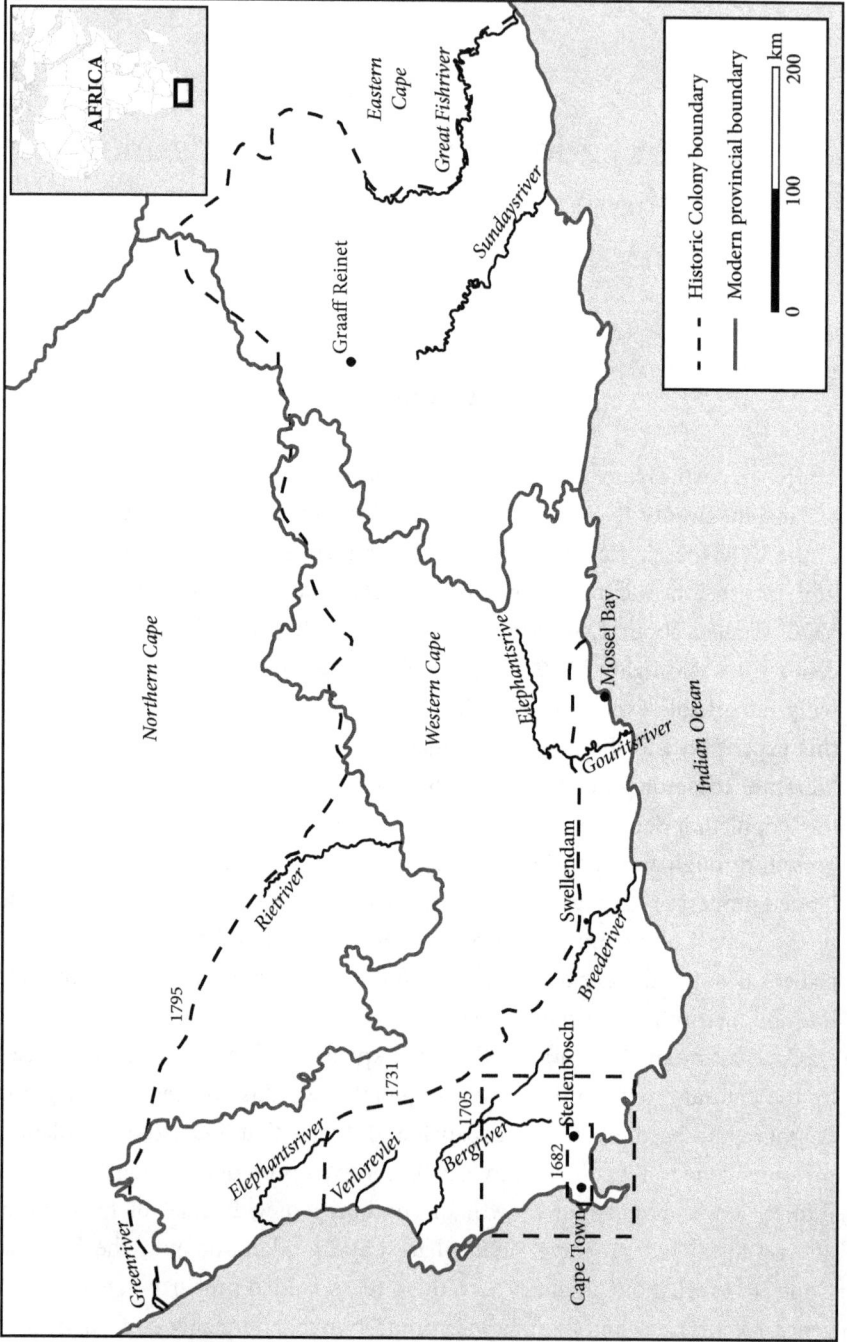

Map 3.1 Map of the Cape Colony, comparing 1682, 1705, 1731 and 1795 boundaries with modern-day boundaries.

seventeenth century, but in combination with more fluid rights to grazing land. Beyond the boundaries of the south-western Cape, settlers eventually got their land registered, but only as leaseholds (locally known as loan farms), and the land was neither surveyed nor properly demarcated. On paper, the VOC could withdraw the leasehold contracts on an annual basis, putting the settlers in the hands of the Company's good will.

I would argue that insecure and fluid landed property rights, together with the practice of the partible inheritance of landed property, encouraged continual expansion of the frontier and extensive economic growth. The question is: why did settlers accept insecure property rights? The reason is found in the fluid and uncertain social orders that characterized the time of open frontiers. The risk of conflicts with the indigenous people who could force settlers to abandon their farms made them unwilling to make any major fixed investments in land, such as buying it or paying the cost of surveying and proper demarcation.

This chapter contributes in three ways to the larger literature on settler economies, factor endowments and property rights. First, the previous literature on settler colonies assumes a one-directional relationship between the factor endowments and the institutional order of a specific society. Factor endowments are taken as given and presumed to have had a significant impact on the shaping of economic institutions. I argue, in contrast, that one must recognize that the relationship is multi-causal. Changes in the relative supply of factors of production can trigger institutional change, but institutions also affect supply and access to economic resources. In this chapter, I argue that the latter mechanism is more important than the former for the understanding of the expansion of the colony's borders. Second, I claim, in contrast to much of the more recent literature on settler economies, that insecure property facilitated rather than impeded extensive economic growth at the Cape. Settler-farmers at the frontier had an interest in keeping the cost of fixed investments as low as possible, given the risk of losing one's property. While the system of insufficiently demarcated loan farms kept the cost of fixed investments low, it also pushed settler-farmers deeper into the interior and thereby increased the likelihood of conflicts with the indigenous people. This leads to the third contribution: my argument that in order to understand how the institutions evolved over time, indigenous agency, largely neglected in the economic literature on settler societies, must be taken into account.

Before I analyse the role of factor endowments, institutions and agency I will briefly summarize the economic development of the seventeenth- and eighteenth-century Cape in order to put the expansion into a proper macroeconomic context.

Economic growth in the Dutch Cape Colony

There is no consensus among historians on how well the Cape economy performed. Scholars such as de Kock (1924), Guelke (1974), Trapido (1990) and Feinstein (2005) describe it as a static, near-subsistence slave economy. Markets were small and were distorted by VOC policies of fixed pricing. Most farmers found it difficult to survive, let alone set up profitable businesses. Many went bankrupt. J. A. de Mist, Commissioner of the Batavian Republic at the Cape, wrote as late as 1801 that

> The embargo on freedom of trade and the difficulty experienced by the farmer in obtaining goods in exchange for the produce which he brought to the Cape Town market in ever increasing quantities, affected the prices of corn and wine so adversely that at times the farmer, arriving at the Cape after many a long day's trek at the slow pace of the ox, through the trackless veld, was unable to obtain a purchaser for his grain, and found himself obliged either to sell it or rather, give it away for next to nothing, or else store it in hired granaries at a considerable loss to himself. Further (with shame be it said) the desperate wine farmer had more than once been seen knocking the pegs out of his barrels and allowing the precious wine to turn to waste in order that the weary oxen might not have to drag the full casks over the veld back to the farm.
>
> (quoted from van Duin and Ross 1987: 6)

The view of the Cape as a backward economy is often derived from anecdotal evidence such as letters from settlers describing the difficulties they were facing. While many settlers probably did find life at the Cape challenging, such evidence could give a biased view of the reality. It was in the interest of the settlers to describe their situation in bleak terms to ensure that they were treated favourably by the colonial authorities.

Quantitative estimates tend to give a much less pessimistic account of the Cape economy. In their groundbreaking book, van Duin and Ross (1987) argue that the Cape economy was fairly dynamic. They use annual tax censuses (*opgaafrollen*) to show how output gradually increased over time. However, as Fourie and van Zanden (2013) have observed, their calculations do not substantiate their conclusion as they do not measure output per capita. Fourie and van Zanden themselves provide the most comprehensive estimates of the performance of the Cape economy, using an output approach and measuring the value added in all sectors of the economy. Their estimates present a middle ground between claims that the Cape economy was backward and claims that

Figure 3.1 GDP per capita (1990 international Geary–Khamis dollars) for the Cape Colony, 1701–93.

Source: Fourie and van Zanden (2013: 473).

it was dynamic. In line with van Duin and Ross, they show that the economy was growing throughout the eighteenth century and, unsurprisingly, that the agricultural sector remained by far the largest part of the economy. However, unlike van Duin and Ross, they also estimate GDP-per-capita growth (see Figure 3.1) and, in per capita terms, find a more ambiguous performance. At the beginning of the eighteenth century, real income at the Cape was on a par with the rate of growth in England, but throughout the eighteenth century, GDP per capita declined. Up to 1770, this decline was fairly modest, but thereafter it became steeper.

These estimates of GDP per capita should, however, be treated with a great deal of caution. The chief problem is that, due to a lack of data, they do not capture the economic activities of the Khoesan. We have no information on their incomes, wealth or consumption, let alone the size of the Khoesan population during the eighteenth century. In an attempt to estimate the size, Fourie and van Zanden use a novel technique. They posit that the number of Khoesan is proportional to how many times they appear before the Court of Justice in Cape Town. This assumption is problematic, however, as appearances before the court would probably have been affected by a number of other factors, such as economic stress, the administrative capacity of the VOC and the extent to which the settlers and the indigenous population regarded the VOC as a legitimate authority. Intuitively, the number who appeared before the court would increase over time – not because of population growth, but because the Khoesan would become increasingly incorporated into the colonial economy.

In a rather eclectic way, Fourie and Green (2015) offer an alternative method, which is to count the number of Khoesan employed on European farms. The methods Fourie and Green use are discussed in detail in Chapter 4. Here, it is sufficient to say that their estimates have the same problem as Fourie and van Zanden's: the size of the indigenous population is probably underestimated as it captures only the Khoesan who were incorporated into the economy as farm labourers and servants. Fourie and Green nevertheless use these estimates to revise the GDP figures and, as one might expect, the revised estimates show a decline in GDP per capita (see Figure 3.2). As a matter of fact, with the revised estimates, the GDP-per-capita levels for the Cape Colony are almost never on a par with those of England.

What do these estimates tell us about the Cape economy? They seem to confirm the general view taken by scholars on long-term economic growth in settler economies. The Cape economy was growing, but the growth was extensive and not driven by major improvements in productivity. The decline in per capita growth was most likely a consequence of the expansion of the frontier marked

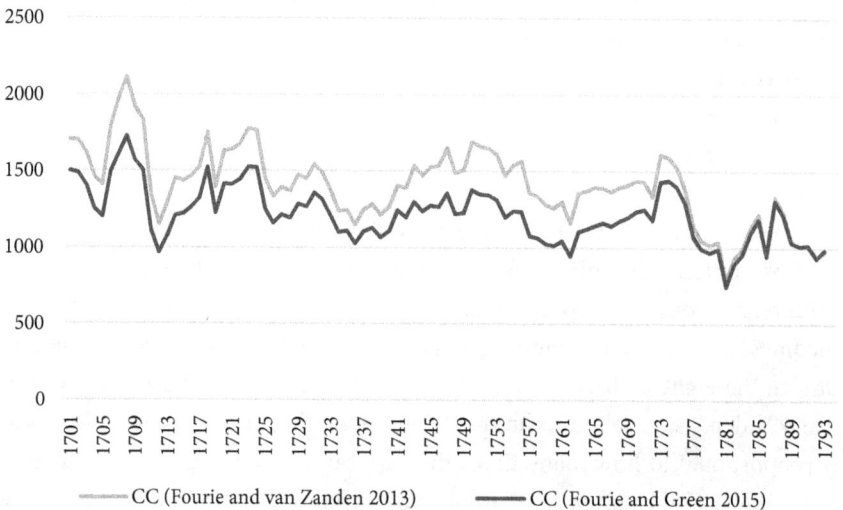

Figure 3.2 Comparison of GDP per capita estimates, 1701–73.

Source: Fourie and Green (2015: 214).

by an increased use of marginal lands for agriculture. This takes us back to the question of why European settlers chose to move farther into the interior.

The expansion of the frontier

As was noted in Chapter 2, the settlers began to move beyond the colonial frontier in the 1660s. The expansion of settler agriculture was briefly held up by the second frontier war, but the borders began expanding again in 1679. The newly appointed governor, Willem Adriaan van der Stel, decided to extend the colony's land claims in order to, once and for all, make the colony self-sufficient in grain. In 1679, the Stellenbosch district, north-east of the Cape Peninsula, was founded, and eight years later the Drakenstein district, just north of Stellenbosch. According to Guelke (1979) the initial expansion was slow. In 1717, there were only four hundred settler farms in an area of 194 km². But despite the low numbers, complaints about land shortages were already being heard from settlers and VOC officials (Giliomee 1981). The expansion of settlers farther into the interior, towards the north and east, continued (see Map 3.2). By 1720, they had reached the Bokkeveld Mountains in the north and Kogmans Kloof in the Langeberg in the east. From 1740, the principal expansion of the frontier took an easterly direction. Settlers went through the Karoo and settled along the northern slopes of the Roggeveld mountains. From there, the expansion continued into the Nieuweld in 1760 and Sneeuberg and Camdeboo in the late 1760s. They then spread southwards to the Sundays and Bushmans Rivers. Here they met with the settlers who had originally moved eastwards between the Langeberg and the south coast and then into the Little Karoo. In 1765, groups of settlers reached the Gamtoos River and in the 1770s they arrived in Camdeboo (van der Merwe [1938] 1995).

Up to the end of the seventeenth century, the VOC was mostly in control of the settler expansion. It even encouraged Europeans to settle in the south-western Cape, by giving them full property rights to the land they took possession of. However, as early as 1702, the VOC had given up the initial plan of a controlled expansion and was allowing settlers to establish farms outside of administrative boundaries (Dye and La Croix 2020). As van Duin and Ross observe, 'By the early years of the eighteenth century the Cape had taken on the pattern that was to last for over a century' (1987: 2). It was a process induced by the settlers' demand for more land. It did not align with the immediate economic interests of the VOC.

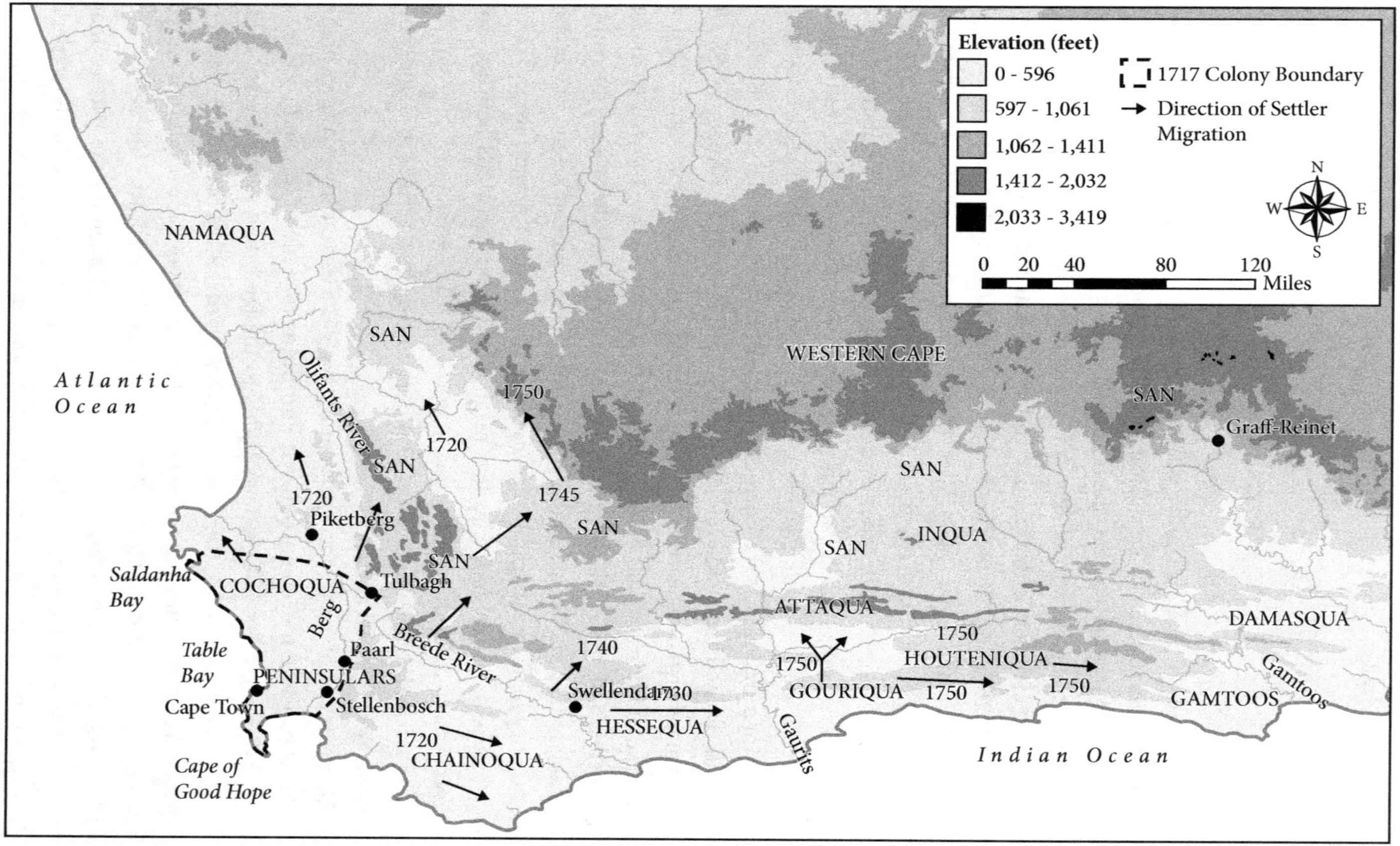

Map 3.2 Settler expansion at the Cape through 1750.

In 1786, the deputy governor, J. W. Cloppenburg, on a tour of the colony, was alarmed by the movement of settlers into the interior and the VOC's lack of control over it. He saw this as 'clearly being a great degeneration of religious faith, of obedience, and as a result, of good behaviour among the present generation' (quoted in van der Merwe [1938] 1995: 111). He asked himself: 'If I found then such folk on a journey, which did not constitute half of the circumference of our possessions, how many more of that rabble shall there be further away? What shall become of them? Troublesome inhabitants, good-for-nothing and dangerous to society' (112). For the VOC the continuous settler expansion into the interior posed a threat to their control over the territory. The question is what drove this settler induced expansion. Could it be population growth leading to scarcity of land or were other factors at play?

Population growth at the Cape

During the first fifty years of the colony the number of Europeans at the Cape remained fairly small. By 1682, thirty years after the establishment of the trading post, there were only 142 adult settlers at the Cape (Guelke 1988). It was in

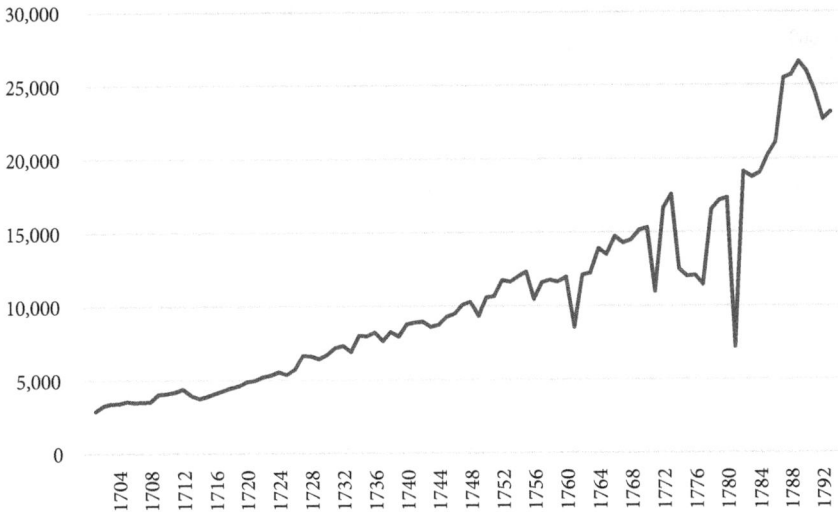

Figure 3.3 European population in the Cape Colony, 1703–93.

Source: Dye and La Croix (2020: 38). Notes on the source: the original data is from van Duin and Ross (1987), which omits the households of the company employees. To deal with that Dyer and La Croix use estimates of average household size from Shell (1986).

the eighteenth century that a significant and stable increase began. Figure 3.3 shows that the number of Europeans increased from roughly three thousand in 1703 to over twenty thousand in 1793. This gives us a population growth rate of about 2.6 per cent per annum. This could be compared with Africa's population growth of 2.52 per cent in 2019.

Despite the growth of the European population, the Cape Colony remained sparsely populated. Guelke's (1985) estimate of roughly 250,000 km² gives us a settler population density of 0.08 people per km² by the end of the eighteenth century. This underestimates the actual population density as it does not include the slave population or the indigenous people. Regarding the former, we have fairly reliable sources. Figure 3.4 shows the European and the slave populations. Including the slaves would give us a population density of roughly 0.18 people per km².

The challenge is to capture the size of the indigenous population. The first proper census taken of the indigenous people, from 1806, estimated that thirty thousand indigenous people were living within the boundaries of the colony (Fourie and Green 2015). Assuming that this estimate roughly represents the size of the indigenous population in the late eighteenth century, the population density reaches 0.3 people per km², which is still strikingly low. As explained in Chapter 2, the biggest challenge is to account for the size of the indigenous people

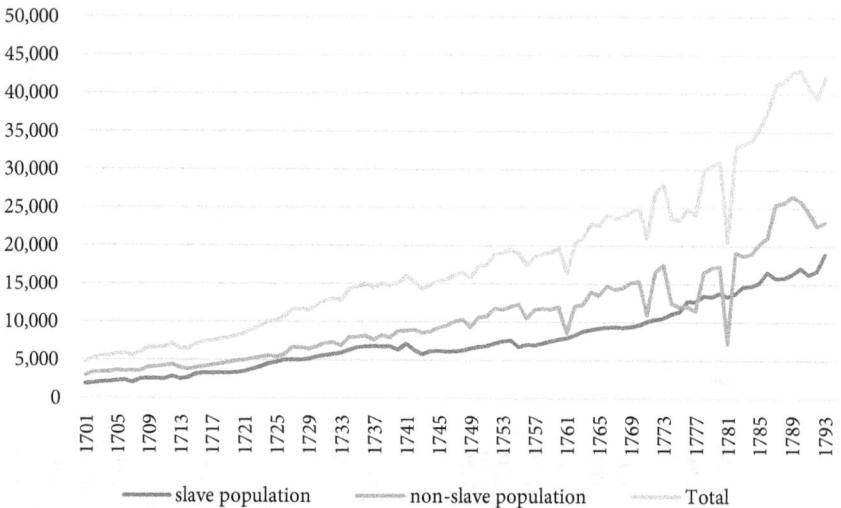

Figure 3.4 European and slave population in the Cape Colony, 1703–93.

Source: Dye and La Croix (2020: 38). Notes on the source: for the European population. Estimates of the slave population are from Shell (1994).

for earlier periods. Several scholars have argued that the size of the Khoesan populations declined throughout the eighteenth century because of the European settler expansion and the outbreaks of smallpox in 1713 and 1755. However, there is no consensus on the pace at which the decline occurred – it depends on which 'estimate' you use as a benchmark. Estimates of the size of the indigenous population in the south-western Cape upon the arrival of the Europeans differ with a factor of 9, from eleven thousand to one hundred thousand (La Croix 2018). If we take the upper bound estimates for the south-western Cape the population density would have been roughly 26 people per km^2 – significantly higher, but not extreme. However, this is probably an overestimate, even if we accept that there could have been a hundred thousand Khoesan in the region. The reason is the Khoesan practised transhumance, a variety of pastoralism in which livestock are moved seasonally between summer and winter pastures, which meant that the Khoesan moved in an area significantly larger than the south-western Cape. Despite the lack of reliable estimates it seems safe to conclude that average Khoesan population densities at the Cape remained low throughout the eighteenth century.

What caused the growth of the settler population? Several Cape historians have acknowledged that, unlike what happened in other settler colonies across the world, immigration to the Cape did not play a decisive role in the expansion of the frontier (van der Merwe [1938] 1995; Guelke 1974; Ross 1993). In 1707, the VOC at the Cape decided not to further encourage immigration, a policy that was reinforced in the 1717 decision that the future of the Cape economy would rely on slave labour and not European immigrant labour. The chief cause of the population growth was the high fertility levels among the settler population. Cilliers and Mariotti (2019) provide the first systematic and longitudinal analysis of fertility levels in the Cape Colony. They find high and stable fertility rates in the colony throughout the eighteenth century that continue in the first half of the nineteenth century. The average settler woman had seven children. Cilliers and Mariotti found no significant differences between regions. Fertility levels were as high in urban Cape Town as in the rural frontier regions. Their estimates are on a par with findings from other settler societies, such as Australia and the United States (Binion 2001 and Moyle 2017). The high fertility rates ensured a steady growth of the settler population at the Cape.

One of the few scholars to question this interpretation is Shell (2005). He argues that if the expansion was due to natural population growth, then we should expect to find an equal sex ratio among the second or third generation of the settler population. Using the annual tax censuses, he finds that from the mid-seventeenth century to the end of the eighteenth century the settler population never had an equal sex ratio; males always predominated. This leads him to argue that immigration must have played an important role in the expansion of the borders. Unfortunately, there are no reliable estimates of immigration to the Cape. Shell therefore uses the number of applications for the status of *vrye burgher* (free citizen) and for loan farms (leaseholds) as proxies. He assumes that on first arriving at the Cape the immigrants offered their services to the Company. Wages were low, but they enabled an immigrant to buy time and become familiar with the region before applying for status as a free burgher and establishing his own farm. The problem is that while Shell finds an increase in the number of both applications to become a free burgher and applications for a loan farm, the numbers remain very low for the years covered (1738–49). The highest number is in 1749 when twenty-five applications for free citizen status were submitted. Further, Shell ignores the steady decline in the sex ratio. By the mid-seventeenth century the ratio was six hundred males to one hundred females, and at the end of the eighteenth century it had dropped to one-hundred-fifty males to one hundred females. In line with Ross (1993) we therefore conclude that while Europeans continued to migrate to the Cape throughout the eighteenth century, the numbers must have been fairly small and not sufficient to explain the growth of the settler population.

The growth of the settler population – independently of its cause – is used to explain why settlers moved farther into the interior. Guelke, for example (1974: 25), concludes that 'the frontier movement was basically demographic in character', while Ross (1993:1) says that 'at the simplest level, the reason for the expansion of white settlement is quite evident. It lies in the immense population increase of the Afrikaners [the white settlers]' (quoted in Shell 2005: 2). Scholars disagree on whether the move into the interior was caused by push or pull factors. Guelke (1974) argues that migration was a last resort for settlers who could no longer access a sufficient amount of land in the closing or closed frontiers. Others, like Neumark (1957), argue instead for pull factors: settlers realized the economic potential in moving towards a new frontier and establishing profitable cattle farms. The two views, as Newton-King (1999) recognizes, are not mutually exclusive. Some may have moved as a survival strategy, while others may have been drawn by the opportunities of setting up profitable agricultural businesses. Estimates by Cilliers and Green (2018), for example, reveal significant wealth differences in the frontier district of Graaff-Reinet: a small group of affluent farmers and a majority who seem to have lived from hand to mouth.

Independently of the motives, both views point to land scarcity to explain settler movements into the interior. The strand of the literature that emphasizes pull factors assumes that there was insufficient land left to establish new farms in the south-western Cape, leaving the settlers with no choice but to try their luck farther inland. Those who emphasize push factors likewise assume that land had become fairly scarce – leaving enough for farms but not enough for profitable agricultural businesses. I do not question that scarcity of land mattered for the expansion of the frontiers. In contradiction of previous literature, however, I argue that the expansion cannot be explained by factor endowments alone but needs to be combined with an institutional perspective. People moved into the interior before land became scarce in the physical sense of the term, because the way that land rights were regulated meant that the farms became widely dispersed and this reinforced the expansion of the frontier.

Factor endowments, institutions and the closing of the south-western frontier

At the turn of the seventeenth century, when settlers were beginning to move beyond the borders of the south-western Cape to establish farms on their own initiative, all the arable land allocated in the south-western Cape was in the form of freehold farms, i.e. private property. The size of the freehold farms was smaller than the plantations in the 'New World', averaging from 35 to 80 hectares (Dye and La Croix 2020). Guelke (1979) estimates that the total size of all freehold farms established in the south-western Cape from 1657 to 1717 equalled 3 per cent of the total land area allocated to farmers (see Table 3.1).

Table 3.1 Freehold land grants, 1657–1717.

District	Number of grants	Area of grants (km^2)	Total area settled (km^2)
Cape	107	45.6	1,300
Stellenbosch	108	53.3	1,300
Drakenstein	189	94.0	3,900
Total	**404**	**192.9**	**6,500**

Source: Guelke (1979: 49).

Fortunately, as the farms in the south-western Cape were clearly demarcated there are archival sources that help us establish their location. Using information from the Deeds records in the Cape Town archives, Guelke, Bonner and Maisoneuve (1987) produced a map which shows the location of the freehold farms and year of establishment. In a pilot study, Fourie and Green (2018) digitized the map and compared the location of farms with soil suitability, access to water and amount and annual variance of rainfall. Unsurprisingly, they found that those who were first to establish farms chose areas more suitable for farming than the latecomers. By 1717, farmers had already gained control over many of the water resources, as can be seen in Map 3.3, which shows farm boundaries (but omits the Cape Peninsula). Large parts of the rivers and perennial streams in the Stellenbosch, Drakenstein and Franschhoek areas were already enclosed by farmland. Although it was becoming more difficult for a prospective farmer to find land with a perennial stream, it would still have been possible to establish a freehold farm, with access to less reliable water resources but in an area with more reliable rainfall and a climate suitable for arable farming. Farther north, in the Land van Waveren (today Tulbagh) and the Swartland, it was still possible to locate farms with secure access to water. Farmers nevertheless went even farther into the east and the north.

To understand why they did this we need to take a closer look at property rights and land control in the south-western Cape. If we consider only the land under freehold tenure, we underestimate the total amount of land under settler control as this neglects the importance of pastoral farming in that part of the colony. Including the amount of land allocated for grazing indicates that land was indeed becoming a scarce resource, as does the way grazing land was regulated differently from arable land, which caused institutionally induced land scarcity.

It is common to distinguish between the south-western Cape and what would become the northern and eastern frontiers of the colony in regard to agricultural activities. It is claimed that the freehold farmers in the south-western Cape engaged mainly in wheat and wine farming, while the frontier settlers engaged in pastoral farming. While this may have been true in the late-eighteenth century Cape, it was not an accurate description of the economic activities of the region during the first eighty years of settlement. During this period pastoral farming was a key industry in the south-western Cape. Table 3.2 shows the estimated average head of cattle and sheep at the Cape. If we focus only on the period 1663 to 1702, when we can be certain that all the farms in the south-western Cape were freehold, we see a significant increase in livestock holdings. In 1662, an

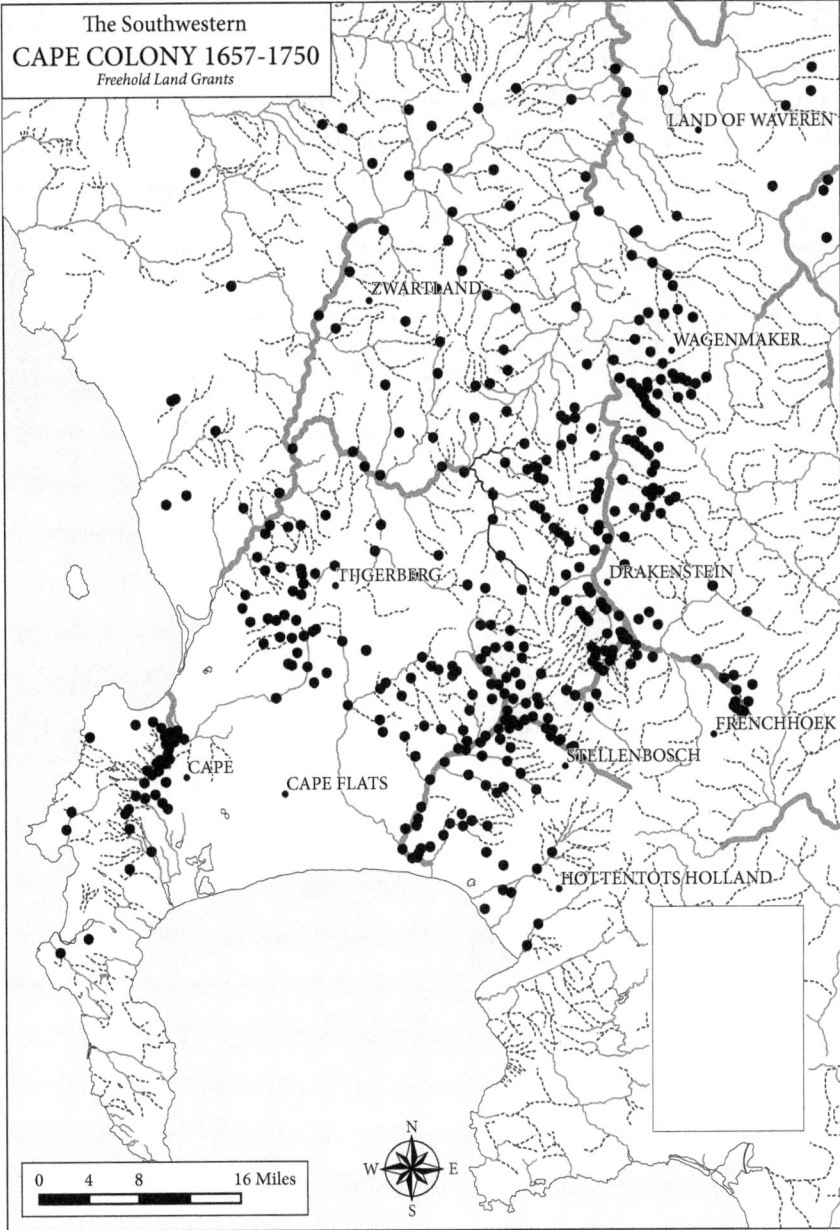

The Southwestern
CAPE COLONY 1657-1750
Freehold Land Grants

LAND OF WAVEREN

ZWARTLAND

WAGENMAKER

TIJGERBERG

DRAKENSTEIN

FRENCHHOEK

CAPE

CAPE FLATS

STELLENBOSCH

HOTTENTOTS HOLLAND

0   4   8   16 Miles

N
W   E
S

Map 3.3 Boundaries of freehold farms at Cape Colony, 1717 (Cape Peninsula excluded).

average settler-farmer had about 12 head of cattle and 45 sheep. Forty years later, this had increased to 37 head of cattle and 201 sheep. This can be compared to the average output of crop production per farm (Table 3.3). Output fluctuated significantly, probably as an effect of changing weather conditions, but shows no clear upward trend. That stock farming played an important role in the early years of settler agriculture is not surprising. It required less investment in labour, which was scarce (see Chapter 4), and the closeness to Cape Town made

Table 3.2 Mean settler livestock holdings at the Cape Colony, 1663–1773 (selected years).

Year	Average no. of cattle per European farm	Average no. of sheep per European farm
1663	11.70	44.74
1670	8.57	134.09
1678	21.40	122.98
1682	15.83	124.73
1685	26.07	170.60
1688	20.34	239.26
1692	22.77	213.00
1695	23.71	145.03
1700	35.08	192.73
1702	37.01	201.20
1712	42.76	281.54
1719	39.09	162.28
1731	42.32	218.54
1738	49.35	221.65
1741	41.35	193.04
1752	29.24	158.84
1757	27.81	150.47
1762	22.87	135.94
1773	23.71	172.29

Source: Fourie and von Fintel (2010b: 21).

Table 3.3 Mean settler production of wine, wheat, rye and barley in the Cape Colony, 1663–1773 (selected years).

Year	Wine (leaguer)	Wheat (muids)	Rye (muids)	Barley (muids)
1663	0	0	0	0
1670	0	0	0	0
1678	0	11.05	1.86	3.02
1682	0	21.28	3.20	12.49
1685	0	18.98	3.19	3.73
1688	0	9.57	2.85	1.69
1692	0	25.89	5.30	7.70
1695	0.56	12.06	1.78	2.16
1700	4.19	14.25	9.15	8.44
1702	3.11	11.54	5.18	4.34
1712	2.65	30.86	1.75	16.87
1719	2.76	29.27	0.61	15.43
1731	2.87	29.28	3.10	18.57
1738	1.44	23.06	1.91	19.58
1741	1.36	38.18	2.70	20.55
1752	2.90	21.66	1.33	16.26
1757	3.32	13.17	0.40	11.97
1762	2.50	18.85	0.48	13.62
1773	4.62	20.74	0.05	9.61

Source: Fourie and von Fintel (2010b: 20).

it reasonably easy and cheap to transport livestock to the market there (van der Merwe [1938] 1995).

It was in the middle of the eighteenth century that settler-farmers in the south-western Cape began increasingly turning to arable farming. Between 1701 and 1740, the total number of cattle in Stellenbosch and Drakenstein, the two main arable farming districts, increased from 5,500 to 24,090 head, an increase of almost 400 per cent (van Duin and Ross 1987: appendix 9). As late as 1748,

40 per cent of all farms in Stellenbosch, for example, were purely pastoral (Ross 1993). But as freehold rights did not provide sufficient grazing land, the farmers grazed their cattle on the common land between the farms and occasionally also beyond their borders.

In order to maintain control of the situation, Governor Simon van der Stel used both sticks and carrots. Already by 1687 he had designated common grazing land in Stellenbosch. At the same time, he forbade settlers to move livestock across district boundaries. The settlers were not even allowed to keep each other's livestock among their own herds for payment (van der Merwe [1938] 1995). Farmers, however, continued to move beyond the frontier. The VOC urged the settlers to keep their livestock no farther away than one day's journey from their freehold properties. But this exhortation had little effect, leading the administration in 1703 to reverse its policy of keeping free grazing land and requiring farmers to apply for grazing permits. These would be issued for free and would give farmers access to grazing land within a specific geographical area. Each grazing post had to be at least one hour's walk from the next grazing post, which in practice meant that a permit holder had an exclusive right to at least 2,420 hectares of grazing land. Officially, a farmer had the right to only one licensed post, but in practice most farmers moved between several (van der Merwe [1938] 1995). We lack information on the number of grazing rights allocated per farm. Rather conservatively, we might assume that each farm had one grazing post. On this basis, we can revise the amount of land allocated for farming in the south-western Cape. Table 3.4 shows the revised estimates.

When grazing land is included, and it is assumed that each farmer had one grazing post, the total area allocated for farming increases, expanding

Table 3.4 Revised estimates of total land allocated for farming, 1657–1717.

District	Number of grants	Area of grants (km²)	Estimated total amount of land allocated for farming[1]	Total area settled (km²)
Cape	107	45.6	450	1,300
Stellenbosch	108	53.3	491.6	1,300
Drakenstein	189	94.0	714.3	3,900
Total	**404**	**192.9**	**1,655.9**	**6,500**

Source: Guelke (1979: 49).
Assuming on average one trading post per farm.[1]

well beyond the borders of the districts. It therefore comes as no surprise that Governor van der Stel stopped further settlement in Stellenbosch as early as 1687. The allocated grazing posts had by this time pushed farmers beyond the district boundaries.

The expansion of pastoral farming in the south-western Cape quickly made land a scarce resource. Although we lack sufficient information, it seems likely that the system of grazing posts favoured early arrivals. The way grazing land was regulated made further settlement difficult. Grazing land was neither demarcated nor surveyed. The location of the grazing post was described only in vague terms. Van der Merwe mentions a licence that gave the farmer the right to graze his livestock in the 'dunes behind the *graauwe heuvel* [burial mounds]' ([1938] 1995: 55). The only regulation imposed, as shown above, was that a farmer could not locate a grazing post nearer than at least one hour's walking distance from the next nearest trading post. In practice, this system favoured the settlers who arrived early. Two farmers who had already settled could position their trading posts so as to prevent a third farmer from accessing pastureland in the area. By locating their grazing posts just less than two hours' walk away from each other, they made sure that there could be no trading post established between the two farms. This gave the two settled farmers access to more pastureland than they were necessarily entitled to, and at the same time prevented competition from other farmers who might want to settle in the area. This system, together with the ability to control water resources, enabled the early arrivals to prevent further settlement even if arable land had not yet become scarce (Guelke 1984).

Property rights and the expansion of the frontier

As land became scarce in physical and institutional terms in the south-western Cape, settlers moved farther north and eastwards. Two things are striking about this mobility: it continued throughout the eighteenth century, and it was marked by a change towards more loosely defined and presumably more insecure property rights. Some, like van der Merwe ([1938] 1995), have argued that the continual movement was part of the culture of the frontier farmers, who were always on the move in search of better land and tended to want to keep the government at arm's length. However, the limited data available do not support this claim. Most of the settler-farmers did not move once they had established a farm. Guelke (1985), for example, notes that an evaluation of the loan farms in 1731 found that the average frontier farm had been occupied for twenty years or more. A more plausible explanation is that the expansion was driven by a combination of the growth of the settler population, the domination of pastoral farming and the vaguely formulated property rights. Physical and institutionally induced scarcity drove the process of continued expansion.

Although the VOC was not in control of this process, it soon realized the economic benefits of expansion. In 1705, Governor Willem Adriaan van der Stel wrote the following in a letter to the seventeen directors of the VOC, the Lords XVII:

> Also it has in truth been discovered and it is well worth understanding that since the freemen with their stock have moved so far inland, where there is much better pasture than hereabouts, the sheep and cattle have increased greatly in numbers, fatness and general condition so that meat at present is better than before and is sold more cheaply; and if the inhabitants were again enjoined from using these areas they would not know where to turn their stock, because the land in Stellenbosch, Drakenstein and also at the Cape for most part have been given out, is occupied and is bare of good pasture; from which it must follow, that livestock in place of multiplying and getting fatter would die and become thin to the great disadvantage of the Hon. Company as meat would certainly then become more expensive.
>
> (quoted in Guelke 1984: 15)

To gain some control over the developments and to increase the economic benefit they brought to the Company, the VOC began to require that farms in the interior be registered as 'loan farms', which meant that they were put under leasehold contracts that theoretically had to be renewed annually. To get a loan farm registered, a farmer had to pay a fixed fee of 12 rixdollars annually, which in 1732 was doubled to 24 rixdollars. This was still a fairly manageable alternative to buying a freehold farm. Before 1770, it was estimated that a settler would need at least 1,650 to 3,300 rixdollars as a down payment to buy a freehold farm. This could be compared with the 330 rixdollars it was estimated that a farmer needed to start up a farm at the frontier, in addition to the annual fee of 24 rixdollars (Guelke 1989). In the late 1770s, a local farmer's wife told the Swedish traveller Sparrman: 'You have already a wagon, oxen, and saddle horses; these are the chief things requisite in order to set up as a farmer; there are yet uncultivated places in the neighbourhood, proper either for pasturage or tillage, so that you may choose out of an extensive tract of land the spot that pleases you the best' (quoted in Neumark 1957: 13).

This is probably an exaggeration of the situation. Yet there is no doubt that a loan farm required less capital than buying freehold land in the south-western

Table 3.5 Net value of arable and pastoral farms (in guilders) at the Cape Colony, 1731–80.

Arable farms				Pastoral farms			
Year	No	Total value	Average value per farm	Year	No	Total Value	Average value per farm
1731–42	33	307,650	9,300	1731–42	24	90,220	3,760
1751–62	18	187,700	10,430	1751–62	36	126,230	3,500
1771–80	20	4,867,640	24,330	1771–80	27	77,000	2,850

Source: Guelke (1989: 94).

Cape. That you needed less capital to invest in pastoral farming in the interior is also reflected in the valuation of arable farms. Table 3.5 shows the average valuation of arable farms in the south-western Cape and pastoral farms at the frontier. The figures should be treated with a great deal of caution as there may be selection biases between the different periods which could affect the temporal trends of the values. The estimates do, however, reveal that throughout most of the eighteenth century, pastoral farms had a much lower value than arable farms. The value of the pastoral frontier farms also declined over time in comparison with the arable farms in the south-western Cape. This probably reflects the fact that less fertile land farther away from the main market in Cape Town was taken up for cultivation.

While farmers in the interior initially needed less capital to set up a farm, they found it much more costly to produce for the market. Cape historians have long debated the extent to which frontier farmers were dependent on selling produce at the market in Cape Town to secure their livelihoods. Some have argued that the typical frontier farmer was semi-nomadic and self-sufficient (Guelke 1989; van der Merwe [1938] 1995); others have held that they could not have survived without the market (Neumark 1957; van Duin and Ross 1987; Newton-King 1999). While scattered evidence for the former position can be found, most historians claim that although the farmers were able to meet some of their basic needs themselves, they were 'never entirely cut off from the exchange economy of the south-western Cape' (Newton-King 1992: 39). They had to have some source of income to pay the recognition fees required to marry, to baptize their children and so on. Indeed, even Guelke (1989: 88) acknowledges that the expansion of this group of frontier farmers could not have taken place without 'guns, gunpowder, wagons and other manufactured items obtainable only in exchange for the produce of the interior'. For these, they needed cash.

Throughout the eighteenth century, Cape Town was the main market. The frontier farmers occasionally took cattle and products such as butter to sell in Cape Town (Smith 1974). One contemporary traveller, Henry Lichtenstein, a German doctor of medicine and philosophy formerly in the Dutch service at the Cape of Good Hope, wrote optimistically about the large profits to be had from stock farming on the frontier. He estimated that some farmers had 'flocks to the amount of six or seven thousand' and reported that the livestock 'gave richer milk than elsewhere, and in greater abundance' with butter 'carried in great quantities to Cape Town', where it was 'always eagerly bought up' (Lichtenstein [1812] 1930: 10).

Meanwhile, the farther the settlers went into the interior, the more costly commercial farming would have become. For farmers who settled on the eastern frontier in the Graaff-Reinet district in the late eighteenth century, it could take three months to get their livestock and goods to Cape Town. They could only do this during the rainy season when there was enough water and pasture for the cattle and sheep they brought to market. In very dry years, of which there were many in the first two decades of the nineteenth century, wagon traffic between Graaff-Reinet and Cape Town almost came to a standstill (Beinart 2003). As Cilliers and Green (2018) show in their study of this district, only a very small proportion of the frontier farmers managed to accumulate significant levels of wealth. Furthermore, the distance to the market favoured pastoral farming over crop farming. Unlike crops, cattle could walk themselves to the market and hence pastoral farming was associated with significantly lower transportation costs compared to crop farming.

What is notable about the expansion of the frontier is that farms tended to be located quite far from each other, which is rather surprising. It is known that settlers commonly moved into the interior in groups (van der Merwe [1938] 1995), probably as a measure of protection from attacks by the Khoesan on the eastern and northern frontiers and the Khoesan and Xhosa on the eastern frontier. It is thus not obvious why farms were established so far apart. Already in the late eighteenth century, Company officials were expressing concerns about the tendency of settlers to disperse and live too far away from each other. The main concern was that this made the settlers vulnerable to attacks from the Khoesan (van der Merwe [1938] 1995). Spatial data that could capture the location of settler farms at the frontier is lacking. Rough estimates, however, show that farmers moved farther into the interior *before* there were signs that pastureland had become scarce. For example, as late as the end of the eighteenth century, there were only 142 farms in the well-endowed Swellendam district east of the south-western Cape. Assuming that the average size of the farms was 2,420 hectares (24.2 km²), that gives us a total farmed area of 3,436 km² within the space of 11,500 km² (the latter figure is taken from Guelke 1979). Given that much of the land in the Swellendam district was suitable for sheep farming, it seems unlikely that the settlers continued to migrate farther into the interior because land had become physically scarce. Still, that is what happened.

One reason for the dispersal is that frontier farmers needed to move their livestock across vast areas as the seasons changed. Although the settlers usually stayed for a long time on the farms they had established, this did not prevent them from moving their livestock. To quote Beinart, 'Afrikaner stockowners [i.e. settlers] are better described as practicing transhumance than nomadism, either sending animals away or moving between two or three fixed points during the year' (2003: 39). Farmers in the Karoo moved their livestock into the mountains during the dry summer months. During the very cold winters in the Sneeuberg in the northern part of Graaff-Reinet, the farmers moved their sheep down to the warm dry plains of Camdeboo (Beinart 2003). The seasonal nature of settler pastoral farming implies that we must treat the idea of strictly regulated property rights at the frontier with caution.

Although ecology and climate mattered, an institutional explanation for the dispersal should not be overlooked. To understand this, one must analyse how the loan-farm system worked in practice – an admittedly challenging task given the lack of accurate information. The loan farm was an extension of the already existing system of granting grazing posts, but became available for people who did not possess a freehold farm. Guelke (1984: 20) believed that the loan-farm system gave a settler 'a large but vaguely defined piece of land which he could use in any manner he saw fit'. The VOC had only a vague idea of the location of the loan farm, and it was not inspected before the grant was awarded. The leaseholder could use the land 'provided that he would not be a bother to someone already herding there' (van der Merwe [1938] 1995: 64). It was this vagueness, together with the quite common practice of owning more than one loan farm, that initially gave settlers enough space to move their livestock seasonally (Mitchell 2002).

Over time, as the number of settlers moving into the interior increased, stricter regulations were brought in to solve land disputes. Using the same principle that had been applied to control grazing posts, it was decided that the walking distance between two homesteads should be at least one hour. As with the grazing land, this meant that a settler could be granted a loan farm between two established farms only if the homesteads of those farms were more than two hours' walking distance apart. The regulation also required that the land of later arrivals be situated away from existing homesteads. This, together with the need to have access to water, meant that the farms were of many different shapes and the distance between homesteads was often much *more* than one hour's walk (van der Merwe [1938] 1995). Guelke (1984: 26) observed that 'the principle of individual grazing rights to land combined with the nature of much of the South African interior led to the dispersal of the stock farmers over an enormous area of land'.

The vague property rights reinforced an already ongoing process of dispersal. Settlers who arrived early at the frontier could take advantage of the system by locating their farms in such a way as to control more grazing land than stipulated by the regulations; those who arrived later were left with no alternative but to move farther into the interior. The question is why there was this shift from a legally secure property rights system in the south-western Cape to a system that was less secure on paper and required the leasehold contract to be renewed annually, thereby giving the settlers less control over their landed property. Intuitively, one would expect the reverse to happen. Insecure property rights would initially dominate as the colony was being established. Gradually, these would be transformed into more secure property rights as the financial and colonial authorities' administrative capacity increased and frontiers were moving towards closure. This did not happen at the Cape. Even more puzzling is that even when the VOC tried to strengthen the de jure rights of the loan-farm system, the settlers resisted. The seasonal nature of pastoral farming is probably part of the story, but here I will argue that in order to understand the preference for more vaguely defined systems at the frontier, one must acknowledge the role of Khoesan agency and the potential cost of conflict at the frontier.

Property rights and landed conflicts

Scholars like Shutte (1989) and Dye and La Croix (2020) argue that the move towards more insecure property rights was a deliberate strategy by the VOC to facilitate further expansion into the interior. By allowing settlers to expand the frontier under the loan-farm system, VOC officials could ensure a sufficient supply of livestock at a low cost. They did not have to invest in expensive and time-consuming land surveying and demarcation. To explain why the settlers accepted this shift, Dye and La Croix distinguish between 'inside' and 'outside' risk. The former refers to land disputes between settlers (for example, between established farmers and later arrivals) and the latter to land disputes between the settlers and the indigenous populations. They argue that the inside risk was smaller the farther the farms were located away from the commercial centre (in this case, Cape Town), while the outside risk was initially greater. However, over time – as the indigenous communities disintegrated and were weakened as a consequence of disease and the expansion of the colonial borders – the outside risk of conflicts over land diminished. The settlers therefore accepted the weakened property rights system as positing the least risk to their interests.

Although this is a valid argument, Dye and La Croix get the history wrong. They overestimate the role of the VOC and underestimate the conflicts over resources between settlers and the indigenous populations at the frontier. They, as well as Shutte (1989), are certainly right that it was in the interests of the VOC to keep the cost of the landed property rights system to a minimum. However, as I shall demonstrate in more depth below, the settlers at the frontier themselves preferred the loan-farm system – but not because the conflicts with the Khoesan had diminished, as Dye and La Croix argue. Quite the contrary: because the risk of such conflicts remained high.

Let us, however, begin with the potential risk of land disputes among settlers. One would assume that if such disputes were common, settlers would demand more secure property rights. Throughout the eighteenth century, there are no indications in the colonial records of serious conflicts over land among the settler population (van der Merwe [1938] 1995). Fisher (1984) concludes that the abundance of land meant that there was little competition over it and hence limited need for secure property rights. But while major conflicts were uncommon, disputes over the location of new farms did break out repeatedly (Guelke 1984; Robertson 1984). When they occurred, a committee consisting of *heemraden* (district officials) was set up for a field inspection of the disputed area. The committee would send its recommendation to the higher authorities, who would have the final say. The system of the loan farms, in which settlers were free to locate their farms where they liked as long as they were at least one hour's walking distance from an existing farm's grazing post, implied that the authorities decided in favour of those already settled. The criterion of one hour's walking distance between the homesteads was not always used to solve the disputes, however. In 1779, Anthony Rink complained to the VOC about Pieter Rossouw, arguing that by leasing a farm close to his own farm, Rossouw had harmed his access to both pasture and water. The VOC went out on an inspection and found that the distance between the homesteads was far enough, but that 'the poor conditions of the pasture on [Rossouw's land] consisting only of brambles and bushes, and without any suitable capacity of grazing nearby the farm in question, must be considered' (van der Merwe [1938] 1995: 66).

Under these conditions, where the rules of the game were uncertain and the system favoured those already settled, new arrivals often decided to locate their farms farther away than the regulated one hour's walk. This was a strategy for avoiding conflicts and the risk of losing the right to the land. In 1806, the travel writer Barrow reported that 'the stakes are so placed that, on an average throughout the colony, the farms are twice the distance, and consequently contain four times the quantity of land allowed by the Government' (quoted in van de Merwe [1938] 1995: 97). In that way, as already noted, the loan-farm system, with its unclear boundaries and the ever-present risk of conflict between settlers over the location of landed property, encouraged the dispersal of the farms and consequently the expansion of the borders. This does not explain why the settlers accepted weak property rights, however. Unlike Dye and La Croix (2020), I argue that the continual threat of clashes with the indigenous people made it rational for the settlers to opt for insecure property rights because they reduced the cost of such conflicts. Buying land was a significant fixed investment that farmers wanted to avoid as long as there was a risk that they may have to abandon their farm.

Dye and La Croix are correct in arguing that the powers of the indigenous people declined over time. In this, they follow a long tradition in Cape historiography. Marais, for example, argued that 'from the year 1689 onwards there was no resistance on the part of the Hottentots to the European advance' and that 'unlike the Bantu, they were surprisingly ready to barter away their cattle in exchange for copper, beads, tobacco and … brandy and arrack' (1957: 6–7). Van der Merwe ([1938] 1995) arrived at a similar conclusion, maintaining that it was only in 1770, when the European settlers first clashed with Xhosa on the eastern frontier, that they began to encounter obstacles to expansion in the form of resistance by indigenous people.

These interpretations, which largely treat the Khoesan as passive victims, have been questioned by scholars who have convincingly shown that Khoesan resistance was far more common than initially believed. As Marks argued, 'The pattern of violence and counter-violence, raid and counter-raid, punctuated every decade of the eighteenth century' (1972: 70). To frame it differently, social and economic conflicts did not disappear with the closing of the frontier; they took different forms. The VOC lacked the capacity to pacify the Khoesan.

As late as 1774, Martinus Adriaan Berg, the *landrost* of the Stellenbosch district, a former frontier area that had been closed for nearly sixty years, instructed Commandant Opperman to reduce the indigenous people to 'a permanent state of peace and quiet, or otherwise, in case of necessity, entirely destroy them' (quoted in Newton-King 1999: 105). The conflicts were not at the level of organized resistance. Rather the clashes occurred between individual Khoesan and settlers about access to grazing land, working conditions and so on. Khoesan farm labourers commonly played a key role in eighteenth-century uprisings against the colonial intruders and could switch during their lifetime from labourer to rebel (Malherbe 1978; Newton-King 1981).

At the frontiers, organized and war-like conflicts were more common and sometimes forced the Europeans to abandon their farms temporarily or permanently. In 1715, for example, a group of Khoesan living in the mountains around Land van Waveren attacked European farmers in an attempt to replenish their herds. They managed to leave with two hundred cattle and several thousand sheep (Newton-King 1999). In the 1730s, after a decade and a half of settler expansion into the Olifants River valley in the northwest of the colony, major conflicts arose between the Khoesan and the colonial intruders. In the early years of settlement in the area, the social relationship between the Khoesan and the settlers had been fluid and relatively peaceful. The Khoesan could continue as pastoralists alongside the Europeans. But as the years went by and more settlers arrived, the relationship became increasingly hierarchical and conflicts over land erupted. This led to organized resistance by the Khoesan. At least ten European farms were attacked and another forty-eight were abandoned in the late 1730s. Another incident occurred in the 1770s, when settlers had reached the Sneeuberg, in what ten years later would form the northern part of Graaff-Reinet district. They were attacked by the Khoesan, and many had to abandon their farms and move farther down south (Cilliers, Green and Ross 2021).

Meanwhile, less organized attacks occurred in parallel on the open frontier. In 1719, for example, seven hundred cattle were stolen from the cattle station at Riviersonderend and in the 1750s several attacks were recorded as the settlers went beyond the borders of Swellendam (Marks 1972; Penn 2005). Rumours of planned Khoesan attacks commonly spread among the settlers. In 1712, it was reported that no fewer than five thousand of the Great Namaqua were moving towards the Olifants River at the northwest frontier. The VOC found no signs of this and the local Khoesan claimed never to have heard of any planned attack (Penn 2005). Such recurrent rumours show that the settler-farmers were aware and afraid of the risk of being attacked.

The settlers were far from innocent. Not only did they give themselves the right to farm on land that was already being used by indigenous pastoral farmers, they also regularly stole cattle from the Khoesan and treated the Khoesan labourers with a significant degree of brutality (Newton-King 1999). The reason I focus on Khoesan resistance and attacks is that it helps us understand why Europeans at the frontier preferred to access land under a loan-farm system rather than under a system of private freehold property rights. The VOC's failed attempt to reform the loan-farm system constitutes evidence of this. In 1732, the authorities introduced a quitrent system. The plan was to further promote settler farming by allowing settlers to extend the size of their loan farms by leasing land annexed to their own farm on a fifteen-year contract. The rent they paid would differ according to the quality of the land. This opportunity was not met with any enthusiasm by the settler-farmers. Only thirty-five grants were issued before the system was abandoned (Fisher 1984).

The pattern of attacks and counter-attacks made it necessary for the settlers to keep the cost of fixed capital investment as low as possible. Where there is a constant risk of losing landed property, a person naturally wishes to reduce the fixed cost of acquiring that property. I thus argue, contrary to the claims made by Dye and La Croix (2020), that it was not the absence of resistance from the Khoesan that made the loan-farm system attractive to the settlers; rather, it was the threat posed by the indigenous people that made the system so attractive that it lasted for more than a hundred years. The reason the VOC failed to make the one-year renewable loan-farm system more secure was that as long as there was a high risk of conflict with the indigenous people, the farmers remained reluctant to sign any long-term leases or to buy land outright, as they would in a system of freehold property.

Expansion and inheritance

As I explained in Chapter 1, the system of inheritance mattered for both the concentration of landed wealth and the dispersal of farms. In Chapter 5, I focus on the former. In this section, I show how the system of partible inheritance further facilitated the expansion of the border. According to the Roman-Dutch law that was used at the Cape, when a husband or wife died, the surviving spouse received one-half to two-thirds of the property and the rest was equally divided among the children. The law gave each heir the right to a 'legitimate portion' of the estate, which prevented property owners from disinheriting heirs (Dooling 2005). The implication of such a system, as explained by Ross (1993: 141), was that

> property was divided and redivided at regular intervals ... This entailed either that the farm as a running concern would be sold, and the proceeds divided among the heirs, or that a valuation would be made of the estate with the heirs receiving their portions in cash. In the latter case, the survivor would in all probability be forced to take out a loan to pay off his or her children and stepchildren.

Subdivision meant that the farms became smaller over time. To avoid this, one of the survivors could buy the entire farm from the other heirs. This required access to credit, which was difficult to obtain without resources to use as collateral, such as farm equipment or slaves. This leads Dooling (2005) to conclude that the practice of settlers buying each other out was uncommon, with the exception of the most affluent, who owned more than one farm. In most cases, the property of the deceased was instead auctioned. Even heirs of fairly affluent owners of freehold farms would auction the whole farm instead of keeping it in the family. Wolwedans, one of the biggest wheat farms in the Stellenbosch district, changed hands nine times between 1751 and 1835. A neighbouring farm faced similar turnover, with five transfers between 1757 and 1815, and the Hoornbosch farms changed hands sixteen times between 1751 to 1835, roughly every fifth year (Dooling 2005).

At the frontiers, where the loan-farm system dominated, subdivision of land was in practice impossible. The loan farm was based on two criteria: a fixed annual rent stipulated in a lease contract between the VOC and an individual settler, and, at least in theory, a fixed size of the farm (a minimum of one hour's walk between the homesteads of two farms). These criteria in effect prevented the subdivision of land. For people at the frontier, there were two alternatives: either to take over a contract and buy others out, or to auction off the farm equipment, including slaves. The latter was the best option for most people if they lacked sufficient capital to buy one another out.

Independently of whether the heirs were bought out or the whole farm was auctioned, the capital received per child would in any case be insufficient to buy a new farm or make significant capital investments, such as purchasing slaves (see Chapter 4 in this book, as well as du Plessis, Jansen and von Fintel 2013). For most people, both those who grew up on freehold farms and those who grew up on loan farms, moving and establishing their own farms was the main option left. As explained above, freehold farms were much more valuable than the loan farms, so it seems reasonable that only a very few of the wealthiest could re-establish themselves by buying a freehold farm. Buying access to a loan farm was easier, but still required access to credit, which was scarce at the time. Instead, the younger generation migrated farther into the interior to establish their own farms.

Property rights and agricultural investments

In 'new' institutional economics and economic history, a well-defined and secure property rights system (i.e. private property rights) is often identified as a key institution for enhancing long-term economic development (North and Thomas 1973; Feder and Feeny 1991; de Soto 2000; Acemoglu, Autor and Lyle 2004). The argument is that secure property rights create incentives for productive investment and facilitate capital accumulation by reducing the risk of getting the land confiscated. With this in mind, one would expect agricultural investments to be significantly lower on the loan farms than on the freehold farms.

The extent to which freehold farms at the Cape provided a more secure form of property rights, and thereby promoted agricultural investments more than loan farms did, is ultimately an empirical question. Scholars like Guelke (1974), Newton-King (1999) and Penn (2005) have argued that in practice there was little difference between the freehold and the loan-farm system. Both provided secure property rights. To quote Penn, 'in practice loan farms became the private and virtually inalienable property of their owners' (2005: 43). Although the lessee did not own the land, he or she had the rights to all improvements made on it, including buildings and agricultural equipment. Confiscation was extremely rare. Even in cases in which farmers did not follow the stipulations and renew their licences on an annual basis, the VOC did not take action to force the farmer to leave the land (van der Merwe [1938] 1995). Smith (1974: 9) notes that 'while the Company did not legally surrender its right to take back a loan farm, this was so seldom done that the *Boers* came to accept that the farms were their own, until they decided to leave; even the failure to pay recognition fees did not result in the revocation of a permit'.

Despite not being exposed to any real threat of confiscation on the part of the VOC, loan farmers at the frontier invested less in their farms than farmers in the south-western Cape did. Guelke (1989: 86) found that the value of houses and other fixed improvements averaged less than 300 to 500 rixdollars on loan farms compared to 1,700 to 3,300 rixdollars on freehold farms. How can we explain this gap? Swanepoel (2017) investigated whether this difference was because the loan-farm property rights system prevented these investments or because loan farmers were on average less wealthy and hence spent less on them. Using probate inventories, she identified types of farms, their value and the farmers' levels of debt. The reports of value were inconsistent and therefore difficult to use, so she used level of debt as a proxy for wealth, assuming that there was a positive correlation between wealth and debt. There are good reasons for this assumption. Several scholars have found that wealthier people in pre-industrial societies were also more indebted (e.g. Muldrew 2012; Ogilvie, Küpker and Maegraith 2012). Swanepoel found that freehold farmers were on average more indebted, which would support the view that it was the de jure rights that mattered. The argument is that a freehold farmer could – unlike a holder of a loan farm – use land as collateral to access credit that could be used for farm investments.

However, as Swanepoel rightly recognized, the reverse may also be true: freehold farmers may have had more debts because they needed credit to buy the farm. It could also be, as argued by Guelke and Malherbe (1989), that if the freehold farmers were wealthier, it was not because of the property rights system, but because of their close proximity to Cape Town. The data did not allow Swanepoel to investigate whether distance to Cape Town was the main factor that determined differences in wealth. However, by using the debt level of the first born, she was able to control the extent to which it was the property rights system that determined levels of wealth. The first born were on average wealthier and when they were included in the regression the correlation between freehold farms and levels of debts became insignificant.

Although we cannot observe this directly, Swanepoel's study does seem to suggest that the difference in property rights systems did not have any major effects on debts. This is something of a puzzle because of the scattered evidence that loan farmers invested less in fixed improvements on their farms. The puzzle can be solved if we shift our focus from the property rights systems per se and look instead at the differences between an open and a closed frontier. I argued earlier that farmers preferred to lease land on an annual basis because they feared losing their property in the event of conflicts with the indigenous populations. For the same reason, investments in fixed equipment like buildings were limited as long as the frontier was open and the economic and political situation uncertain. Credit was instead used for other types of agriculture-related investments and for smoothing out consumption patterns among the pastoral farmers at the frontier. Long distances to the market meant that wealthier farmers invested more in mobile assets like carts, wagons and horses, as Cilliers and Green (2018) argue was the case in Graaff-Reinet.

To conclude, there is little evidence that loan farms – the less secure property rights system – impeded agricultural investment, probably because the risk of land being confiscated by the VOC was very low. The difference in the pattern of investments probably reflected the fact that most of the loan farms were located on the open frontier, where farmers were at risk of losing property in times of conflict with the Khoesan, rather than differences in the property rights systems.

Conclusion

As with settler societies in other parts of the world, the history of the Cape Colony was to a large extent the history of expanding frontiers. Scholars have argued that the expansion of the borders of settler colonies was an effect of the continuous immigration of Europeans to the colonies. The growth of the population made land scarce, forcing arriving settlers to move past the existing frontier in search of fresh land. The inflow of Europeans and the ability to expand the land frontier enabled settler economies to pursue a path of extensive economic growth. Cape historians paint a similar picture of the first 150 years of the colony, with one modification: that the expansion of the frontier was caused not by immigration but by an extensive growth in the settler population already present in the colony. While I do not question the importance of population growth for understanding the expansion of the frontier, I argue in this chapter that the explanation needs to be modified. Factor endowments and geography played an important role in the dispersion of settler-farmers, but to fully grasp the dynamics we also have to take the evolution of property rights systems into account.

It is tempting to see this expansion as a planned process whereby the VOC sought to enlarge the territory it controlled in order to enhance its profits. Such a claim lacks historical evidence. As I argue in Chapter 6, the VOC never managed to make the Cape Colony a profitable enterprise. On the contrary, the Company hardly managed to make ends meet. So how would we then explain the expansion of the colonial frontier? In our case, it was largely a process induced by the settlers, but in which the actions of the Khoesan played a part. A major reason for the continued expansion was the fluid landed property rights system. With the exception of the south-western Cape, the property rights were on paper insecure and in practice fluid. Farmers leased land on an annual basis with a risk – in theory – that the VOC would withdraw the contract. In practice, this never happened, and one should not exaggerate the insecurity of the leasehold system. Contracts were hardly ever cancelled. What mattered was the fluidity. Land was not surveyed or clearly demarcated. This made the borders between farms fuzzy. In order to avoid land disputes, settler-farmers spread themselves out over vast areas.

The VOC's weak administrative and financial capacity can explain why the system of property rights evolved as it did in the initial years, but not why it persisted throughout the 150 years that the VOC governed the colony. Although it remained poor, the VOC's administrative capacity did improve over time. The persistence of the insecure and fluid system was instead a consequence of the potential risk the settler-farmers faced in being chased away by the indigenous people. As long as the frontier was not completely closed, this was a real risk. The many frontier wars bear witness to this. Under these circumstances, settler-farmers wanted to keep the fixed investments in land as low as possible. Buying land or getting your leasehold converted to clearly demarcated freehold property was costly. Settler-farmers were not ready to make such investments as long as they faced a risk that they could lose their land. The consequence was a continued dispersion of settler farms and a continuous expansion of the colonial frontier.

4

Was the Cape Colony a slave economy?

Introduction

Shortly after the VOC established its trading post, it began to import slaves. Between 1652 and 1808, about sixty-three thousand slaves were imported from Asia and elsewhere in Africa. Numerous scholars have argued that the use of slaves constituted a major contribution to the growth of European settlement at the Cape (Legassick 1980; Worden 1985; Armstrong and Worden 1989; Feinstein 2005; Worden and Groenewald 2005). In order to explain the widespread use of slavery, authors point at the prevailing factor endowments: the abundance of land and the scarcity of labour (Worden 1985; Feinstein 2005; Green 2014). Though scholars do not always refer to it explicitly, this reasoning is inspired by the so-called Nieboer-Domar hypothesis (Nieboer 1900; Domar 1970). This hypothesis holds that in cases of land abundance and an absence of barriers for people to access land, people will take up farming instead of selling their labour, forcing landlords in need of additional labour to pay wages so high that it eats up any potential profits. Landlords will thus instead resort to the use of coercion (slavery) to access labour. As the enslavement of the Khoesan was not allowed, settler-farmers instead became dependent upon the use of imported slave labour.

In this chapter, I reassess the economic role of slavery at the Cape and argue that previous literature partly exaggerates the role of slave labour and simultaneously underestimates the importance of indigenous Khoesan labour. The profitability of using slaves depended upon how it could be combined with other forms of labour, including Khoesan wage labour. Further, the economic role of slavery cannot be narrowly understood in terms of labour input. While land–labour ratios can explain the emergence of slavery in part, its persistence cannot fully be grasped through a narrow focus on slavery as labour. Inspired by recent research by Martins (2020b) and Martins and Green (2021), I make the case in this chapter that we need to acknowledge the role of slaves as not simply another coercive labour arrangement, but as a system that gave slaveholders a complete right over a mobile property. This allowed the owners not only to extract labour from the slaves, but also to use it to access capital. The latter is key to understanding the spread and persistence of slavery at the Cape.

The Cape as a slave economy

There is a consensus in the scholarly literature that the Cape was a slave economy and that slaves played a crucial role in the growth of settler agriculture (Worden 1985; Armstrong and Worden 1989; Feinstein 2005; Worden and Groenewald 2005; Legassick and Ross 2012). I have no reason to question the importance of slavery at the Cape. Having the right to own people was an integral part of Cape society and contributed decisively to shaping the cultural, social and political fabric of the colony. Yet the fact that slavery existed and was practiced does not automatically mean that the Cape Colony was a *slave economy* as such. To quote Garnsey (1996: 2):

> There have been slaves in many societies, but very few slave societies. In a genuine slave society (as distinct from a society with slaves, or a slave-owning society), slaves are numerous, but the crucial issue is not slave numbers, but whether slaves play a vital role in production.

Nieboer (1900) distinguished between slavery in general and slavery as an industrial system, the latter referring to a system in which slavery was required for the establishment and persistence of profitable farming. The question is: was this the case for the Cape Colony? In scholarly work on the economics of slavery, the plantation economies of the Americas are often seen as classic examples of agricultural and slave-based settler economies. In them, landowners ran their plantations, producing goods for the world market, with a large-scale use of slaves who lived apart from the landowner and his family in separate compounds (Engerman and Sokoloff 2005). Taking the Americas as a point of departure, we find that the Cape Colony was similar in some regards, but also strikingly different. Just as in the slave economies of the Americas, slave ownership in the Cape was widespread. In 1773, 96.5 per cent of all farmers in the Cape district had at least one slave, while in Stellenbosch and Drakenstein it was around 70 per cent. The farther farms were located away from Cape Town, the fewer the number of slaves in them. In Swellendam district, west of the south-western Cape, 51 per cent had at least one slave. On the eastern frontier, less than 30 per cent of the settlers were in possession of slaves by the end of the eighteenth century. These figures could be compared with 1860 South Carolina and Mississippi, the two American states with the most widespread use of slaves, where about one-half of the free population were slaveholders (Worden 1985). Furthermore, the size of the slave population relative to the entire settler population in the Cape was high. In 1701, slaves accounted for 63 per cent of the total settler/slave population. By 1741, it had dropped to 42 per cent. Thereafter it increased modestly and constituted 45 per cent of the settler/slave population at the end of the century (calculations made by author based on estimates from van Duin and Ross 1987 and Shell 1994). The share is similar to those in South Carolina (Worden 1985).

Yet, when one looks at the average number of slaves per farm at the Cape, the similarities with the plantations in the Americas disappears. On average, the number of slaves per farm at the Cape was small. By the mid-eighteenth century more than 50 per cent of farmers held fewer than five slaves. This could be compared with the 'median sugar estate' in Jamaica, which between 1741 and 1745 held an average of 99 slaves, increasing to 204 for the years 1771 to 1775 (Fourie 2013b). In the United States, on the other hand, a little less than half of the slaveholders in the American South held five slaves or less (Inter-university Consortium for Political and Social Research 2005).

Following Nieboer's (1900) definition of a slave economy, one would expect slavery to significantly contribute to surplus production at the Cape. Armstrong and Worden (1989) suggest a strong positive correlation between slave ownership and yields of wine and wheat. Not only Cape historians but also earlier observers highlighted the importance of slavery for the economy. Mentzel, a visitor to the Cape, stated in the 1730s that 'the expansion of the colony demands an ever increasing number of slaves. Every farmer requires many more slaves than members of his own household to grow his crops and develop his land' (Mentzel 1925–44 vol. II: 126). Meanwhile, estimates provided by Fourie (2013b) reveal that growth in the number of slaves outpaced the growth of agricultural output throughout the eighteenth century, and that settlers' investment in slavery was not, necessarily, essential to agricultural growth.

Worden (1985) is the only scholar to have analysed the economics of slavery at the Cape in detail. His findings are interesting as they stand in contradiction with what we would expect to find. He begins by making the case that many factors militated against the profitable exploitation of slave labour. First, pastoral farming played an important role, as I showed in Chapter 3. In a pastoral economy, the demand for slaves would be limited due to overall low demand of labour and high enforcement costs as the slaves could easily escape their captivity when they are out herding livestock. Second, an extensive slack season in crop farming at the Cape made the use of slave labour expensive. As a fixed investment, the farmer had to ensure that the slaves were kept as busy as possible throughout the year. One possibility was to explore economies of scope by employing slaves in proto-industrial activities (Fourie 2013a). This certainly happened but most of the proto-industrial production was used for consumption and not sold on the market. Lastly, as the farms were comparatively small, the Cape settlers could not benefit from economies of scale to the same extent as could plantation owners in America. Together, these factors led Worden to conclude that it is far from obvious that slave labour at the Cape would have been profitable. This is echoed in Nieboer's (1900) own work, in which he concludes that slavery, independently of land–labour ratios, is less likely to exist or persist in agricultural societies that mainly produce cereals and have limited export markets.

Having said that, Worden's calculations find that the rate of return for slaves in the Cape was on par with estimates from the plantations in the New World (1985; see also in more detail below). This high rate of return is surprising given the factors that Worden himself lists, which suggest that it would have been difficult to exploit slaves profitably. In what follows, I show that Worden's calculations likely overestimate the productivity of slave labour as they ignore the role played by indigenous people. I will argue that the profitability of slave labour was partly determined by how this form of labour could be combined with indigenous labour. Equally important, and partly at odds with previous literature, I argue that the profitability of slavery at the Cape cannot be captured by narrowly focusing on slaves as a labour input. Equally important was the role of slaves as a capital investment.

The rise of slavery at the Cape

While the Nieboer-Domar hypothesis correctly identified that slavery and/ or forced labour is more likely to exist and persist in societies characterized by low land–labour ratios, it cannot explain why slavery develops in the first place. Nieboer himself admits that the theory depends on slavery already being 'invented' (1900: 425). This implies that slavery as a political, social and/or cultural institution must already be present in a society for it to develop into an economic institution as Nieboer defined it.

This is confirmed in the case of the Cape. As Shell (1994) showed, slaves were initially brought to the Cape not to be employed as farm workers but as VOC labourers. The VOC used the slaves in the construction of its fort and buildings, but also for fishing, saltworks and brickmaking and domestic tasks (Böesken 1977; Armstrong 1979). Of the 230 slaves who arrived in the Cape in 1659, seventy-nine were sold to settlers, of which only a minority were farmers (Schoeman 2007). In 1670, the VOC had 310 slaves while the settlers in total possessed 191 slaves. The majority of the slave-owning settlers were involved in trade and basic urban services. It was not until after 1700, when European settler agriculture took off and the frontier expanded, that the number of slaves possessed by settlers first exceeded those held by the Company. By 1750, settlers' slaves outnumbered Company slaves by more than ten to one (Armstrong 1979). That the use of slaves as farm labourers would not take off until settler farming began its expansion is expected and does not refute the Nieboer-Domar hypothesis. However, that slavery became an important solution to the labour shortages that settler-farmers faced partly depended on the fact that slavery as an institution was already present at the Cape. It was far from obvious in the mid-seventeenth century that importation of slaves would become a strategy of the VOC.

The use of imported slaves was not the only option considered by the VOC in the early colonial years, or even the preferred alternative. At an early stage, bringing in European and Chinese labourers was discussed as a possible solution. European immigrants were indeed employed as VOC servants, but it was soon concluded that Europeans constituted a relative expensive form of labour. Large-scale immigration of Chinese contractual workers was also turned down by the Lords XVII as it was argued that few Chinese would be interested and those who did sign up were likely to leave for Batavia to become traders as soon as the contractual period was over (Worden 1985: 8–9). A third alternative proposed by the VOC in 1654 was to enslave the indigenous Cape population. This came out of the frustration of failing to establish regular trading contacts with the Khoesan. As shall be shown in more detail below, the use of coercion to control Khoesan labour was not uncommon, but the Lords XVII strictly forbade the VOC in the Cape to enslave the indigenous population (Worden 1985). The chief reason was the calculation that this would endanger the trade with the Khoe, which in turn would reduce the supply of provisions for passing ships.

Lacking reliable alternatives, Governor van Riebeck began to ask the Lords XVII for permission to import slaves. While slave trading was not a major economic activity of the Company, its operatives nonetheless did participate in enslavement – to various degrees – in all of their Asian possessions (Armstrong 1979). The first three governors of the Cape – van Riebeeck, Wagenaer and van der Stel – had all lived and worked for the VOC in the East and had therefore come into contact and had some knowledge of slavery and the slave trade (Schoeman 2007). Given that they could not afford to employ European immigrants, were not supported in their attempts to attract Chinese contract workers and were forbidden to enslave the indigenous population, they suggested that the importation of slaves could be the solution to the labour problems the VOC faced. The Lords XVII were reluctant, arguing that slaves were needed in Batavia instead. But the governors van Riebeeck, Wagenaer and van der Stel did not give up and were eventually allowed to import slaves, though on a small scale. Initially, the slaves were imported from Dahomey, which lay within the monopoly area of the Dutch East Indian Company. A few slaves were also imported from Angola. After 1658, slaves were mainly imported from Madagascar, Mozambique, the East African coast and Zanzibar (Armstrong and Worden 1989). Reliance on imported slaves was far from optimal for the VOC. Their rate of mortality was high. Between the years 1667 to 1678, mortality among the imported slaves was as high as 39 per cent per year (Armstrong and Worden 1989).

Settler farmers began to invest in slavery once settler farming began to yield profits. It is far from obvious whether this would have happened if the VOC at the Cape had not already begun importing slaves. The Company's already-existing slave-trade activities were an important precondition for the rise of slavery as an economic institution in the colony. The reliance on slave imports from the VOC was temporary. Most settlers did not buy slaves through VOC channels during the eighteenth century. Instead, they were allowed to import slaves privately upon payment of a fee to the *fiscal*, the Company's law officer. The VOC imported in total about three thousand slaves during the eighteenth century. This could be compared with the 58,500 slaves that were privately imported from the colony's inception in 1652 until slave imports were banned in 1807 (Legassick and Ross 2012).

Following Nieboer's prediction, we should expect slaves to be more common on arable than on pastoral farms. We lack data for the entire colony, but the

Table 4.1 Mean holding of adult male slaves by district and farming types, 1705–99/1800 (selected years).

Year	Cape district			Stellenbosch district			Drakenstein district			Swellendam district
	All farmers	Arable farmers	Pastoral farmers	All farmers	Arable farmers	Pastoral farmers	All farmers	Arable farmers	Pastoral farmers	Pastoral farmers
1705	6.85	8.35	2.37	2.42	2.62	0.25	0.88	1.00	0.08	
1723	11.49	15.86	4.34	3.80	6.14	0.4	2.89	3.59	0.45	
1731	12.88	14.68	5.66	6.17	7.38	1.2	3.8	4.87	1.56	
1741	19.34	22.07	7.26	6.29	8.45	2.64	3.93	5.51	2.11	
1752	11.31	12.65	5.36	5.09	7.02	1.52	3.5	4.57	1.65	1.65
1762	11.41	14.17	5.50	6.76	9.98	1.84	3.65	6.00	1.93	1.78
1773	11.68	12.89	7.06	5.41	8.33	2.16	3.65	6.51	1.89	1.84
1797/8				6.58	9.01	2.25	4.84	7.84	1.71	
1799/1800	15.75	16.5	11.96							

Source: Worden (1985: 29).

data we do have largely confirms this view. Table 4.1 shows the distribution of slaveholding on arable and pastoral farms in the Cape and in the Stellenbosch, Drakenstein and Swellendam districts from 1705 to 1800. In all districts, the mean holding of adult male slaves is indeed lower on the pastoral farms than on the arable farms.

Table 4.1 also reveals that the closer the farms were, geographically, to Cape Town (at the time, the only market for agricultural produce in the colony), the larger the mean size of slaveholding. Indeed, the mean holding of slaves on pastoral farms in the Cape district was larger than for the arable farms in Drakenstein. Farther away, at the frontier, the mean holding of slaves were even smaller. In Graaff-Reinet – a district established in 1786 at the eastern frontier – the mean number of slaves remained around one per farm for the period from 1798 to 1828 (Cilliers and Green 2018). This is also in line with expectations as farms in the commercial south-western Cape on average were more profitable than those farther into the interior.

It seems intuitive to assume that wealthier farmers were likely to have more slaves. Yet it is difficult to establish this empirically, as most studies that analyse wealth distribution across the settler population include slaves as a wealth variable (Guelke and Shell 1983; Ross 1999; Dooling 2005; Fourie and von Fintel 2010a, 2011; Cilliers and Green 2018). What can be determined for certain, as I discuss in Chapter 5, is that the settler farming community was highly stratified. This is also noted in the uneven distribution of slaveholdings, as shown in Table 4.2. The vast majority owned nine slaves or less, while only a tiny number of settlers were in possession of more than twenty slaves each. Over time, the largest slaveholders and those who held between ten and nineteen slaves increased in proportion to the smallest slaveowners, which indicates that some managed to accumulate more slaves.

So far, it seems that the case of Cape Colony largely confirms the Nieboer-Domar hypothesis. Due to low land–labour ratios, slavery gradually developed into a viable solution to the problem of labour shortages. Initially, only the wealthiest could afford to invest in slaves, but over time more and more farmers became slaveholders, although at a modest scale. The crucial question is: did these investments make economic sense from the landholders' point of view? Given the factors mentioned by Worden (1985) – dominance of pastoral farming, fairly small farms and limited demand on the world market for Cape produce – it is far from obvious that investments in slave labour were profitable.

Table 4.2 Percentage distribution of holdings of adult male slaves by district, 1705–99/1800 (selected years).

Year	Cape district			Stellenbosch district			Drakenstein district		
	1 to 9	10 to 19	> 20	1 to 9	10 to 19	> 20	1 to 9	10 to 19	> 20
1705	85.8	10.7	3.5	84.2	15.8	0	97.5	2.5	0
1723	61.5	25.0	13.5	77.1	12.5	10.4	94.2	4.8	1.0
1731	53.3	27.6	19.1	70.8	16.9	12.3	88.3	10.4	1.3
1741	54.3	31.1	23.6	73.2	15.5	11.3	87.6	10.0	2.4
1752	55.0	24.8	20.2	83.7	11.9	4.4	92.1	6.4	1.5
1762	56.0	31.4	12.6	76.3	15.0	8.7	90.5	9.1	0.4
1773	53.0	31.8	15.2	83.3	12.1	4.6	87.3	12.1	0.6
1797/8				70.6	20.7	8.7	76	19.5	4.5
1799/1800	31.8	41.6	26.6						

Source: Worden (1985: 32).

The economics of slave labour

Scholars writing on slavery at the Cape have often argued that it was the preferred system because the cost of slaves was significantly lower than the cost of employing European labour. This view is also echoed in VOC reports. In 1717, Fiscal Cornelis van Beaumont wrote:

> Each labourer's wage was reckoned at the rate of a soldier's pay – ƒ9 per month – for he would hardly accept less even for work done by slaves, add to this the cost of his board and further emoluments, and a great difference will be found, as a slave cost annually (everything included) about ƒ40. Set against this the fact that the emoluments of a soldier vary from 8 to 10 gulden, let alone the wages which the Company would have to pay. Further, one will not find Europeans of nearly as much use as slaves, especially in the daily menial tasks; besides it is more fitting that slaves rather than Europeans should be used.
>
> (quoted in Schoeman 2007: 196)

The latter point – the unwillingness of Europeans to perform the hard work of slaves – was repeatedly brought up. In 1699, Captain-Lieutenant K. J. Slotsboo remarked that 'no matter how poor a [European] is, he will not accustom himself to perform the work of the slaves, as he thinks in this way to distinguish himself from a slave. Moreover, the fact that they have left their country makes them think that they should lead an easier life than at home' (quoted in Schoeman 2007: 197). A hundred years later, Fiscal W. W. van Rijneveld concluded that slavery had become a 'necessary evil, that cannot be removed without sacrificing the Colony, and perhaps the poor slaves themselves that are in it' (quoted in Schoeman 2012: 324).

Not everyone agreed that slave labour was cheap. Captain Dominique Pasques de Chavonnes, the nephew of the Governor, concluded in the late seventeenth century that European labour would be cheaper. He argued that an ordinary slave would cost 80 to 150 rixdollars and for an enslaved herdsman the price would be 150 to 300 rixdollars. To this there were additional costs of clothing and feeding as well as 'the never-ending sickness, accidents, maimings, deaths and burials and whatever is stolen by this class or person, and the fact that three slaves are required to do the work of two Europeans' (quoted in Schoeman 2007: 198). A few observers claimed that slavery made Europeans lazy and hindered the Cape's economic development. In 1743, Baron von Imhoff, a minor nobleman who had spent sixteen years in service of the Company, claimed that 'a carpenter each earns from eight to nine schellingen a day and in addition receives food and drink, and withal does not do as much as a half-trained artisan in Europe'. This was, according to him, a 'burden that the Colony could not bear'. It was devastating, especially for the development of agriculture in the colony. It would have been much better, according to Imhoff, if the colony in its early years had tried to attract European labourers, instead of importing slaves (Schoeman 2012: 326–7). These two examples represent exceptions, however. Most contemporary witnesses agreed on the benefits of using imported slaves over European immigrants as a source of farm labour.

That slaves were cheaper than European labour does not mean that it was inexpensive for farmers to acquire them. Data on slave prices are imperfect. The best source available are the auction rolls, which give the price of slaves that were sold upon the death of his or her owner. Unfortunately, the auction rolls do not provide information on the health and status of the slave sold. They do, however, provide the prices of all slaves sold at the farm, which enable us to identify the price range for each year. Table 4.3 shows the percentage distribution and median price of slaves from the auction rolls. The price of slaves varied significantly across time and space. The price changes were, according to Worden, closely

Table 4.3 Percentage distribution and median price of adult male slaves sold at rural auctions in rixdollars, 1682–1795.

Year	Total number	1–99	100–99	200–99	300–99	400–99	500–99	600–99	700–99	800–99	900–99	> 1,000
1692–1714	103	29.1	62.1	8.8	0	0	0	0	0	0	0	103
1715–21	67	16.4	50.7	28.3	4.6	0	0	0	0	0	0	130
1722–9	131	38.2	48.8	12.2	0.8	0	0	0	0	0	0	105
1730–7	197	21.3	58.8	13.2	5.0	1.0	0	0.7	0	0	0	134
1738–47	151	32.4	44.4	16.5	5.9	0.8	0	0	0	0	0	120
1748–56	123	17.8	40.6	30.9	6.5	1.8	0	0	0	0	0	192
1757–64	123	17.0	52.0	17.9	4.1	6.5	1.6	0.9	0	0	0	156
1765–72	219	18.7	47.5	20.1	9.1	4.1	0.5	0	0	0	0	163
1773–9	175	13.7	35.4	28.0	14.9	4.6	3.4	0	0	0	0	195
1780–4	189	3.3	16.6	23.2	19.8	14.4	7.2	6.1	2.2	0	5.5	310
1785–90	199	6.5	19.1	19.1	23.1	14.6	4.5	7.6	1.5	1.5	2.5	305
1791–5	201	5.4	21.9	21.9	26.4	16.9	6	2.5	1.5	0.5	1.0	345

Source: Worden (1985: 74).

related to factors of demand and supply. The median price rose gradually until 1740 and more sharply in the 1740s and 1750s due to a shortage of supply caused by increased slave mortality as a result of an epidemic of gastroenteritis and possibly also measles. The price increase in the 1780s was caused by inflation together with a cutback in slave imports (Worden 1985).

To put the prices of slaves in context, we can compare them with the average incomes of the settler-farmers. We lack reliable data on settler farm incomes, but rough estimates by Fourie and von Fintel (2010a) show an average annual income of 192 rixdollars in 1723 and 107 rixdollars in 1757. This would allow the purchase of roughly one slave of 'lower quality'. Income stratification was significant (see the more detailed discussion of this in Chapter 5) and groups of farmers earned significantly above the average income. However, for the broad masses of settler-farmers, buying a slave represented a considerable investment.

The long-term trend of slave prices reveals a significant increase, which has to be understood in the context of the VOC's mercantilist trade policies. As I discuss in Chapter 6, the VOC bought some of the wine, wheat and livestock at administratively set prices while the rest was purchased by individual settlers with which it contracted. The price offered by the VOC was stable for wine while it modestly declined for wheat during the eighteenth century. Prices paid by the contractors fluctuated more. The price of wheat was lower than the VOC price throughout the period, while the price of wine was higher after 1740. While the prices paid by the VOC stagnated, the prices paid by the contracted traders did not increase at the same rate as the price of slaves (see Table 4.4), suggesting that the returns to slave labour decreased over time.

This begs the question: why continue to invest in slaves that were expensive and whose returns decreased over time? It seems plausible that farmers would not have continued to practice enslavement if slaves were not a profitable investment. But it is difficult to establish any precise estimate of the profitability of slaves, for two reasons. First, we do not know for sure what type of work the slaves were doing. Some qualitative evidence gives us examples of the farm tasks slaves were engaged in, but it is difficult to generalize from these observations. Second, our knowledge of the role of indigenous Khoesan farm workers is rather limited. Due to lack of quantifiable data, scholars have until recently excluded them from any assessment of the profitability of slaves.

Worden (1985) is to my knowledge the only scholar who has tried to systematically assess the productivity of slave labour at the Cape on a few

Table 4.4 Average price of agrarian produce at public auctions and Official Company price (in rixdollars), 1716–1800 (selected years).

Year	Price			
	Wheat (per muid)		White wine (per leaguer)	
	Auction	VOC	Auction	VOC
1716	2.0	2.6	21	27
1720	2.2	2.6	22	27
1730	2.4	2.6	26	27
1740	2.4	2.6	28	27
1750	1.6	2.5	30	27
1760	1.5	2.5	38	27
1770	1.0	2.5	22	27
1780	2.4	2.5	38	27
1790	2.6	2.5	35	27
1800	2.8	2.5	30	27

Source: Worden (1985: 69).

selected farms for which contemporary sources do exist. These estimates reveal rates of return of between 5 and 11 per cent, which equal those found in the Caribbean and in the American South. However, as Worden himself admits, the estimates must be treated with a great deal of caution, for two reasons. First, the few selected farms represent the larger and more profitable ones, producing on large scale for the market, and possibly achieving economies of scale. Second, not all costs of production are always included. For some farms, for example, the cost of hired European labour, (*knechts*) personal expenses and maintaining the household are excluded. To deal with this, Worden creates three different types of model farms (for a detailed overview of his methods, see Worden 1985: chap. 6). Like the contemporary sources, the model farms reveal a rate of return of between 5 and 12 per cent. Although not a linear relationship, larger farms on average show greater returns per slave. The existence of economies of scale has been supported by some scholars (Guelke and Shell 1983; Fourie and von Fintel 2010a) and questioned by others (Williams 2013).

Meanwhile, a fundamental and partly overlooked problem with Worden's calculations is that while they do include the employment of European farm labourers (*knechts*), they neglect the role of Khoesan labourers. In fact, Khoesan labourers are not included at all in the equation employed for the model farms. It seems plausible to assume that the European workers were not assigned the same work tasks as the slaves, while the Khoesan would have worked side by side with the slaves. This phenomenon distinguished the Cape Colony from the slave societies of the New World (Worden and Groenewald 2005). In a census that includes indigenous farm labourers in Stellenbosch and Drakenstein districts in 1806 it is recorded that indigenous labour accounted for about 30 per cent of the total labour force. These were the two districts where slave-based agriculture was most widespread. In the pastoral frontier districts, the proportions were greater. In Graaf-Reinet in 1798, for example, the average farmer employed eight Khoesan and fewer than one slave (Cilliers and Green 2018).

Khoesan labour

European settlers may have regarded slavery as preferable to European wage labour. It is less clear whether they regarded slave labour as superior to the employment of Khoesan labour. It seems plausible to assume that it was initially difficult to rely on Khoesan labour as long as land was in abundance, but that this changed over time as the settler community expanded and the Khoesan lost access to land and livestock, forcing them to seek employment on European farms. Given their experience as pastoralists and their knowledge of the region, they were commonly employed as herders (Penn 2005). Court records also show that the Khoesan were often permanently attached to the arable farms in the south-western part of the colony, especially in Stellenbosch and Drakenstein, two districts where the use of slaves is known to have been widespread. The Khoesan must have lived and worked alongside the slaves (Worden 1985). This suggests that there is little evidence to warrant the exclusion of the Khoesan from earlier quantitative estimates.

The VOC had been reluctant to employ Khoesan to work on their pastoral and arable farms. In the former case, the company feared theft; in the latter, it was believed Khoesan lacked the necessary skills to till the land. Settlers, however, seem to have been less reluctant to employ Khoesan. European settlers who moved into Stellenbosch and Drakenstein districts in the very early years of frontier expansion in general lacked the means to buy sufficient numbers of slaves. In 1695, there were 0.65 slaves for every European settler in Stellenbosch and only 0.27 in Drakenstein. To fill the gap, the farmers recruited Khoesan labourers. By 1688, Khoesan labourers on farms had reached such numbers that Governor Simon van der Stel compared them to the influx of migrant workers from Westphalia into the Netherlands (Guelke and Shell 1983). According to Elphick, most Khoesan men in the south-western Cape were by the end of the seventeenth century either in service in Cape Town or on the European farms (1979). The work of the indigenous people was often described in appreciative terms. In 1695, Johannes Willem de Grevenbock referred to the Khoesan labour rather enthusiastically:

> They train oxen for use in ploughing [...] and are found exceedingly quick at inspanning or outspanning or guiding teams. Some of them are very accomplished riders, and have learned to break horses and master them [...]. They make trusty bearers, porters, carriers, postboys and couriers. They chop wood, mind the fire, work in the kitchen, prune vines, gather grapes, or work the wine press industriously [...]. Without relaxation they plough, sow, and harrow.
> (Elphick and Malherbe 1989: 17)

In 1713, the Cape experienced a devastating smallpox epidemic. There is no consensus as to how badly the Khoesan were affected. Worden argues that almost 90 per cent of the Khoesan population died (1985), while Ross (1977) produces a much lower estimate of 30 per cent or less. The truth may be somewhere in the middle of these two estimates. Regardless, the epidemic led to a significant reduction in the Khoesan population. This in turn led to a significant increase in slave imports as settlers needed to replace the Khoesan labourers who had died in the epidemic (Armstrong 1979). This reveals that Khoesan early on played an important role as farm labourers and that the use of slave labour was far from always the preferred choice among the settler-farmers. One could speculate about what would happen if the Cape had not been hit by the smallpox epidemic in 1713. It is not unreasonable to assume that the importation of slave labour would have been significantly lower.

Despite the increased labour shortages caused by the epidemic, there are good reasons to believe that Khoesan labour continued to play an important role throughout the eighteenth century. Worden (1985) assumes that most of the Khoesan migrated as a consequence of primitive accumulation. Scholars like Elphick (1977), Penn (1989) and Fourie and Green (2015), however, claim the contrary, that the processes of primitive accumulation caused an *increase* in the supply of indigenous labour over time.

We lack reliable estimates of the total size of the Khoesan population living within the boundaries of the colony. The first estimates of the number of Khoesan on European farms date to 1806. Johan Fourie and Jan Luiten van

Zanden (2013) have constructed a GDP series for the Cape Colony based on the consumption patterns of four population groups: settlers, VOC employees, slaves and Khoesan. To account for the latter, they use a novel technique: they assume that the number of indigenous people was proportional to the number of Khoesan who appeared before the Court of Justice in Cape Town. Using the Court of Justice records, they are able to estimate the size of the Khoesan population. Figure 4.1 shows the estimates. Khoesan numbers are much lower than those of the other three population groups, though their growth rate is much the same. By the mid-1720s, the rate of Khoesan population growth increases considerably, followed by a temporary and modest decline from 1740 to 1750; it then continues to increase to reach more than ten thousand in 1795.

There is a fundamental problem with this account. The number of Khoesan who appeared in court may simply have been a function of how developed the court system was and how willing people were to take matters to court or solve them by themselves. Rather than being a useful proxy for the size of the Khoesan population living in the colony, Fourie and van Zanden's estimates should be read as an attempt to measure the number of Khoesan that were incorporated in the colonial economy. Their estimates confirm what we would expect. As the frontier closed, the number of Khoesan operating under the radar of the colonial authorities decreased.

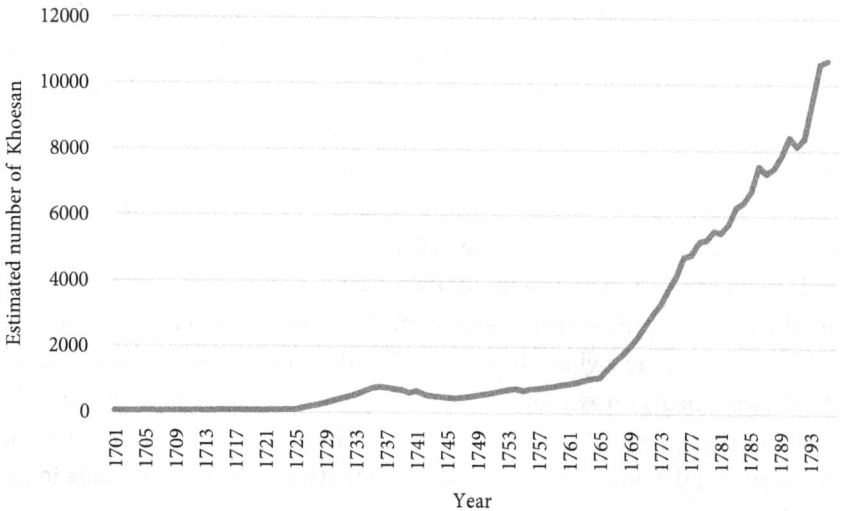

Figure 4.1 Estimated number of Khoesan, 1701–95 (based on their presence in court records).

Source: Fourie and van Zanden (2013: 472).

In an attempt to improve these estimates, Fourie and Green (2015) use another method, not to calculate the size of the indigenous population in total, but rather the numbers of Khoesan working on European farms. Assuming that only Khoesan were used for pastoral farming, and estimating their productivity by relying on a few travellers' accounts that give the number of Khoesan present on individual farms that they identify in the annual tax censuses, they are able to estimate the size of the Khoesan labour force as a function of number of cattle on the European farms. The estimates are found in Table 4.5.

Table 4.5 Estimated number of Khoesan and slaves by region, 1663–1773 (selected years).

	All regions		Cape, Stellenbosch and Drakenstein districts		Swellendam*	
Year	Khoesan	Slaves	Khoesan	Slaves	Khoesan	Slaves
1663	0	19	0	19		
1682	0	192	0	192		
1685	122	222	122	222		
1692	406	303	406	303		
1695	380	533	380	533		
1700	526	807	526	807		
1709	1338	1582	1398	1582		
1712	1298	1766	1298	1766		
1719	1076	2317	1076	2317		
1723	1434	2508	1434	2508		
1731	2016	3590	2016	3590		
1738	2724	4769	2724	4769		
1741	2617	4495	2617	4495		
1757	5359	5007	2123	4711	3236	296
1773	6843	7101	3296	6369	3547	732
Total	**26136**	**35211**	**19354**	**34183**	**6783**	**1028**

*Swellendam was only proclaimed as a separate district in 1754.
Source: Fourie and Green (2015: 205).

Their estimates show that, in all three of the districts they studied, the number of Khoesan working on European farms increased over time. In Cape, Stellenbosch and Drakenstein, where arable farming dominated, they never outnumbered the slaves, with the exception of the year 1692. In Swellendam, where pastoral farming was more common, the number of Khoesan outnumbered the slaves. That said, Khoesan labour nonetheless played an important role in all three districts. Including only Khoesan and slave labourers, the former constituted 35 per cent of the total labour force in 1685. By 1773, their share had increased to almost 50 per cent.

It should be noted that the estimates provided by Fourie and Green are conservative, as they assume that no indigenous people were employed in arable farming. Scattered evidence suggests, however, that they were, in fact, employed in arable as well as pastoral farming. In 1706, it was reported that the Khoesan moved in gangs from farm to farm in the south-western Cape in search of temporary wage employment on the arable farms (Shell 1994). In 1744, settler-farmers complained that they were being forced to limit the size of their crops because of shortages of Khoesan labour (Worden 1985). Estimates of population and production that the colonial authorities recorded in 1790 for the Cape, Stellenbosch, Graaff-Reinet and Swellendam districts (see Table 4.6) largely confirm Green and Fourie's calculations. According to these estimates, there were no Khoesan recorded as living in the Cape district, which is in line with the assumptions made by Fourie and Green. The number of Khoesan in Stellenbosch is estimated at five thousand, which is well above the estimates provided by Fourie and Green. Not all of these were necessarily employed on farms, but it is likely that a far majority was, including the children. In line with our expectations, the number of Khoesan living in the eastern frontier district of

Table 4.6 Estimates of population in various districts in Cape Colony, 1790.

	Cape	Stellenbosch	Swellendam	Graaff-Reinet	Total
Christians*	6,261	7,256	3,667	4,126	21,310
Slaves	11,891	1,073	2,196	964	16,124
Khoesan	0	5,000	800	9,083	14,883
Total	18,152	13,329	6,663	14,173	38,144

Source: Fourie and Green (2015: 206).
* Christians is the term used for European settlers.

Graaf-Reinet was higher than in the south-western Stellenbosch district. Graaf-Reinet was officially declared a district as late as in 1786, while Stellenbosch district had been closed – in other words, had become an integrated part of the colony, for more than eighty years. Having said that, the Khoesan outnumbered the number of slaves even in Stellenbosch at the end of the eighteenth century, as the estimates show.

Although the data is incomplete, we have numerous indications of Khoesan being present and most likely playing an important role in the Cape economy. Naturally, as the frontier expanded, the absolute numbers of Khoesan attached to the colonial economy increased. On the farm level, however, we have reasons to believe that the Khoesan played an important role as labourers from the very early years of the establishment of European settler farming at the Cape. This begs the question: what would happen to Worden's calculations of the productivity of slave labour if we were to include the input of Khoesan labour in the equation?

The productivity of slave labour revisited

As shown above, Worden's calculations suggest that slavery in the Cape was as profitable as in the Caribbean and the Antebellum American South. Fourie and Green (2015) use the same method as Worden to calculate the productivity of slaves but include their conservative estimates of the indigenous labour working on the European farms. Tables 4.7, 4.8 and 4.9 show that including the Khoesan has a significant effect on Worden's estimates of slave productivity.

To further analyse the effects on slave productivity when Khoesan labour is included, one can distinguish between farms according to the size of their

Table 4.7 Estimated slave productivity with and without Khoesan labour on wheat farms in various districts.

	No.	Without Khoesan	With Khoesan
Cape district	126	12.5	12.5
Stellenbosch district	38	18.4	8.1
Drakenstein district	206	15.1	5.6
Total	**370**	**14.5**	**8.2**

Source: Fourie and Green (2015: 209).

Table 4.8 Estimated slave productivity with and without Khoesan labour on wine farms in various districts.

	No.	Without Khoesan	With Khoesan
Cape district	114	0.8	0.8
Stellenbosch district	54	3.3	2.3
Drakenstein district	152	4.1	2.3
Total	**320**	**2.8**	**1.7**

Source: Fourie and Green (2015: 209).

Table 4.9 Estimated slave productivity with and without Khoesan labour on mixed farms.

		Wheat productivity			Wine productivity		
	No.	Without Khoesan	With Khoesan	% growth	Without Khoesan	With Khoesan	% growth
Cape district	321	7.7	7.7	0	0.5	0.5	0
Stellenbosch district	207	9.7	4.9	−49.5	1.6	1	−34.5
Drakenstein district	567	9.5	3.7	−61	1.8	1	−47.6
Total	1096	9	5.1	−43.4	1.4	0.9	−39.4

Source: Fourie and Green (2015: 211).

slaveholdings. Fourie and Green do that; their estimates are presented in Table 4.10. They show that slave productivity declined more on farms with relatively small slaveholdings, which is expected as they proportionally would rely more on Khoesan than would the large slaveholders.

Worden's initial scepticism towards the efficiency of using slave labour is to some extent confirmed in Fourie and Green's revised estimates. The productivity of slave labour is significantly lower than that of the slave economies in the New World. Contemporary observers also expressed concerns about the productivity and profitability of slave labour in the Cape. In 1806, Barrow noted, for example, that:

> There is not, perhaps, any part of the world, out of Europe, where the introduction of slavery was less necessary than the Cape of Good Hope ... To encourage the native Hottentot in useful labour, by giving them an interest in the produce of that labour, to make them experience the comforts of civilized life, and to feel

Table 4.10 Slave productivity with and without Khoesan labour, all arable farmers split by the number of slaves.

| | Between 1 to 5 slaves | | | | | More than 5 slaves | | | |
| | Wheat productivity | | Wine productivity | | | Wheat productivity | | Wine productivity | |
No.	Without Khoesan	With Khoesan	Without Khoesan	With Khoesan	No.	Without Khoesan	With Khoesan	Without Khoesan	With Khoesan
111	10.7	10.7	0.6	0.6	210	6.1	6.1	0.5	0.5
131	12.3	5.8	1.6	1.1	76	5.2	3.6	1.6	1.2
422	10.4	3.6	1.9	1	145	7.1	4.1	1.5	1
644	10.8	5.2	1.7	0.9	432	6.3	5	1	0.8

Source: Fourie and Green (2015: 211).

they have a place and value in society ... would be the sure means of diminishing and, in time, of entirely removing the necessity of slavery.

(quoted in Ulrich 2013: 1)

Not only were slaves expensive; they were also not extraordinarily productive. A key reason why slaves may not have been the preferred choice in arable farming has to with the length of the slack season, that is, the part of the agricultural season when the need for labour is low. Wheat farming required a heavy concentration of labour during the period of ploughing and sowing. The former took place from May to July, but also involved preparation of the land in April. The ground was often hard, so heavy ploughs were needed, which made the ploughing labour intensive. Mentzel observed in 1785 that a grain farmer at the Cape required more labour than in Europe. At least three men were needed for every plough drawn by six to twelve oxen (Worden 1985). December to March was the threshing and harvesting period. The grain had to be quickly harvested before the strong south-eastern winds came and threatened to flatten a field of ripe corn. In 1795, van Ryneveld (1797: article 4) claimed that winds required 'a double number of hands to get the corn speedily cut down and gathered'. Between these two periods, the demand for farm labour was limited. A farmer could choose to keep far more slaves than were needed during the slack season in order to ensure sufficient supplies of labourers during the peak season. This would be very costly, especially as there was little scope for farmers to establish profitable proto-industries (see above) to keep the slaves busy during the slack season. Alternatively, a farmer could invest in relatively few slaves and employ additional Khoesan labourers during the peak season (Green 2014). The latter would be the preferred choice if the settler-farmers could ensure that there was a sufficient supply of Khoesan labourers ready to work during the peak season. One way of ensuring that, as has been discussed in Chapter 3 and will be in Chapter 5, was to allow the Khoesan to herd on the settler's grazing land in exchange for their labour.

Labour demand on vineyards also fluctuated, but not to the same extent as on grain farms. Between July and September the vines had to be pruned and cut and the soil needed to be fertilized. Meanwhile, new vine stocks were planted between July and August. In October and November, weeds were removed, stocks propped and soils regularly hoed. In January and February, labourers were used, albeit in smaller numbers, to keep birds and stray animals out of the vineyards as the grapes were growing. The peak period followed immediately after the harvest, when the grapes were picked and pressed to make wine (Worden 1985). In that regard, the annual volatility in labour demand was less severe on vineyards than on grain farms, which made slavery a more suitable system for vineyard owners. This can in part explain why the use of slaves was more prevalent in viticulture than in grain farming.

The differences in the annual fluctuations in labour demand between viticulture and wheat farming make possible a third strategy for a more efficient use of slave labour, namely wheat farming and viticulture, perhaps also together with keeping livestock. Armstrong and Worden (1989: 137) note: 'Although there were fluctuations, depending on the success of the annual crop as well as the accuracy of census recording, it is apparent that farmers producing both wine and grain had the closest correlations, and hence were the most efficient in exploiting their slaves, largely because they made more intensive use of them throughout the year'. Worden's (1985) estimates largely confirm this. Mixed farms, on average, showed higher rates of return for slave labour.

The revised estimates of slave productivity have to be understood in the context of the increasing cost of acquiring slaves. Not only did the prices of agricultural output fall behind the price of acquiring slaves; the slave population never managed to reproduce itself. Table 4.11 shows the number of slave men, women and children in the Cape Colony in 1687–1793. Although the table shows a declining sex ratio, it remained high throughout the period. At the end of the eighteenth century, the number of slave women made up not more than 28 per cent of the total adult slave population. Further, and unlike the plantations in the Americas, most settler-farmers at the Cape had too few slaves to exploit opportunities of economies of scale.

The question then is why, after all, slaves were used. Part of the explanation is likely to involve non-economic factors. As Genovese (1965) argued in his work on plantation societies in the New World, once established, slavery will persist even when it makes less economic sense, due to the fact that it gives the slaveholders social and political prestige. Still, it is difficult to see how slavery could persist in the context of the Cape Colony – where the average farmer was poorer than in the New World – if it was not of economic use. To understand why slavery persisted in the rural Cape, we need to recognize that slaves were not only used as labour, but also as a means to access much needed capital.

Table 4.11 Number of slave men, women and children in Cape Colony, 1687–1793 (selected years).

Year	Men	Women	Children	Sex ratio	% of W to M
1687	230	44	36	5,23	18
1691	285	57	44	5,00	17
1701	702	109	80	6,44	13
1711	1,232	290	249	4,25	19
1723	2,224	408	290	5,45	16
1733	3,384	711	614	4,76	17
1743	3,804	815	742	4,67	18
1753	4,137	1,031	877	4,01	20
1763	5,072	1,214	929	4,18	19
1773	6,102	1,707	1,093	3,57	22
1783	7,808	2,533	1,609	3,08	24
1793	9,046	3,590	2,111	2,52	28

Source: Worden (1985: 53).

Slaves as capital at the Cape

Labour was not the only challenge settler-farmers faced. Capital was also a constraint. Credit has played an important role in most agricultural economies, and the Cape Colony was no exception. Ross (1986) argues that the most important source of finance stemmed from the formation of capital on the farms. Yet, as he also acknowledges, it is difficult to see how especially the larger landholdings would survive without an external source of capital. The location of the Cape in the global trade network of the Dutch Empire made the role of credit even more important, since there was a chronic shortage of Dutch rixdollars.

A number of scholars have noted that a significant share of the settlers in the Cape Colony were highly indebted and used this observation to make the claim that the average farmer was poor and could hardly make ends meet (e.g. Guelke 1989; Schoeman 2012). Contemporary witnesses shared this view. In 1795, for example, right before the British annexed the Cape Colony, the concerned farmer Johannes Frederik Kirsten wrote to the British government, complaining that 'by far the greater part of the Farmers and Inhabitants of the Town are Bankrupts [*sic*], the rest have their property under Sequester, and every individual looks forward to impending ruin' (quoted in Swanepoel 2017: 21). There is ample evidence that farmers struggled from time to time. But Swanepoel finds that wealthier farmers at the Cape tended to be more indebted than poorer ones. Using auction rolls from 1663 to 1784, she finds that credit played an important role for settler-farmers (65 per cent of her sample were involved in credit transactions) and that farmers who had more slaves, which she uses as a proxy of wealth, also tended to be more indebted. This is, moreover, in line with findings from pre-industrial Europe (Thoen and Soens 2009). It is worth noting that the majority of the credit was used for investments in production rather than consumption. Of all the credit in the sample, 56 per cent was used for production, 21 per cent was allocated for consumption and the rest was used to fund donations, taxes, accounts and inheritance. This underscores the importance of credit for settler farming at the Cape.

The formal credit market was limited and dominated by major players like the Company, the Orphan Chamber, churches and a few Company employees (Guelke 1989; Ross 1989; Schoeman 2012). Together, these institutions and individuals made up a small share of the credit transactions at the Cape. In total, 90 per cent of the lenders at the eighteenth-century Cape were individual settlers (Swanepoel 2017). It is for these transactions that slaves played an important role. The majority of settlers, who leased land under the loan-farm system, could use neither land nor houses or buildings as collateral. Theoretically, they could make use of farm equipment as collateral, but its value was in general too small to enable settlers to access any significant levels of credit.

Farmers did, however, possess one asset they could use as collateral: slaves. Slaves were the most liquid and mobile assets in the colony, serving for 'creditors [to] gauge a debtor's riskiness' (Swanepoel 2017: 42). In 1713, for example, slaveholder Johannes Craa mortgaged his slaves to receive credit from the Dutch Reformed Church. Evidence suggests that from that point on, this practice became widespread since short-term credit was essential to the operation of slaveholding estates (Shell 1994; Dooling 2006). In her study, Swanepoel (2017; see also Fourie and Swanepoel 2018) finds that slave ownership was the only significant characteristic used to determine debt. Especially for older slaveholders, the slaves 'were their bank' (Shell 1994: 109). The use of slaves as collateral was in no way unique to the Cape. In cases like precolonial Nigeria (Fenske 2012) and Brazil (Schulz 2008), for example, slaves were used as security in credit transactions. Just as it was at the Cape, de jure landed property rights were weak in these three cases, making it difficult for farmers to use their land as collateral. Even when de jure landed property rights were strong, as they were in the United States, slaves there were commonly used as collateral simply because they were moveable assets (Kilbourne 2014).

Slaves were not only used as collateral. There is ample evidence of slaveholders leasing out their slaves to others. This made a lot of sense given the different agricultural seasons prevailing in wheat farming and viticulture. The lease market for slaves meant that large slaveholders could lease out part of their slave labour force during their slack season to farmers who had fewer slaves and needed additional labour during their peak season. The importance of leasing for the slaveholder was acknowledged by the VOC. In 1786, the Council of Policy wrote:

> The acquisition of slaves having increased by means of the great profits, part of them being used to extend the vineyards, while another part belongs to such people as make a living by hiring them out, so that they are bound to lose their source of income on the death of these slaves or are burdened with their support when they can no longer be hired out.
>
> (quoted in Schoeman 2012: 323–34)

The VOC published a recommended price for hiring slaves, indicating that the practice had become institutionalized in Cape society. In 1775, the rate was 4 rixdollars per month plus food and tobacco. By 1783, the price had increased to 6 rixdollars plus food and tobacco as an effect of the increasing price of purchasing slaves. Hiring out slaves was a profitable enterprise. For example, Jan Nel, a vigneron from Stellenbosch, hired out two slaves for the period from March 1730 to November 1737. In return, he was paid 225 rixdollars, which is almost equivalent to what he would have earned by selling them at auction. The VOC itself hired slaves from slaveholders and spent a substantial amount in doing so. In 1787–8, for example, the Company allocated no less than 22,000 rixdollars for this expense (Armstrong 1979; Shell 1994).

The possibility of using slaves to acquire capital is manifested in the effects of the slave emancipation in 1834. The emancipation happened forty years after the period covered by this book, so I will not discuss it in any detail. But it needs to be mentioned as it bears witness to the importance slaves played for slaveholders' access to capital. It has been argued that the emancipation led to an agrarian crisis for the settler farming community as labour withdrawal caused a decline in output (Dooling 2006; Worden 2017). Meanwhile, one needs to acknowledge the limited choices facing the freed slaves. The vast majority remained within the districts and were left with no alternative other than to provide their labour services to the settler-farmers. This has led scholars like Shell (1994) to conclude that the post-emancipation crisis was short lived. Still, how can one explain the crisis, short-lived or not, if the slaves were not in a position to leave their former masters? In a recent study, Martins (2020) offers the explanation that the decline in output was to a great extent an effect of the capital losses the settler-farmers faced due to the emancipation of slaves. No longer being their property, the settlers could no longer make use of slaves to access capital. Martins estimates that 70 per cent of the variation in grain output and 20 per cent of the variation in wine output after the emancipation can be explained by the capital losses that farmers faced.

Conclusion

The central question asked in this chapter was whether the Cape Colony was a 'slave economy' in Nieboer's sense of the term, that is, whether slavery was a key institution for the growth and surplus production of the settler farming sector at the Cape. My conclusion is that it was indeed a slave economy, but not necessarily in the way described in prior literature. In this chapter, I have made the case that previous scholarship has exaggerated the role of slaves as labour and at the same time has neglected the importance of Khoesan labourers. Rather than being a superior form of labour, slaves paid a key role in the Cape economy as they gave settler-farmers access to both labour *and* capital.

Despite the many factors that theoretically would prevent the profitable use of slaves, the general conclusion is that slave labour was a key element in the growth of settler agriculture in the colony. My conclusion in this chapter – based on estimates that admittedly should be treated with a great deal of caution – is that prior studies have overestimated the productivity of slave labour. Recognizing the importance of Khoesan labour and including it in the equation causes estimates of slave labour productivity to fall significantly. With the Khoesan included, the productivity of slave labour at the Cape is shown to be far lower than that of slaves in the New World. To make matters worse, the cost of slave labour increased over time because of the way the Cape market for agricultural produce was organized.

Why then was slave ownership so widespread at the Cape? Was it simply that owning a slave was associated with social status? That probably was one factor, but equally important was the fact that it gave farmers access to much-needed capital. Large slaveholders could accumulate capital by speculation on the slave market, but also by leasing out their slaves to other settlers who could make use of them. Further, in the absence of secure, de jure property rights in land, slaves played a key role as collateral enabling the capital-constrained settlers to access resources needed to keep their businesses afloat. The Nieboer-Domar hypothesis rightly points to the role of factor endowments but focuses too narrowly on land–labour ratios. To understand slavery as an economic institution, we need to include capital into the equation. Slavery was not just a form of coerced labour, but a system that gave the slaveholder complete rights over a mobile property, a system that allowed the owner not only to extract labour, but also access capital.

5

Unequal we stand

Introduction

A central concern in the rational-choice political economy (RPE) literature on settler colonialism is the divergent levels of inequality across settler colonies and its impact on long-term economic development. The literature argues that inequality levels remained relatively low in regions where the Europeans settled in greater numbers (Acemoglu, Johnson and Robinson 2002; Engerman and Sokoloff 2005; Angeles 2007). Because of their large numbers, the Europeans constituted a critical mass that pressured the colonial authorities to implement so-called 'developmental' or 'inclusive' institutions that guaranteed broad access to economic and political markets, secured property rights (for the settlers) and used tax revenues for the provision of public goods. In regions where the number of European settlers was lower, settlers instead persuaded the colonial authorities to implement extractive institutions that enabled them to extract economic rents through the exploitation of human and natural resources and at the same time prevent settlers who arrived later to do the same. RPE scholars further argue that initial levels of inequality have persisted over time and can explain current income gaps between former settler colonies.

While the recent literature on settler economies has had a significant impact on our understanding of differences in inequality among those colonies, they do not provide a systematic empirical analysis of the evolution of inequality. In this chapter, I use the Cape as a case study to contribute to the debate on settler colonialism, its institutional order and its effects on inequality. The Cape Colony does not easily fit with either side of the dichotomy proposed by RPE. On the one hand, the number of Europeans was, in relative terms, large and the average size of the settler farms was comparatively small. In that respect, the Cape resembles North America, in which European family farms dominated, leading to low levels of inequality and an inclusive institutional order. On the other hand, as I explain below, inequality levels were high at the Cape and the institutional order – which entailed slavery, weak de jure property rights and regulated markets – was extractive if we follow the classification proposed in the RPE literature.

This chapter will make use of rich historical sources, enabling micro-level longitudinal analysis of the evolution of inequality at the Cape to ask a fundamental question: what factors enabled some settlers to accumulate wealth more quickly than others? Previous work on the Cape has highlighted a range of factors to explain inequality during this period, including uneven access to fertile land, slave ownership and differences in human capital. While all of these factors mattered, I will argue that differences in accessing and controlling labour were the most important. There were two ways of accumulating capital in the initial years. First, we have a group of settlers who initially gained wealth through non-farming activities. This wealth was invested in land and eventually in purchases of slaves. This group made up a small proportion of the richest farmers. The larger share of relatively wealthy farmers initially accumulated their wealth through farming, whose profitability during the first fifty years depended on the ability to access and control indigenous Khoesan labour. Operating in an open frontier, the European intruders initially used a range of methods to ensure a sufficient number of indigenous labourers, including brute force and other kinds of coercion. However, coercion could not be employed on a systematic basis. Instead, the first wave of settlers took control of more land than they had the means to put into productive use. This was done in order to attract pastoral Khoesan to stay on the land as tenants. The wealth they then accumulated through the use of Khoesan labour could be invested in slaves, and over the years having large slaveholdings became a key characteristic of the settler farming elite.

This chapter looks at inequality in the settler population, rather than among the Khoesan, for two reasons. First, we lack reliable information about income and wealth among the Khoesan. It is not controversial to assume that the Khoesan – as a group – was significantly poorer than the settlers. However, we do not have enough information on the wealth/income of the Khoesan to systematically study changes in the differences in income/wealth between various Khoesan groups and the settlers. Second, the recent research on inequality and economic development in settler colonies has primarily concerned itself with stratification among the settlers. So, while our narrow focus on the settlers can rightly be blamed for being Eurocentric, it can still provide important insights about the current debates on the legacy of settler colonialism.

Explaining inequality in pre-industrial colonial societies

Economic historians have long been interested in explaining differences in inequality over time and space. Economic growth in general and paths of structural change in particular have been highlighted as key factors determining inequality trends. A prominent contribution stems from the work of Simon Kuznets (1955) and his famous inverted U-shaped inequality curve. Kuznets related changes in inequality to the structural transformation of the economy, that is, a shift away from an economy dominated by low-productive sectors (in most cases agriculture) to one in which high-productive sectors (commonly manufacturing) increased their share of GDP. During the initial phase of this transformation, the wage gap between the low- and high-productive sectors would lead to increased inequality. Over time, however, inequality will decrease as more people move into the high-productive sectors, while the wage levels converge between the sectors as labour shortages in the former low-productive sectors stimulate labour-saving technological changes. Kuznets himself admitted that one should refrain from generalizing as each case, with its own institutional mix, would affect the pattern. This is also confirmed in later research that shows mixed results (Lindert and Williamson 1985; Lindert 1986; Feinstein 1988; Bourguignon and Morrison 2002; Milanovic, Lindert and Williamson 2010). Acemoglu and Robinson (2002) offer one explanation for the mixed results, arguing that the existence of a U-shape inequality curve depends on political factors. In line with Kuznets, they argue that industrialization led to increased inequality but at the same time facilitated an increased geographical concentration of the workforce. This reduced the cost to that workforce of mobilizing protests against the economic and political elite. The threat posed by an organized working class would, under certain circumstances, make the elites willing to implement redistributive policies leading to a decline in inequality. This is what happened in Western Europe but, for example, not in Latin America, according to the authors. In the latter case, initial inequality was high and civil society relatively weak, so pressure to change the system was likewise weak. This begs the question: why was initial inequality much higher in certain regions than in others?

The Kuznets' inverted U-shape curve implicitly assumes that pre-industrial societies were characterized by relative low levels of inequality. This is at odds with more recent research showing high levels of inequality in various pre-industrial societies, of which most of the cases come from Europe (see Alfani 2021 for an overview). It is also widely accepted that inequality levels were quite high in pre-industrial settler colonies. This is commonly explained by political factors. The settlers were a privileged group who, under the protection of the colonial authorities, could ensure the implementation of economic and social policies that favoured them at the expense of indigenous populations and/or late-arriving immigrants (Elkins and Pedersen 2005). Alternatively, although this is seldom discussed in the literature, one could explain the high levels of inequality in settler colonies as a consequence of population growth and an extension of the land frontier. The growth of population would lead to the opening of marginal land for cultivation, leading to so-called Ricardian rents. According to the classic economist Ricardo ([1821] 2004), the rent is the difference in the yield of a plot of superior land as compared to the yields produced on marginal lands. This would lead to an 'early-arrival premium' in which late arrivals would earn lower incomes (Cilliers, Green and Ross 2021). Inequality would increase as long as population growth continued and the land frontier expanded.

A key focus in the RPE literature on colonialism is how inequality differs among colonies. To account for the differences, RPE scholars offer a modified political explanation. Keeping the assumption that levels of inequality are driven by the interests of the settlers, RPE scholars argue that the size of the settler population determined the institutional order that was established and therefore also the degree of income and wealth inequality. In areas with few settlers, they would rely on extracting economic rents and prevent further settler immigration. This created high levels of inequality that have persisted over time. In cases where Europeans settled in greater numbers, they became a political force for equal opportunities (for the settlers) and inclusive institutions (for the settlers), which creates societies of relatively low levels of inequality (Engermann and Sokoloff 2000; Acemoglu, Johnson and Robinson 2002). Latin America and North America epitomize a different path. In the former, settlers remained few and levels of inequality high, while in the latter the number of settlers was greater and levels of inequality smaller. This interpretation of inequality has – directly or indirectly – influenced a great deal of work on colonialism and inequality among economic historians and economists over the past two decades (Baker, Brunnschweiler and Bulte 2008; Bruhn and Gallego 2008; Putterman and Weil 2010; Easterly and Levine 2012).

A basic problem with this line of inquiry, however, is that, in the words of Gonzalez and Montero, it is 'a basically anti-empirical way of reasoning' (2010: 255). Instead of investigating levels of economic inequality the authors assume that it was higher in certain parts of the colonial world, an assumption they substantiate by identifying the existence of certain institutions, such as the hacienda plantations in Latin America. No actual figures on land distribution between regions are offered (Frankema 2009). The few scholars who have tried to empirically investigate economic inequality in the Americas have found little evidence that Latin America and North America differed to any significant degree during the colonial period (Coatsworth 2008; Williamson 2015). It was during the commodity boom in the late nineteenth and early twentieth centuries that the two regions first began to diverge in terms of inequality.

The negative correlation between number of settlers and inequality can also be questioned when one looks at the African experience. Scholars on colonialism in Africa convincingly make the case that inequality was higher and extraction more pervasive in settler colonies than in non-settler colonies (Acemoglu and Robinson 2012; Frankema, Green and Hillbom 2016). Excluding Australia, Canada, New Zealand and the United States, where the indigenous populations were merely eliminated, the same pattern seems to exist for most former colonies, as Angeles (2007) has shown.

To understand the evolution of inequality over time, we have to return to the framework used in this book, which suggests that the institutions governing an open frontier are not the same as would be found in a closed one. At the Cape, there were two major avenues for generating wealth: trade or farming. The former created significant wealth, but only for a very small elite, as I show in the final chapter. The majority invested in farming. One's ability to generate wealth from farming was a combined effect of the quality of the land and the farmer's capacity to access and control a sufficient number of labourers. The frontier being open, one would expect the first wave of settlers to establish their farms in the climatologically most favourable locations, if this was not prevented by resistance from the indigenous populations. However, climatological differences would not be translated into different capacities to generate wealth as long as the settlers did not have a sufficient number of labourers to work the land. This has been recognized by a great number of Cape historians and is one of the reasons why many argue that slavery played such an important role for the economy (see Chapter 4).

In Chapter 4, I argued that much of the existing research has exaggerated the role of imported slave labour. Slaves played a crucial role and over time a strong correlation between slave ownership and wealth developed at the Cape. However, to be able to purchase slaves one already had to be able to accumulate sufficient capital as slaves were expensive. This was done by ensuring a sufficient supply of Khoesan labourers. Those who established farms first had an advantage as they were allowed to take control of as much land as they wished. They commonly managed to gain control of more land than they needed or had the resources to cultivate. In this way, they could attract Khoesan to herd their cattle in exchange for labour. Those arriving later had no choice but to move farther into the interior. The farmers in the interior lived farther away from the market and found it more challenging to access and control sufficient numbers of Khoesan labourers. It is therefore not surprising that on average the frontier farmers were less wealthy. There was a significant level of persistence in the distribution of wealth. The wealth created was passed on to the next generation through inheritance, which may seem contradictory given the practice of partible inheritance of property. That system enabled affluent farmers to consolidate land holdings through marriage strategies. The latter implies a clear gender dimension to the process of wealth accumulation and inequality.

Inequality trends in the eighteenth-century Cape Colony

Thanks to recent research, we have a fairly accurate picture of inequality trends among the settler farming community of the eighteenth-century Cape Colony. Far less is known about degrees of inequality between the settlers and the indigenous population and information regarding urban residents and/or non-farmer Europeans is scant.

The three most important secondary sources providing inequality estimates are Guelke and Shell (1983) and Fourie and von Fintel (2010a, 2011). Guelke and Shell use annual tax censuses, loan-farm records, property deeds and probates to estimate the distribution of land and wealth among the settler population for selected years in the early colonial period (1682–1731; see Tables 5.1 and 5.2). Their estimates reveal significant levels of stratification among the settler farming community already by 1682 – before the take-off of settler farming. Of 102 census households, twelve held more than 50 per cent of the *knechts* (European servants), slaves and livestock and they produced most of the colony's wheat, barley and rye. These farmers often owned several farms and cattle posts. In 1731, more than half of the farms in the colony were owned by 7 per cent of the settler population, of whom most owned three or more farms (Guelke and Shell 1983).

In 1705, the richest 20 per cent of the settlers controlled nearly 59 per cent of the total wealth (measured in land and slaves). Meanwhile, returns to capital were significantly higher among the poorer settlers with smaller farms, according to Guelke and Shell's estimates. The poorest quintile showed a return to capital of 35 per cent compared with 14 per cent for the richest quintile. Guelke and Shell therefore conclude that the early period of settler expansion was relatively favourable for smaller farms, which could easily find land to cultivate at a low cost due to an abundance of land and access to cheap Khoesan labour.

Despite that fact that the poorer farmers enjoyed higher returns on capital, the gap was already too large between the wealthier farmers and the poorer ones to be closed. By 1731, wealth inequality had increased even further. The wealthiest 20 per cent then controlled 60 per cent of total wealth while the poorest share had declined to 2 per cent. The rates of return had declined for all groups but continued to be higher among the poorer quintiles. Guelke and Shell argue that the declining rate of returns indicates that the initial economic boom during the period from 1682 to 1705 had come to an end. The demand for agricultural produce and livestock did not keep up with the growing number of settler farms being established. Meanwhile, the closing of the south-western Cape frontier was marked by an increased concentration of landed wealth. Whereas in 1705, the richest 20 per cent had controlled 56 per cent of land value, by 1731, the percentage had increased to 67 per cent.

Guelke and Shell only provide a few snapshots and for a limited period of time. Fourie and von Fintel (2010a) use the annual tax censuses to extend the

Table 5.1 European settler-farmers, 1705: capital and income.

Quintiles	Capital assets (in guilders*)			Income (in guilders*)	Returns on capital	
	Land	Livestock	Total	Livestock and produce	Average of individuals (%)	Group average (%)
1	15,000	20,000	35,000	12,000	36	35
2	37,000	41,000	78,000	17,000	22	22
3	82,000	59,000	142,000	22,000	16	15
4	156,000	105,000	260,000	39,000	15	15
5	367,000	360,000	727,000	99,000	14	14
Total	**657,000**	**585,000**	**1,242,000**	**189,000**	21	15

* rounded to nearest thousand. Note on sample: 210 of 567 census households with agricultural income of 72 guilders or more.
Source: Guelke and Shell (1983: 270).

Table 5.2 European settler-farmers, 1731: capital and income.

Quintiles	Capital assets (in guilders*)			Income (in guilders*)	Returns on capital	
	Land	Livestock	Total	Livestock and produce	Average of individuals (%)	Group average (%)
1	5,000	89,000	94,000	14,000	14	15
2	40,000	196,000	236,000	26,000	11	12
3	216,000	242,000	458,000	48,000	10	10
4	516,000	459,000	975,000	92,000	9	9
5	1,571,000	997,000	2,568,000	230,000	9	8
Total	**2,348,000**	**1,983,000**	**4,331,000**	**400,000**	**11**	**10**

* rounded to nearest thousand. Note on sample: 210 of 567 census households with agricultural income of 72 guilders or more.
Source: Guelke and Shell (1983: 275).

inequality estimates to 1757 by estimating changes in the Gini-coefficient, which measures the value of a frequency distribution. A Gini-coefficient of 1 expresses maximum inequality, i.e. one person in a given society controls all wealth/income, while a coefficient of 0 marks a society where everybody is equally rich/poor. Their estimates are shown in Figure 5.1. Just like Guelke and Shell, they find that wealth inequality remained comparatively high during the first half of the eighteenth century. Thereafter, and differently from Guelke and Shell, their estimates show a decline in inequality to 1740, when it began to increase again. According to Fourie and von Fintel, this is because of a slowdown in immigration, implying that the bottom end of the distribution was no longer filled with newly arrived Europeans.

A major limitation of both Guelke and Shell's and Fourie and von Fintel's work is that it only captures wealth inequality among settler-farmers. Fourie and von Fintel do include slaves and European *knechts*, but given the nature of their sources, these are recorded as having zero assets. In another paper (2011) they include European wage earners as well as slaves by constructing estimates of income inequality using three cross-sections: 1700, 1723 and 1757. This not only allows them to capture a larger population but also to compare the Cape with estimates of income inequality in other parts of the pre-industrial world. The authors emphasize that estimates should be treated with a great deal

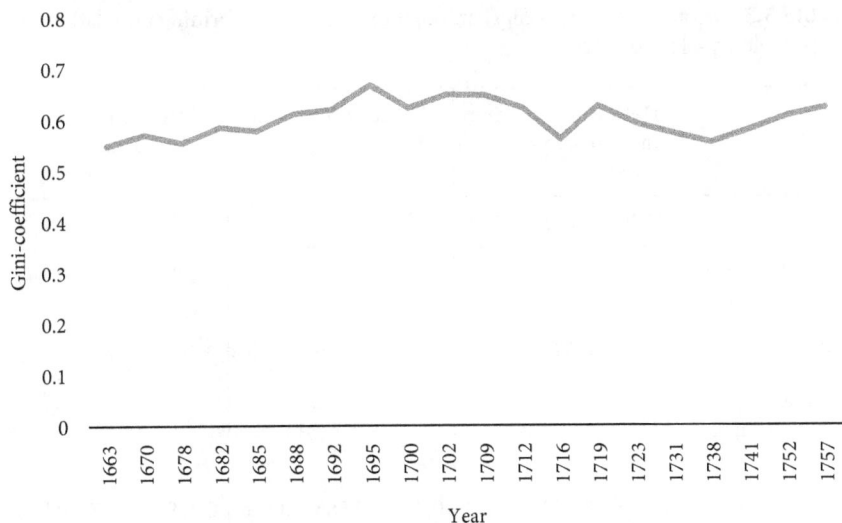

Figure 5.1 Wealth inequality among settler-farmers in Cape Colony, 1663–1757.

Source: Fourie and von Fintel (2010a: 253).

of caution due to data limitations and the assumption that they are forced to make in order to derive incomes for as many groups as possible. Having said that, their measurement of income inequality between groups reveals high but declining levels of inequality, on average. Their estimates are presented in Table 5.3. Depending on the measurement strategy employed, the Gini for 1700 varies between 0.79 and 0.84. It then declines and by 1757 the income inequality varies from 0.71 to 0.74.

According to the authors, the decline is to a large extent driven by declining incomes from so-called *pachters* – settlers who were granted a licence by the VOC to trade domestically and to supply passing ships with provisions (see the more detailed discussion of this in Chapter 6). Only a handful of settlers were granted these rights, so in practice they held monopsonostic positions and could thus generate substantial profits from this trade. Excluding the *pachters* leads the income inequality levels to drop significantly and remain fairly stable over time. A possible reason for this pattern is that they assume that slave incomes are stable over time. To control for this, they also exclude both *pachters* and slaves from their estimate of the Gini for the population. This brings levels of income inequality down further, but they then increase over time. This pattern is confirmed in the measurement of within-group inequality. For non-farming settlers, the income inequality levels remain fairly stable, although it increases

Table 5.3 Income inequality (Gini) among European settler farming population in Cape Colony, selected years.

	Deflation of settler income by price index			Settler income in 1700 prices			Settler income in 1757 prices		
	1700	1723	1757	1700	1723	1757	1700	1723	1757
Whole settler population	0.792	0.761	0.742	0.792	0.713	0.713	0.837	0.816	0.744
Whole settler population (excluding incomes from pachts)	0.569	0.592	0.559	0.569	0.626	0.626	0.543	0.582	0.555
Whole settler population (excluding incomes from slaves and pachts)	0.475	0.563	0.578	0.477	0.586	0.586	0.479	0.587	0.575
Within group inequality									
VOC employees	0.284	0.31	0.297	0.284	0.31	0.297	0.284	0.31	0.297
Farming settlers	0.554	0.625	0.625	0.554	0.636	0.652	0.565	0.659	0.689
Other settlers	0.402	0.576	0.576	0.402	0.568	0.426	0.417	0.546	0.433

Source: Fourie and von Fintel (2011: 43).

within the group of European settler-farmers. Table 5.4 reveals that the increased inequality among the farmers was mainly driven by a concentration of incomes among the richest farmers. All except the top quantile experienced declining incomes.

A major constraint of the data above is that it only covers the period up to 1757. For the remaining part of the eighteenth century we only have estimates of wealth inequality beginning in the 1780s and they only cover the Stellenbosch and Graaff-Reinet districts. With that in mind, the estimates show that inequality remained high in Stellenbosch with a Gini index of just above 0.7. In Graaf-Reinet, inequality was somewhat lower, with a Gini of 0.6, and it fluctuated more. The latter is expected as the district was founded as late as 1786 and continued to see an inflow of settlers throughout the century. Some of these newly arrived

Table 5.4 Percentage change of real incomes at various percentiles among the European settler farming population in the Cape Colony, 1700–57.

Quintile	1700–23	1723–57
1	−95.2	1488.6
5	−73.3	19.5
10	−46.0	−39
25	−37.9	−57.2
50	−30.3	−59.2
75	−31.0	−40.9
90	−14.4	−30.2
95	14.1	−35.8
99	−23.9	−12.8

Source: Fourie and von Fintel (2011: 42).

immigrants had already managed to accumulate a degree of wealth while others came more or less empty-handed (Cilliers and Green 2018; Martins 2020a). This scattered evidence does, in combination with estimates for previous periods, suggest that wealth inequality among settlers increased throughout the latter half of the eighteenth century.

Another major concern is that we lack data for the indigenous populations. Up to 1800, we do not have any direct estimates of the size of the population, let alone their economic activities, wealth or incomes. The only available estimates of the wealth of an 'independent' group of Khoesan is from Swellendam district in 1825 (Links, Green and von Fintel 2018). This is beyond the period studied in this book but can serve as an example in the absence of any alternative. Table 5.5 shows the average wealth of the group compared with the average wealth of the settlers in Swellendam district. As one would expect, the differences are huge. The Khoesan in the sample were on average much poorer than the Europeans. Meanwhile, looking at only the Khoesan, we find high levels of within-group inequality. The estimates should be treated with a great deal of care. I do not know why this data was collected for this group, let alone the extent to which the group is representative of an independent Khoesan society. It is likely that the levels of inequality would be even higher if we were able to accurately include the wealth and incomes of the Khoesan.

Table 5.5 Wealth and inequality of settlers and Khoesan population in Swellendam, 1825.

Group	Average wealth	Gini
Farming settlers with land and slaves	894.38	0.47
Farming settlers with land and no slaves	214.63	0.38
Farming Khoesan	42.56	0.57

Source: Links, Green and von Fintel (2018).

What can we make of these estimates? If we focus on the settler farming community, the estimates reveal high levels of both income and wealth inequality. The long-run trend seems to be towards an increased concentration of wealth and income over time among the wealthiest settlers. This is a fascinating finding. The fact that most farms were smaller than those found in the New World, the practice of partible inheritance, which in theory meant that farms were subdivided for each generation, along with the fact that factor endowments did not allow for large-scale production of tropical products as they did in the New World, would all seem to militate in favour of relatively low levels of inequality. Why do we find the opposite?

Explaining inequality trends among the settler farming population

Previous research has identified different drivers of inequality at the Cape. Inspired by Engerman and Sokoloff (2005), Fourie and von Fintel (2010a) argue that changes in immigration policies can explain how inequality evolved over time. In the early years, wealth inequality among the settler-farmers was low, as the majority of the newly arrived immigrants were poor with no possessions. As they began to invest in land, they managed to accumulate more wealth while at the same time there was a continued inflow of poor migrants. Under these conditions, wealth inequality grew. After 1700, immigration to the Cape declined, leading to a diminishing share of people at the bottom tail of the wealth distribution. Wealth inequality consequently decreased. The increase in inequality after 1740 was mainly driven by changes in the upper tail, where a group of farmers managed to accumulate wealth at a faster pace than the average. According to Fourie and von Fintel, this was because the first generation of immigrants had been able to establish viable farms that were successfully taken over by the second generation. Those who were relatively better off could reap the benefits of economies of scale by employing more slaves (see also Gulke and Shell 1983 and Worden 1985).

There is a fairly large literature from the 1980s that implicitly analyses wealth distribution by focusing on the rise of a specific group of European settlers, the Cape gentry. The interest stems from work done by the German immigrant O. F. Mentzel, who lived at the Cape in the 1730s. Mentzel divided the European settlers at the Cape into four groups. First, there were the poorest, who were pastoral farmers living in the interior. Above them he identified crop farmers who owned few slaves and worked hard to make a living. They were, in Mentzel's terms, both 'master and *knecht*'. The second wealthiest group were settlers who operated profitable farms, while the richest group consisted of Europeans living in Cape Town and owning several profitable farms (Guelke and Shell 1983: 277). The latter Mentzel describes as 'capitalists … who live in town but own estates in the country, which are worked by slaves and managed by an overseer or steward who has to render a proper account periodically to his employer' (1925–1944, vol. 2: 85). It is this second wealthiest group of settlers that Mentzel defined as a gentry. Mentzel referred to them as settlers who live in the south-western Cape and 'who possess excellent farms, paid for and lucrative, who live on these farms and produce more than they consume' (vol. 3: 98–101).

Although Mentzel's classification was vague, it has nevertheless inspired a number of scholars to critically analyse the factors that explain their rise. Ross (1983) refers to the gentry as a group of farmers who produced for the markets on an extensive scale and contends that they constituted the broad mass of farmers rather than a small elite. Guelke (1979), on the other hand, defines the gentry as a small group of farmers that had relatively large farms that they operated by using slaves. The problem with this is that slave ownership was widespread among farmers (see Chapter 4) and Guelke failed to provide a definition of a large farm in the context of Cape settler agriculture. Dooling (2005) similarly defines the 'gentry' in terms of having access to large landholdings and slaves. To this he adds that the gentry had a certain degree of influence over local politics (I discuss this in more depth in Chapter 6).

Williams (2013) rightly points out that having access to large tracts of land does not necessarily put farmers into a certain class in the economic sense of the term. Farmers need sufficient labourers to put the land into productive use and it is their differential access to labourers that should define them into different classes. Given the importance of slaves, both as labour and capital, it would make sense to distinguish the gentry from other groups of settler-farmers in terms of number of slaves owned. This is in line with Giliomee (2003), who defines the 'gentry' as farmers who owned sixteen slaves or more. Following this definition and using Worden's (1985) estimate of the distribution of slave ownership (see Chapter 4) we can see that in the south-western Cape, the size of the gentry class increased over time.

The question is: what enabled the growth of the gentry? To answer that, one must differentiate between the initial conditions enabling a group of farmers to accumulate wealth and the factors that enabled them to sustain this accumulation over time. Starting with the former, it seems likely that the first mover advantage played a role. In Chapter 3, we saw that the first wave of settlers to grant freehold land rights located their farms in more suitable areas than groups coming later. Explorative work by Cilliers, Green and Ross (2021) suggests that the first mover advantage continued to play a role as the colony expanded geographically.

But, again, having access to the best land means little if you lack the capacity to utilize it productively. Fourie and von Fintel (2012) argue that Huguenots from wine-producing areas of France who arrived as refugees at the Cape in 1688 had a comparative advantage in viticulture. Controlling for labour, soil quality and other important factors, they argue that these farmers on average produced more wine than other settlers. They do not associate the rise of viticulture in the Cape with gentry farmers explicitly, but argue that by the end of the eighteenth century these wine producers were among the wealthiest vignerons in the Cape.

I have no reason to question this interpretation, but two factors lead me to argue for modifying the role of human capital in it. First, wine played a marginal role in wealth accumulation until the second half of the eighteenth century. Exports of wine were small and of low quality. Wine travelled badly and Cape wine had a poor reputation abroad. Passing ships wanted to purchase brandy, not wine (Theal [1922] 1964; Ross 1993). Exports of Cape wine did not start to grow until the 1740s, when it began to be exported annually to Batavia (Guelke 1989; Boshoff and Fourie 2010). In the 1770s, wine surpassed wheat as the major export crop (van Duin and Ross 1987). Before that, the money one could make out of viticulture was limited and it is not surprising that Boshoff and Fourie (2010) find no correlation between passing ships and the production of wine. Instead, as I showed in Chapter 3, the most important source of wealth in the first seventy years of settler farming was investing in cattle and slave labour.

As discussed above, access to slaves correlated strongly with farmers' wealth. This was true in the eighteenth century when the use of slave labour first took off. Before that, the number of slaves remained low. In Chapter 4, I showed that slaves were expensive and required farmers to have access to sufficient capital. The number of settlers with large slaveholdings was very small until the second decade of the eighteenth century. In 1682, only 2 per cent of settlers had more than fifteen slaves and none had more than twenty. By 1702, 3 per cent had more than fifteen slaves, while 2 per cent had between fifteen and twenty slaves and 1 per cent had more than twenty-five. It was not until 1710 that the share of settlers with more than fifteen slaves began to grow and by 1731, 12 per cent had between fifteen and twenty slaves while 8 per cent had between twenty to twenty-five and 6 per cent had more than twenty-five (Fourie and von Fintel 2010a). In other words, the size of the gentry class – if defined in terms of number of slaves – was negligible until 1710. To understand the drivers of inequality, we thus need to take one step back and ask how the settlers managed to accumulate enough capital to invest in slaves in the first place.

Inequality and initial sources of capital

It is generally agreed that most of the European immigrants to the Cape were poor, although exceptions existed. High death rates and the low wages offered by the VOC made it difficult to attract wealthy Europeans. Most of the immigrants were farmers, skilled artisans or labourers (Guelke 1989). Once the VOC decided to promote European agriculture, the immigrants were initially offered favourable conditions. They were allowed to cultivate as much land as they could, and they were provided agricultural implements, seed and cattle on credit (Theal [1922] 1964). To turn agriculture into a profitable business, however, they needed labour, an input that was *not* subsidized by the VOC. One possibility was to invest in slaves, but this required capital, which had to be generated from non-farm activities.

As Worden (1985) and Williams (2013) have shown, many farmers did not initially accumulate wealth from farming, but by engaging in trade, transport and other non-farm activities. Investing in the tertiary sector was an important source of income for many Europeans. Passing ships and their crew brought money to Cape Town that was spent on lodging, food, drink, prostitution and minor trade. According to van Duin and Ross (1987) this 'may indeed have contributed, through the multiplier effect, to the prosperity of [the] Colony in ways we have been unable to measure' (quoted in Boshoff and Fourie 2010: 473).

A large portion of the activities in the urban tertiary sector indeed went unrecorded, but a survey of occupations in Cape Town in 1732 reveals that about

20 per cent of the settlers were employed in the service sector, while another 40 per cent were recorded as 'uncertain' (Boshoff and Fourie 2010). Having said that, by far the most profitable business was to gain control of domestic trade. In order to trade, a licence (*pacht*) from the VOC was needed. Only a few settler-farmers were granted such rights (see Chapter 6). This monopsony power over local trade generated substantial profits (Groenewald 2007).

There are several examples of wealthy farmers who began their careers outside of agriculture. H. O. Eksteen, for example, initially accumulated his wealth by getting a licence to trade in alcohol. The money he made through trading he invested in farming. By 1731, he had acquired a total of seven freehold farms, six loan farms and one hundred slaves (Groenewald 2007). Investing in pastoral farming and viticulture was especially profitable for this group as it could be integrated with their trading businesses and ownership of slaughterhouses. In that regard, as Williams (2013) has observed, their advantages did not lie in productive farming per se, but in their control over the markets. Some of the businessmen would become absent landlords and not a landed gentry as defined in the literature, while others would move out of Cape Town to become full-time farmers.

Most settlers, however, lacked the financial capital and, equally important, the political connections to the VOC to get a trading licence. Instead, they gradually accumulated wealth by investing in agriculture. As shown above and in Chapter 3, investment in viticulture was initially relatively modest and not very profitable. The market for wheat was better, but growth in wheat production was slow until the 1720s. What initially became a chief source of accumulation was pastoral farming. The demand for meat was initially comparatively high and remained stable in the seventeenth and early eighteenth centuries. According to Robertson (1984: 114), the combination of freehold tenure and the associated right to access pastureland gave individual settler-farmers an opportunity to accumulate wealth at a rapid pace, and this led to increased inequality among the settlers. He concludes that:

> it was in the stock farming and/or bartering or otherwise acquiring stock from the Hottentots, fattening it, and supplying the more buoyant markets for animal products, that exceptional wealth would seem to have accumulated most rapidly in the hands of a limited number of farmer-butchers, whose wealth was not necessarily reflected – or was only partially (and secondarily) reflected – in extensive freehold properties.

In sum, the wealthiest livestock farmers were those who had the capacity to also take control of the local meat trade and/or industry. Over time, they increased their investments in arable farming, most notably viticulture (Williams 2013). The gentry, on the other hand, were those who invested mainly in livestock that they sold in Cape Town, to the VOC or sometimes directly to passing ships.

Labour and accumulation in the seventeenth-century Cape Colony

Until 1717, early arrivals generally managed to access the most suitable lands as a consequence of the VOC policy of first-come, first-served. They also benefited from the vague formulation of property rights with regard to pastureland, which allowed them to gain control of rather vast land areas (see Chapter 3). This led to a concentration of land ownership that benefited early arrivals over latecomers (Guelke and Shell 1983).

As already mentioned, land concentration per se would have limited effect on wealth inequality if farmers lacked access to the sufficient number of labourers needed to make productive use of the land under their control. Slave labour was in part a solution, but investing in slaves was expensive and only an option for the few wealthy settlers who could invest in non-farming activities. The majority had to gradually build up their wealth by investing in agriculture, which, again, would generate profits if the settlers could manage to access and control sufficient numbers of Khoesan labourers.

According to Elphick (1977), settlers were initially reluctant to employ Khoesan labourers. They mistrusted the Khoesan as herders as they feared that they would steal the cattle. They also considered the Khoesan to be inefficient as farm workers as they lacked skills in arable farming. As the settlers expanded beyond the Cape Peninsula, however, the need for labour became acute. Buying slaves or hiring *knechts* was initially not an option for most farmers because they lacked sufficient capital. To operate their farms, they needed access to Khoesan labour (Penn 2005). Low population densities, the nomadic lifestyle of the Khoesan and most likely a general dislike of the Europeans among them made it challenging for the settlers to find sufficient supply of labourers. In his racist and prejudiced terms, Theal ([1922] 1964: 351) summarized the situation well as it was perceived by the VOC and some settlers:

> The colonists would gladly have employed some hundreds of Hottentots [i.e. Khoe], if they could have been induced to take service, but the men loved their wild, free, idle life too well to exchange it for one of toil. They had no objection, however, to do light work occasionally to earn tobacco and spirits, and in

harvesting especially they were useful. They were willing also to hire out their female children, and by this means a few household servants were obtained and knowledge of the Dutch language was spread. None of them had yet progressed so far in civilization as to make gardens for themselves, or in any way to cultivate the ground.

But it was not that the Khoesan people were lazy that made it challenging for the settlers to employ them as farm workers. Instead, it made little sense for them to work for the settler-farmers as long as they could continue as independent pastoral farmers selling cattle directly to the settlers or the VOC. The situation was partly eased by the expansion of the Europeans and the hostility between the various Khoesan societies that this caused. This gave some settlers the opportunity to employ Khoesan who found themselves bereft of cattle as a result of infighting. It was commonly reported in the seventeenth century that groups of Khoesan moved in gangs from farm to farm (Elphick 1977). They used temporary employment as a strategy to gain the means to restock their herds. From the landlords' perspective, however, this source of labour was inherently unreliable. Settlers could never be sure that sufficient numbers of Khoesan labourers would be around in time for the peak seasons or finish their tasks before they left. Although often treated harshly, the Khoesan gang labourers therefore operated with some degree of freedom. To make matters worse, the settler-farmers competed with the VOC over Khoesan labour, as shown in Chapter 4. It seems plausible to assume that the Khoesan would prefer to be employed by the VOC as the Company could offer better protection and possibly also higher levels of remuneration.

The settler-farmers consequently needed to take certain measures to obtain the service of sufficient numbers of Khoesan. The use of direct coercive measures on a systematic level was not possible. This resembles the situation of European settlers in twentieth-century colonial Africa. Europeans in the latter era depended on the colonial authorities to take measures to ensure a process of primitive accumulation. The authorities were able to increase the opportunity cost of African farming to the extent that Africans were willing to sell their labour to the European landlords (Arrighi 1970; Frankema, Green and Hillbom 2016; Fibaek and Green 2019). With the exception of allowing settlers to establish farms on land already occupied by Khoesan, no explicit measures were taken by the VOC to facilitate an increase in the supply of Khoesan labourers. They were not taxed, they were not removed to special designated areas, and control of their mobility was not introduced until the nineteenth century. Even though land was already scarce in the south-western Cape by the end of the eighteenth century (see Chapter 3), Khoesan who were still in possession of cattle theoretically had the option to move farther into the interior.

By the end of the seventeenth century, the expansion of the frontier had not yet gone far enough to completely disintegrate the Khoesan in the south-western Cape and its environs. Neither the economic nor the political forces were strong enough to invoke a full-scale process of primitive accumulation and turn the pastoral Khoesan into a proletariat. This did not mean that the Khoesan were untouched by the development that did occur. Their nomadic pastoral economy lost access to valuable land as Europeans brought the south-western Cape under their control. This, together with the cattle trade and the wars against the European intruders (see Chapter 2), put the two societies under pressure as it strained their capacity to build up their herds.

The strain the Khoesan experienced is best exemplified by the experience of two groups: the Chainouqua, who dwelled on the rich pastures of the southern plain west of the colonial frontier, and the Cochoqua, present at the south-western Cape. Together with the Hessequa, farther west, the Chainouqua were likely among the wealthiest Khoesan societies in the mid-seventeenth century. This wealth temporarily gave the Chainouqua the upper hand in conflicts with other Khoesan societies like the Cochoqua. Fifty years later, its prosperity and power had diminished considerably.

The Chainouqua were involved in a continual feud with the Cochoqua. At the height of the second frontier war (1671-7), their alliance with the VOC enabled them to severely weaken the latter group. This alliance came at a cost, however, as the Chainouqua, in exchange, had to ensure a steady supply of livestock to the VOC. In 1693, Governor Simon van der Stel, under pressure from enemies of the Chainouqua, abandoned his friendship with them. The Chainouqua were already weakened due to diminishing herds caused by the intensive trade with the VOC (Ross 1989). The once-powerful society was on the verge of disintegrating. No longer protected by the alliance with the VOC, many of its members sought employment as labourers for the settler-farmers.

While temporary losses of cattle could be dealt with on a societal level, individual Khoesan families found it increasingly difficult to manage major losses. Those who owned just a small number of livestock were vulnerable to exogenous shocks like theft or disease as the supply of cattle within their communities was reduced through intensive trading and warfare. The European settler-farmers could take advantage of this vulnerability by offering Khoesan the hope of regaining their stock the way that had often been used traditionally: by herding for someone else. We lack reliable records of remuneration, but according to Elphick (1977), the wages received by the Khoesan who worked as casual labourers for settler-farmers were likely too low to enable them to restock and return to their weakened *kraals* (villages). Instead, the Khoesan would settle on the farms and work as herders as well as farm labourers for an extended period of time. For this, they were often paid in livestock and were allowed to herd it on the settlers' land. This was the possibility available to the Khoesan to rebuild their herds in the shortest time possible (Viljoen 2001; Penn 2005).

By the beginning of the 1680s, settler-farmers in the south-western Cape began to encourage the Khoesan to come and live on their farms. Although evidence is only scattered and prevents any quantification of the Khoesan who did this, there are numerous references to Khoesan families living on European farms in the latter part of the seventeenth century (Elpick 1977; van de Merwe [1938] 1995). This patron–client relationship provided the settlers with a partial solution to the high enforcement costs associated with employing Khoesan on short-term contracts. It was quite easy for casual workers to desert their employment when they needed to. Their *kraals* were not very far away, and the VOC lacked the capacity to police them (Ross 1993). Tying the Khoesan to the farms on long-term contracts (in which they were paid in livestock and also allowed to herd their own cattle and sheep) lowered the incentives for them to run away. In 1688, a VOC captain reported that the Khoesan were living side by side with the Europeans in the south-western Cape. In rather enthusiastic terms, he described 'their love and affection toward us growing more and more, so that at the present during the pressure of harvest and plowing time, they slip down among us just like the Westphalians in the Netherlands' (quoted in van de Merwe [1938] 1995: 24).

The first quantitative observation we have of livestock ownership among Khoesan workers is from 1798, almost 150 years after the establishment of the colony, when the expansion of the colony's borders had weakened the Khoesan to the point that very few could still live independently. At that point, the average Khoesan residing on a European farm had five cattle and twenty-three sheep (Ross 1993). It is likely that the numbers were larger at the end of the seventeenth century, when Khoesan societies had not yet collapsed.

The need to tie Khoesan labour to the farm created incentives for the settlers in the south-western Cape to control more pastureland than they actually needed for their own farming. This not only facilitated dispersion farther into the interior, as we saw in Chapter 3, but also created the increased concentration of land and other assets that Guelke and Shell (1983) observed. As the settlers lacked the economic and political capacity to push the Khoesan out on the labour market, those who had the means gained control over larger amounts of land in order to pull Khoesan to their farms as herders. These farmers would eventually constitute an important part of the Cape gentry.

Gender, inheritance and wealth accumulation

To what extent did the wealthy manage to keep their fortunes within their families across generations? The factors that explain the initial accumulation of capital are not the same as those that explain their persistence. To understand the continuity of wealth, we need to draw our attention to inheritance practices at the Cape. The Cape followed the Dutch model of partible inheritance. The implication of this system was described in Chapter 3. Ross (1993: 141) summarizes it in this way:

> property was divided and redivided at regular intervals ... This entailed either that the farm as a running concern would be sold, and the proceeds divided among the heirs, or that a valuation would be made of the estate with the heirs receiving their portions in cash. In the latter case, the survivor would in all probability be forced to take out a loan to pay off his or her children and stepchildren.

The system of partible inheritance made it more difficult to pass on wealth across generations than was the case in primogeniture systems, in which wealth was bequeathed to the oldest child (most commonly the son). Scholars like Fourie and von Fintel (2010a) also emphasize the negative effects the system of inheritance could have on wealth accumulation. Notably, it led to smaller farms. Conflicts over productive resources among family members were common, often ending with one or more members moving farther into the interior in search of fresh land (see Chapter 3).

The farmers in the south-western Cape owned their farms, while settlers farther into the interior leased their land from the VOC on an annual basis (see Chapter 3). Their land could not be subdivided or sold. Loan farmers did own permanent buildings, farm equipment and slaves, however, and these could be auctioned after the death of a farmer. In practice, buying the permanent buildings gave the purchaser the right to take over the lease contract.

Contemporary witnesses argued that if the inheritance system allowed farms to be sold off or subdivided, it would stymie long-term accumulation. In the early nineteenth century, a British merchant at the Cape made the following claim about the system:

> if, as is very frequently the case, there is a large family of children, and several of them are still minors, the whole property must be exposed to public sale, in order that it may be realized in money to effect its division into, perhaps, eight or ten equal shares. By these means the family farm either falls into new hands or if purchased back by one of the heirs, it is now reoccupied, either with funds inadequate to its full cultivation, or upon capital borrowed at the rate of six, or perhaps eight, per cent interest; which presses as a dead weight upon the new possessor, probably, for half his lifetime. The rest of the sons either purchase farms on credit, and enter upon them in the same embarrassed state; or, if they cannot effect this, they migrate to the frontier districts, and become graziers.
>
> (quoted in Ross 1993: 143–4)

This observation seems to suggest declining wealth inequality among settler-farmers over time, which is at odds with the inequality estimates provided by Guelke and Shell (1983) and Fourie and von Fintel (2010a, 2011). Swanepoel (2017) even found significant levels of upward mobility among the settler farming population. Sons managed to have equal amounts and sometimes even more land and slaves than their fathers had. Scattered evidence also indicates that many of the settlers who were wealthy in the early years of the colony remained so throughout the eighteenth century. Ross (1983), for example, shows that among the fifty-three families that were the leading wine producers in Stellenbosch in 1731, nineteen remained in 1825. To quote Dooling (2005: 149), 'It is clear, for instance, that there was significant continuity amongst large landed families of the southwestern Cape through the eighteenth and until the beginning of the nineteenth centuries, yet it is not at all clear how and why such continuity was maintained or what factors undermined it.'

This seems counterintuitive given the practice of partible inheritance. How was wealth maintained across generations despite the sales and parcelling out of property? How do we account for this paradox? Dooling (2005) argues that much of the literature on wealth and inheritance in pre-industrial rural economies narrowly employs an Anglocentric model in which primogeniture forms the basis of land stability and wealth accumulation. In order to understand the development of landed elites at the Cape, we have to separate individual families from specific pieces of land. Instead, wealth was accumulated through *marriage*. This gave women in general and widows in particular an important role in wealth accumulation. Dooling (2005: 40) explains: 'Women (and widows in particular) were central to ensuring the preservation of landed and slave wealth ... Partible inheritance gave [settler women] control over significant amount of property, both landed and human, and it was their control over such property that secured the stability of the Cape's landed elite.'

Land may have changed hands regularly, but owners were frequently related to each other through marriage. Marriage was thus an important part of wealth accumulation. It was used in various ways to keep wealth within the family (Dooling 2005). Marriage between close relatives could, in particular, be used to avoid the effects of land fragmentation. As Mitchell (2007: 8) notes,

> In a family with six children, at the death of a parent, the surviving spouse would inherit half the estate and the children would split the other half equally. One-twelfth of a farm was not likely to maintain subsistence, let alone be a stepping stone to prosperity. If, however, a pair of siblings was to cooperate with siblings from another family, an equitable exchange was possible that would put both couples on a better footing.

According to Mitchell (2007), familial unions made up a considerable part of the recognized marriages at the Cape, which suggests that inheritance negotiations must have played an important part in marital decisions. Women were significantly younger than the men, in most cases, when they got married. There was also a significant sex imbalance throughout the eighteenth century. It was greater at the frontier, where there were 227 men for every 100 women, as compared to 174 men for every 100 women in Cape Town and the immediate surroundings (Cilliers 2012). The age gap between men and women at marriage meant that widowhood was virtually guaranteed for women and remarriages were fairly common, while the sex imbalances made it fairly easy for widows to get remarried. It even happened that women remarried more than once (du Plessis, Jansen and von Fintel 2013).

The farm Wolwedans can be used as an illustrative example. As noted in Chapter 3, the farm was sold no less than nine times between 1751 and 1835. Who were the new owners? In 1757, the owner of the farm Jacobus van Aarden sold it to his brother-in-law Dirk Verwey. Twenty-five years later the farm was transferred to Dirk Verwey's son Dirk Gysbert Verwey. By then the farm was owned by Jan Jurgen Cotze. He was none other than the second husband of Dirk Verwey's widow, Susanna Francina van Aarden. In 1797, the farm was sold again, this time to one Jacobus Gideon. Gideon was Dirk Gysbert Verwey's brother-in-law who had married Martha Angelina Verwey in 1765. What this shows is that all owners of the farm between 1751 to 1810 were connected through marriage (Dooling 2005).

The Cape Colony was a patriarchal economy where all major economic decisions were taken by the men (Ross 1999). Yet, the system of inheritance gave individual women a key role for long-run accumulation of capital within families. Their social and economic position was in that regard in many ways stronger than in for example Western Europe. As there were fewer females than males at the Cape, women commonly married someone belonging to a better social class. This in turn meant that women who had remarried several times often managed to improve their financial status substantially (Giliomee 2003; du Plessis, Jansen and von Fintel 2013). In a few cases marrying a widow also enabled settler men to gain access to substantial amounts of wealth, although the practice remained rather uncommon (Ross 1993; Williams 2013). For example, one of the wealthiest settlers in the Stellenbosch district of the mid-eighteenth century, Jan Blignault, accessed the farm by marrying widow Anna Rossouw in 1725, just two years upon his arrival at the Cape (du Plessis, Jansen and von Fintel 2013). Another example is Martin Melck. He was a German immigrant who arrived at the Cape in the eighteenth century. He initially worked as a *knecht* for the VOC. With the money he used, he managed to buy two farms and then married Margaretha Hop, a very wealthy widow. At his death in 1781 he was the richest man in the Cape, owning no less than 204 slaves and with investments in the lucrative wine trade (Giliomee 2003; Groenewald 2011). What all these examples show is that marriage alliance played a significant role in both creating and sustaining wealth. It was used to ensure that wealth was kept within the family despite the system of partible inheritance. Farms changed hands, while wealth stayed within the family across generations.

Conclusion

Much of the previous research on inequality in settler-colonial societies has focused on political factors, but institutional factors explain levels of inequality and their persistence. Historians have argued that inequality levels were a function of the economic and political interests of the settlers. In this chapter, I use the Cape Colony as a case study for understanding the evolution and persistence of inequality from an economic perspective. As I show, the evolution of inequality is complex. One not only must differentiate between the factors that explain the rise of inequality and those that explain its persistence; one also needs to understand which income and/or wealth classes are driving the inequality trends, how groups initially accumulated wealth and to what extent this wealth was kept within families across generations. This can hardly be done by trying to identify one or two determinants of inequality. In brief, the Cape Colony represents a case of high levels of inequality that increased over time. From the middle of the eighteenth century, this was mainly driven by a concentration of wealth and/or incomes among the wealthiest farmers.

Much of the previous literature on inequality in settler economies emphasized the distribution of land. Being able to take control of large tracts of fertile land was an important but not sufficient factor to explain inequality in a pre-industrial settler-colonial context. The key to understanding initial differences in wealth accumulation was to what extent different settler groups were able to make productive use of the land. Settlers' access and control over labour was in this regard key to understanding income and wealth accumulation. Cape historians have recognized the importance of labour for the growth of settler farming in the colony, but their focus has largely been on the role of slave labour. Access to slave labour was indeed essential for farmers' wealth and income accumulation in the long run, but that does not help us understand why some farmers were initially able to purchase more slaves than others. Investing in slaves was expensive and for most settlers initially not a viable option.

The minority who early on were able to invest in slaves were those who managed to invest in off-farm activities, namely, trading and/or urban services. It is no coincidence that among the wealthier settlers at the Cape many were involved in both farming, trading and urban economic activities. Making such investments required a licence from the VOC. This avenue for wealth accumulation was only open to a very small group of settlers who had established good contacts with the VOC. In that regard, political factors mattered for inequality at the Cape (see the more detailed discussion of this in Chapter 6).

The other option, available to the majority of settlers, was to accumulate income by attaching indigenous Khoesan labour to their farms. Coercion was used to control the Khoesan, but not on a systematic level, as that was not supported by the VOC. Instead, the first group of settlers to establish farms in the south-western Cape took advantage of the fact that they could acquire vast tracts of land, including pastureland, at a low cost. They used this opportunity to take control of more land than they could make productive use of. This created a situation of artificial scarcity that not only prevented competing settlers from establishing farms in the south-western Cape, but also enabled them to attract weakened groups of Khoesan to stay on their farms and rebuild their herding stocks in exchange for labour.

While access to Khoesan labour and off-farm economic opportunities can explain the initial accumulation of capital, marriage strategies are key to understanding how wealthy settlers kept their wealth within families across generations. Although weak property rights and the practice of partible inheritance would theoretically hamper the persistence of an economic elite, marriage alliance enabled elite families to retain their farms and wealth.

This chapter has shown that while factors like land distribution and slave ownership can be used to identify long-term patterns of inequality, they do not help us understand its evolution. The chapter has also demonstrated that rather than imposing European institutions and destroying the indigenous communities with ease, Dutch settler-farmers at the Cape had to adapt to local circumstances and take the agency of the Khoesan into account in order to make productive use of the land.

As we saw earlier, RPE scholars place a great deal of emphasis on the role of politics as a means of understanding the persistence of inequality. Some argue that elites could maintain their economic status by ensuring that policies are implemented to limit other people's access to resources and markets. In the next chapter, I focus specifically on the role of the VOC in shaping the Cape economy. I analyse whether the Company's mercantilistic policies hampered the development of profitable settler agriculture and discuss whether and to what extent the VOC represented the interests of the landed elite.

6

Elites, coalitions and settler resistance

Introduction

A fundamental question in the scholarly work on European settler economies is the extent to which the colonial authorities represented the interests of the settlers. Much of the previous literature on the Cape Colony assumes that the VOC had almost complete control over the territories and implemented policies in favour of the settlers in general or elites among the settlers in particular. In this chapter, I take issue with this interpretation by combining an understanding of the frontier with the concepts of social contracts and elite coalitions. As discussed in Chapter 1, an open frontier is characterized by a fluid social order. This has profound effects on the relationship between the settlers and the colonial authorities. Neither was entirely in control of events, even (as explained in previous chapters) in cases in which their interests were clearly aligned. The divergent interests among the settler population, the agency of the Khoesan and the administratively and financially weak VOC were all key factors that need to be considered if we are to understand the political economy of the Cape Colony.

To make sense of these complexities, I take as my point of departure the theoretical work of North, Wallis and Weingast (2009) on states and elites that I introduced in Chapter 1. This means that we treat the VOC conceptually as a specific form of a so-called natural state – a state that is weak and dependent on stable coalitions of elite groups. These authors focus on the transition from one type of a state to another. While the descriptions of 'open' states and transitions between states have been criticized, the theory of 'natural' states has seen strong levels of support (e.g. Bates 2010). In short, a natural state is inherently fragile, and its existence depends on the capacity to extract rents that are unevenly distributed among a small elite. In that regard, the Cape Colony was held together by not giving the population at large open access to politics and markets, but by granting that access only to a few. If the size of the coalition grew too fast, or its ability to extract rents diminished, the system would fall apart, either gradually or in a more dramatic way. This implies that a natural state is inherently fragile. As long as the frontier is open and expanding, new competing elites may arise as the economy evolves. These new elites either have to be included in the coalition or repressed. If we accept this argument, then we cannot portray the relationship between colonial settler elites and the authorities as static.

To tease out the changing relationship between the VOC, the settler farming community and the Khoesan, I begin with Nugent's classification of social contracts. In his article 'States and social contracts in Africa' (2010), Nugent critically reviews studies on states in Africa and concludes that they ignore the way the relationships between the states and the populations vary. To capture the variation, Nugent proposes three different contracts: coercive, productive and permissive. A coercive contract is one in which the right to govern is predicated on the rulers' capacity to make life miserable for the subjects. In extreme cases, the ruled give away their political voice in exchange for not being exposed to predatory acts from the authorities. A productive contract represents the opposite of a coercive one. In this case, the rulers and the ruled have, through negotiations, agreed that the rulers will have the right to govern as long as they improve the life of the ruled. Lastly, the permissive contract represents a situation in which the government has the capacity to be coercive but exercises restraint in order to ensure some kind of de facto compliance.

Although Nugent's classification scheme allows for a more complex picture of the African colonial and postcolonial state, it has some limitations. First, when identifying the social contracts, Nugent largely focuses on the relationship between the government and certain sections of the population. In the case of Ghana, for example, the focus is on the relationship between the authorities and the cocoa growers, the latter being crucial for the colonial economy, but nevertheless constituting a minority of the population. Second, Nugent does not allow for several social contracts to exist in parallel. It could be that the existence of one contract between the state and parts of the population is predicated on the presence of another contract between the state and other parts of the population. To take an extreme example, one may conclude that the relationship between the government and the white minority in apartheid South Africa was based on a productive contract that relied heavily on a coercive contract between the government and the majority of the black African population. Lastly, Nugent does not take into account that contracts may change over time as a consequence of shifting power balances between the authorities and the various segments of the population as well as among those different segments.

In this chapter, I build on Nugent's notion of social contracts by allowing for all three types to exist in parallel and to depend upon one another. I also allow for contracts to change over time. Using the existence of multiple social contracts and taking the limitations of the VOC's powers, the divergent interests of the settlers and the agency of the Khoesan into account, this chapter provides an analysis of the political economy of the Cape Colony.

Typologies of settler colonialism

A number of scholars have pointed out that settler colonies became relatively independent of metropolitan rule. This autonomy is often used to distinguish between settler colonies and other forms of colonialism (see Veracini 2013). Settlers used their relative independence to assert control over the colonial authorities and ensure that an institutional order was established that acted in their interests (Arrighi 1970; Frankema, Green and Hillbom 2016). Mosley (1983) and Osterhammel (1997) argue that what distinguished settler from non-settler colonies in twentieth-century Africa was not the number of settlers, but whether settlers' interests had representatives in the local colonial government. In short, a precondition for a settler colony to emerge and sustain itself was that the settlers' interests were protected by the local colonial authorities.

Elkins and Pedersen (2005) sketch what they refer to as a 'beginning of a typology' of settler colonialism in an attempt to move beyond the assumption of a generically strong relationship between settlers and local authorities. The typology concentrates on four variables: high and low levels of institutionalization of settler privilege and high and low levels of the incorporation of settlers into governance. Figure 6.1 summarizes this typology and shows where Elkins and Pedersen place different settler colonies. What the typology suggests is that there are cases where settlers have been privileged yet had no influence over local administration (e.g. Nazi Germany's occupation of Eastern Europe). There are also cases in which settlers have been part of the local government but have not experienced favourable treatment (e.g. Northern Ireland). There are even cases where the settlers have been neither represented nor privileged (e.g. Japan's colonies in Asia).

Unlike Elkins and Pedersen's cases from the twentieth century, the Cape was governed by a Company and was not a nation state. A chartered company's

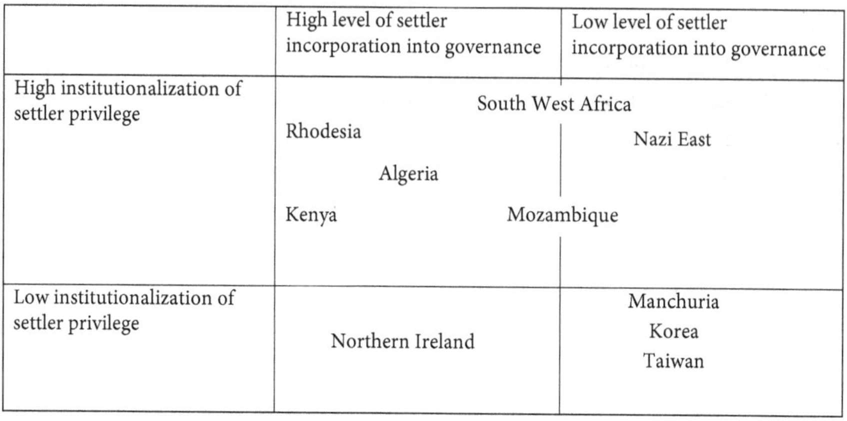

	High level of settler incorporation into governance	Low level of settler incorporation into governance
High institutionalization of settler privilege	South West Africa Rhodesia Algeria Kenya	Nazi East Mozambique
Low institutionalization of settler privilege	Northern Ireland	Manchuria Korea Taiwan

Figure 6.1 Graph of settler privilege and incorporation into governance.

Source: Elkins and Pedersen (2005: 5).

chief objective is to create profits for its shareholders by engaging in global trade. The financial interests of the Company were always the overall priority. For a chartered company, control over territory is never an objective in itself, but can be deemed necessary to make trade profitable. Furthermore, the Cape Colony was not a source of the lucrative spices and other trade goods which Asian settlements offered. It was merely a transit point for Asian luxury goods (Baartman 2015). To avoid expenses, the Lords XVII of the VOC pushed the local authorities to keep the colony's recurrent running costs as low as possible. In a way, the VOC represented an extreme form of a 'gate-keeping state', a concept introduced by the African historian Frederick Cooper in 2002 to describe a colonial and postcolonial African state that is administratively and financially weak and whose existence depends on making revenues by taxing trade, or 'guarding the gate'. To make the Cape Colony a profitable enterprise, the VOC had to ensure that European settlers produced a surplus and that it would, to a large extent, control the profits.

Using Elkins and Pedersen's typology, one would place the Cape Colony in the same position as Kenya and Southern Rhodesia. The expansion of the Cape Colony and its borders was not part of a long-term, planned process. Further, the financial capacity of the local authorities was severely limited because the managing Lords XVII remained unwilling to make any major investments in the colony and, throughout the eighteenth century, the income from exports was not sufficient to make ends meet (as discussed further below). While this made the colony financially weak, it also meant that the settlers could act either relatively independently of the local colonial authorities and the VOC headquarters in Amsterdam or could influence the local authorities to ensure that they worked in the settlers' interests, although the settlers lacked formal representation beyond the district levels.

Given that we are dealing with a frontier economy, we need to recognize the importance of indigenous agency. The fact that both the VOC and the settlers initially depended on the Khoesan for trade and labour made the situation delicate. To avoid losing a major trading partner, the VOC needed to ensure that the Khoesan societies did not completely collapse, though at the same time it was weakening their pastoral economies by depleting their livestock and employing them as labourers.

To analyse the political economy at the Cape we thus need to take into account a web of different interests. To understand these we first need to look at the fiscal capacity of the VOC. The Company's restricted financial and administrative capacity is an essential element for understanding the political economy of the Cape.

The fiscal capacity of the VOC

As the VOC was a shareholder company, short-term profitability was important to it. This profitability would be ensured through control of trade rather than long-term investment in productive activities. Control of territories was thus never an aim per se, although that was sometimes deemed necessary as a means of stimulating trade. To enable it to compete economically with the Portuguese and Spanish in the East Indies, the VOC was granted the right to monopolize all interregional trade in the East Indies and to control trade in all other areas that were under its control, including the Cape Colony (Fourie, Jansen and Siebrits 2013).

As mentioned in Chapter 2, the Lords XVII never planned to establish a permanent European settlement at the Cape. They intended only to found a small permanent station at the Cape of Good Hope to further facilitate trade with the Khoesan and passing ships. They never considered the Cape station to be commercially profitable for the VOC and consequently the Cape was not one of the Company's priorities (Ross 1989). Once the expansion of the colonial borders began, it was left to the VOC at the Cape to fund its own recurrent costs. Its main source of revenue came from trade, but revenues from exports remained low. Wheat was primarily exported to factories in Asia where it was

Table 6.1 Revenues, expenditures and deficits (in guilders) as percentages of GDP.

Year	Revenue	Expenditure	Deficit	GDP	Revenue/GDP ratio	Expenditure/ GDP ratio	Deficit/GDP ratio
1777	200,000	454,000	254,000	2,391,000	8%	19%	11%
1787	282,000	1,586,000	1,304,000	4,014,000	7%	40%	32%
1789	341,000	1,744,000	1,403,000	3,472,000	10%	50%	40%
1791	...	1,300,000	...	3,499,000	...	37%	...
1792	416,000	758,000	342,000	3,253,000	13%	23%	11%
1794	588,000	818,000	230,000	...	...	...	...

Source: de Kock (1924: 78).

made into bread for European traders, while wine produced at the Cape was long regarded as inferior and was not in demand in Europe or Asia. Exports of livestock products were limited. Salted meat could be sold as provisions for passing ships, but there was no export market as there was no technology for keeping the meat fresh for long periods of time (Ross 1989). The limited revenue from trade, in combination with an inefficient system of collecting taxes, meant that throughout its period of rule, the VOC was running on budget deficits (Ross 1989). Or, to quote Groenewald (2012: 1), the VOC at the Cape 'ran at an enormous loss'. Estimates by de Kock (1924) for the late eighteenth century, shown in Table 6.1, confirm this view.

To manage the situation, the VOC had to keep their recurrent expenditures as low as possible. In 1795, total expenditure was 790,000 guilders, of which 44 per cent went to law and order, 43 per cent to the military and the remainder to maintenance of the trading posts (de Kock 1924). The districts were expected to be self-financing. District authorities were responsible for infrastructure (maintenance of roads, bridges and churches) and remuneration (salaries for those employed by the district). The district authorities commonly ran deficits. Table 6.2 shows estimates of accumulated debt for selected years in the Stellenbosch and Swellendam districts. Worth noting is the substantial increase in debt in Stellenbosch, the home of many of the wealthier farmers at the Cape.

The financially weak VOC resembles the 'gate-keeping' states of twentieth-century colonial Africa (Cooper 2002). Its existence depended on the possibility

Table 6.2 Accumulated debt of Stellenbosch and Swellendam districts in selected years, 1702–93.

Stellenbosch		Swellendam	
Year	Guilders	Year	Rixdollars
1702	4,025	1760	4,333
1720	2,000	1770	4,333
1729	4,000	1780	4,333
1740	4,000		
1753	9,000		
1766	18,500		
1794	13,000		

Source: P. J. Venter (1960: 157), taken from Fourie, Jansen and Siebrits (2013: 64).

of making revenue by controlling trade. Being a 'natural state', this in turn required the creation of a coalition between the authorities and the settler elites.

Trade, profits and the settler elites

The Cape Colony differed from other possessions under VOC control in a crucial way: its economy over time became dependent on establishing profitable European agriculture. With the exception of the Banda archipelago in the Dutch East Indies, there were no other areas controlled by the VOC where a large number of European settlers organized agricultural production. Although the role of the Cape in the global economy was primarily to provision passing ships, it was a key concern of the VOC to earn as much revenue as possible from this trade. The initial idea of ensuring provisions through trade with the Khoesan was gradually abandoned as Europeans became the main suppliers of meat, grain and wine (Ross and Schrikker 2012).

In *An Inquiry Into the Nature and Causes of the Wealth of Nations*, Adam Smith criticized the Dutch practice of governing their colonies through private monopolies, saying that: 'Of all the expedients that can well be contrived to stunt the natural growth of a new Colony, that of an exclusive company is undoubtedly the most effectual' ([1776] 1982: 44). This criticism was grounded in his firm belief that free trade was fundamental for long-term economic growth as it would spur the division of labour. For him, the VOC's practices represented the very opposite, as he assumed that they had a monopoly over trade in the territories under their control. A number of scholars working on the Cape have confirmed this overall negative impression. The VOC used its monopsony power over trade at the Cape to buy European settler produce at prices that it set. It then sold the produce to the passing ships at much inflated prices (Worden 1985; Fourie, Jansen and Siebrits 2013). This would imply the existence of a coercive contract that enabled the VOC to extract rents from the settler-farmers. As expected, and as will be discussed below, this created tensions between the VOC and parts of the settler community.

The VOC's control over trade should not, however, be exaggerated (Ross 1983, 1989). As van Duin and Ross (1987) pointed out, if the VOC extracted profits from farmers by setting low prices and if the level of extraction increased over time, we would likely see a decline in agricultural production. This was not the case, as I showed in Chapter 3. Instead, production increased throughout the eighteenth century. Van Duin and Ross (1987) conclude that historians in general have tended to uncritically accept the views of the VOC's opponents, most notably the Cape Patriots, who complained about VOC control over the market and its pricing policies (see the further discussion below). The Patriots did not necessarily represent the interests of the settler-farmers at large.

In reality the VOC's ability to control trade was restricted. It had no direct control over imports, which were in the hands of private traders (Ross and Schrikker 2012). Its control over exports was only partial. In the 1770s, the VOC directly controlled only one-fifth of the wine market and half of the meat market. The rest was in the hands of licensed private traders (*pachters*) who sold the wine and meat either on the local market or to passing foreign ships. The VOC did, however, dominate the wheat market (van Duin and Ross 1987). Its control of the domestic market was partial and indirect, but nevertheless lucrative. Instead of directly engaging in trade, the VOC controlled the revenue stream by selling trading licences (*pachts*) to the settlers, which brought in substantial revenue, as Table 6.3 shows. Being able to grant one of these licences allowed individual settlers to accumulate significant amounts of wealth (as seen in Chapter 5). It was a system in which the authorities managed to establish a coalition between the VOC and the settler elites, regulated by a productive social contract from which both parties benefited.

In general, the prices paid by *pachters* on the auction floors were lower than those paid by the VOC. This is partly due to the nature of the trade. The settlers bought produce at the auctions that took place throughout the colony, while the VOC only bought produce at the Cape Town market. When selling to the VOC, the settler-farmers covered their own transport costs, while these were deducted by the private traders buying agricultural output at auction. As we do not know the locations of the various auctions, it is impossible to calculate the transport costs. Rather than comparing levels, we can look into price trends. Worden's (1985) estimates of prices at the auctions show that auction prices of

Table 6.3 VOC income from *pacht* as proportion of total revenues (selected years).

Year	Proportion of *pacht* income (%)
1777	41.1
1787	68.9
1789	65.2
1792	30.6

Source: van Duin and Ross (1987: 148–9).

wine remained fairly stable over time, while wheat prices declined significantly in the period from 1741 through the 1770s. The same did not happen with the wheat prices paid by the VOC, which remained stable throughout the period (see Table 6.4). The declining prices at auction require an explanation. Was the market saturated, as Guelke and Shell (1983) have claimed, or was the decline a consequence of local traders' increased ability to extract a larger share of profits from the wheat farmers, using non-market measures?

The period in which prices for wheat declined on the auctions coincided with the period when tax evasion peaked. One possible reason for the increased tax evasion was the wheat farmers' deteriorating financial situation. In the 1740s, they began to complain to the VOC about the Company's irregular demand for wheat. The farmers often had to stockpile produce before it could be sold (van Duin and Ross 1987). I have no evidence that the number of auctions declined during the period or that there was a declining demand for wheat on the export market. On the contrary, van Duin and Ross's estimates show that the demand for wheat increased by a factor of 5–6 between 1704 and 1793. Although difficult to substantiate empirically, one possible reason for the declining prices is that the private traders could use the irregular demand for wheat from the VOC to their advantage. They were willing and able to trade regularly with the wheat farmers, but only at declining prices.

Table 6.4 Average price of wheat (per muid) and wine (per leaguer) in rixdollars paid by VOC and at the auction floors.

Year	Wheat (per muid)	White wine (per leaguer)
1716	2.0	21
1720	2.2	22
1730	2.4	26
1740	2.4	28
1750	1.6	30
1760	1.5	38
1770	1.0	22
1780	2.4	38
1790	2.6	35
1800	2.8	30
Official Company price	2.6 (to 1741) 2.5 (after 1741)	27

Source: Worden (1985: 69).

The system of trade regulations that gave the VOC only indirect control created a strong coalition between the ruling and economic elites at the Cape. As I argued in Chapter 5, it was the wealthiest settlers who had the means and resources to control domestic trade by buying trading licences. This gave them the opportunity to extract rents from the majority of the settler-farmers. The VOC generated substantial revenues from this system, and the coalition of elites lasted only as long as the VOC benefited from it financially. Meanwhile, the system generated revenues only as long as a broad group of settlers could produce a surplus to be sold on the domestic markets, which in turn depended to a large extent on their ability to access and control enough labourers.

Landlords and labour: Productive or permissive contracts?

As I have shown in the preceding chapters, a fundamental driver of settler agriculture was European farmers' access to labour. In Chapters 4 and 5, I argued that there are good reasons to believe that the Khoesan played a more important role – for both the establishment and subsequent expansion of settler agriculture at the Cape – than previously acknowledged. To understand how the indigenous people were incorporated into the Cape settler economy in general and how the settlers managed to make productive use of them, I analyse the implicit contracts regulating the relationship between the Khoesan and the settlers.

During the eighteenth century, the VOC instituted legislation that limited the freedom of the Khoesan. Gradually, informal ways of controlling Khoesan labour were formalized through various legislative measures (Elphick and Giliomee 1989b). That is, over time, the contract between the VOC and the larger group of settlers was transformed from permissive to productive. This development may seem puzzling. Why was the VOC not prepared to provide legislation to support the coercion of Khoesan labour in the initial years, when Khoesan communities were still fairly independent? And why did it move towards more repressive legislation in the latter half of the eighteenth century when most of the Khoesan communities had already lost their independence and had little choice other than to be incorporated into the colonial economy? I argue that several factors explain the VOC's behaviour, but in more general terms it was only when the frontier was closing that the VOC achieved the capability to step in and legally back the labour relations already in place on the settler farms.

The VOC's power consisted of exercising jurisdiction not over territory but over people, in this case its employees and the settlers. It did not attempt to exercise judicial control over the Khoesan people, with the exception of those who were tied to the colonial economy and who thus interacted with the Europeans. In practice, this meant that the Khoesan could seek assistance through the VOC court system only in relational disputes with the Europeans. While the VOC could interfere in matters of labour disputes and the theft of livestock, it did not protect the rights of the Khoesan to access land. Without rights to land, the very existence of the Khoesan societies was under threat as the Europeans expanded their territory. This set in motion a process in which the Khoesan gradually went from being independent to a condition 'not far removed from that of serfs' (Elphick and Giliomee 1989b: 540).

Travellers to the Cape Colony were divided on how the Khoesan were treated by the settler-farmers. Some described the farmers as brutal, with no sense of humanity when it came to their Khoesan labourers; others reported that the Khoesan received fair and considerate treatment. The farmers themselves, unsurprisingly, leaned towards the latter description. They often blamed the Khoesan for being unreliable and for deserting. The Khoesan, on the other hand, blamed the settlers for mistreatment, violence and withholding agreed wages. The court records put the Khoesan in the right. They reveal high levels of violence on the employers' part and depict the existence of a master-servant relationship (Elphick and Malherbe 1989). As one would expect, though, the lack of any regulations tended to favour the more powerful, in this case the European farmers. Viljoen (2001: 49) describes the situation:

> After the Cape authorities ostensibly distanced themselves from matters concerning labor relations, colonists took recruitment and control of their labor force into their own hands to suit their operational needs. Since no legal contracts bound master and servant, colonists always maintained an advantage in verbal agreement.

The settlers quite early on requested legal support from the VOC to strengthen their control over Khoesan labour. In 1721, a group of farmers in Stellenbosch petitioned the Council of Policy for the right to apprentice the children of a 'free' Khoesan woman and a slave man. The Council turned down the request as the VOC believed that such measures would create tension between the Khoesan and the settlers (Elphick and Malherbe 1989). The Company was clearly aware that its political position at the Cape remained fragile. It was only in the latter half of the eighteenth century that the VOC took action to formalize limitations on the freedom of the Khoesan. In 1775, the governor approved a regulation in Stellenbosch that gave the right to settler-farmers to apprentice the children of a slave-Khoesan couple up to the age of twenty-five. Locally the system was known as *inboekstelsel*. In practice this meant that children of a free Khoesan woman and a slave man were born in temporary slavery, which also gave the settler-farmers increased control over the mother's mobility. According to Giliomee (1981: 85), 'The indentured system can be regarded as a quasi-institutional form of labour'. While it legalized the indenturing of previously free children, it did not regulate the settler's obligations towards the Khoesan child and the child's rights. The settler was obliged to provide the child with food and lodging, but there were no regulations for the use of these children as labourers. In 1787, the Council issued legislation that further limited the freedom of the Khoesan by forbidding them to live in the south-western Cape or to move around without carrying an identity document. In 1797, the same legislation was introduced in Swellendam and in 1798 in Graaff-Reinet on the eastern frontier (Elphick and Giliomee 1989b).

It seems puzzling that this piece of legislation was introduced 120 years after the establishment of colonial rule. By that time, most Khoesan had lost their independence and been co-opted into the labour market, so there would have been little need for it. It is also puzzling that it was at first applied only in the south-western Cape, since several historians have argued that the settlers treated the Khoesan more brutally at the frontier (Newton-King 1999; Penn 2005).

Elphick (1979) offers one way of understanding this puzzle. He argues that the transition towards more coercive legislation with regard to Khoesan labour did not derive only from settlers' demands. The legislation was passed in a period of military crises. The wars in Europe and North America increased the risk of the Cape Colony being attacked by foreign enemies. The VOC therefore decided to restrict the mobility of the Khoesan to make it easier to mobilize them for defence. The military crises further affected the supply of labour at the Cape as they led to a reduction in slave imports. Between the years 1787 and 1795, no slaves were imported into the colony. The shortfall had to be filled with Khoesan labour, which further created a need for the VOC to reduce Khoesan mobility. At the same time, the expansion of the colonial frontier had come to a halt as the Europeans faced severe conflict with the Xhosa (who often allied with the Khoesan) in the east and the Khoesan in the north. In the south-western Cape, these conflicts made the settlers, as well as the VOC, increasingly fearful of Khoesan resistance even in the commercial heart of the colony. Rumours of

Khoesan conspiring to kill all the colonists spread among the settler community (Elphick and Giliomee 1989).

While this is likely to be part of the story, the changes in legislation must also be understood in more generic terms as part of the process of frontier closure. In the early years of the colony, any legislation that backed coercive methods to be used by the settlers would have put the VOC at a great deal of risk. As shown in Chapter 2, the Khoesan had proven to be capable of resisting the European intruders in efficient and organized ways. In the very early years, they were not far from forcing the VOC to leave the Cape. The VOC was aware of the strength of the Khoesan and for this reason did not allow the local authorities to enslave them. Instead, given its weak financial and administrative capacities, the Company laid much of the responsibility on the settlers themselves. In that way, the VOC and settler interaction was based on a partially permissive contract up to the second half of the eighteenth century. Moving towards frontier closure, the VOC started to formally recognize settlers' use of various coercive or semi-coercive methods to control Khoesan labour. At the frontier, the situation remained more fragile, but eventually the VOC could not delay the application of judicial regulations in the commercial centre at the Cape. By the end of the eighteenth century, the contract between the VOC and the settlers with regard to Khoesan labour had been transformed from permissive to productive.

The limited political influence of the gentry

I showed above how strong ties developed at an early stage between the VOC and the wealthiest farmers and merchants. The VOC needed them to keep domestic trade under control, while the elites gained considerably as they were granted control over local trade. But what about the gentry – the wealthy, but not the wealthiest, commercially oriented farmers, often described in the literature as the backbone of the settler economy – did this leave them politically marginalized? Not entirely. They could also influence politics – not on a colony-wide level, but within the districts. The VOC's control extended only to trade. In other matters, its actual power was limited and diminished over time as the colony's frontiers expanded. It was in the arena of local politics that the gentry could exercise an influence.

The Company expected the districts to be self-financing. No provisions were made for intergovernmental transfers. Instead, local expenditures had to be financed by tax collection, mainly poll, livestock and house taxes (Fourie, Jansen and Siebrits 2013). Locally, it was the *landrost* who was at the top. He was a civil magistrate whose main role was to take care of the daily administrative duties and ensure that the laws were obeyed in the district. The *landrost* reported directly to the governor. He was supported by a court made up of local officials, the *heemraden*, who were mostly the richest farmers in the district. They were 'the rural elite in each of the districts and monopolised the positions of authority within the civil – and indeed military and ecclesiastical – administration' (Ross 1993: 196; see also Ross 1989).

Initially, the powers of the *landrost* and *heemraden* were circumscribed because the VOC required that all court cases be settled in Cape Town. With the expansion of the frontier, this system became increasingly inefficient, and, over time, the VOC delegated more of its powers to the local authorities, including allowing them to handle more substantial court cases. This gave the local settler elites greater power to protect their interests, especially when it came to their relations with Khoesan labourers (Ross 1983; Viljoen 2001; Dooling 2005).

An illustrative example is the settler-farmers' resistance to the VOC's attempt to regulate Khoesan labour contracts by requiring written contracts (Ross 1993). I discussed earlier that already in 1720 settler-farmers in the south-western Cape were demanding that indentureship be made legal. Settler-farmers on the frontier did not make the same demand. On the contrary, they preferred that the system not be formalized legally as they feared that this would limit their ability to use coercive and semi-coercive methods to control labour (Newton-King 1999). This concern seems to have been partly justified. Once indentureship was legalized in the late eighteenth century, the VOC began to raise concerns about the tendency to apprentice children for longer periods than allowed. To prevent this, the farmers were required to report the birth year of the Khoesan children on the farm. The farmers at the frontier objected to this and successfully used their influence over local authorities to persuade the *landrosts* to abuse the system by changing the year of birth or in some cases not keep a proper register. In fact, keeping a proper register was more the exception than the rule. In Graaff-Reinet, for example, the *landrost* did not keep a register until 1821 (Malherbe 1978).

It is difficult to provide sufficient empirical evidence of the local elites being systematically favoured by the district administrations. Historians nevertheless agree that the gentry were overrepresented in local offices and we have no reason to believe they would not have used this position to their benefit.

Clashes between the VOC and the settlers

I argued above that the trade regulations imposed by the VOC at the Cape favoured a settler elite. At the same time, the settler elites were also those who most strongly opposed VOC policies, indicating that the relationship was not necessarily stable. To reveal the complex bonds between the settlers and the Company, I zoom in on three events where groups of settler-farmers actively opposed its policies. These were the attempts to get rid of Governor Willem Adriaan van der Stel; the Barbier Rebellion; and the rise of the Cape Patriot movement. The aim is to show that the settlers were a diversified group with different economic and political interests, while the colonial system was kept intact by a coalition of the VOC and the settler elites.

Willem Adriaan van der Stel became governor at the Cape in 1699. He was the son of the famous governor Simon van der Stel, who had generally been praised by the settlers. Initially van der Stel issued a number of policies that the Europeans welcomed. He abandoned the prohibition on settlers bartering livestock with the Khoesan and he issued grazing licences allowing settler-farmers to graze in the Land van Waveren, the area that later became the Tulbagh district. Both policies were aimed at increasing the supply of meat for passing ships. He also took steps in a direction that the wealthier settlers feared threatened their positions. Just as his predecessors had done, he used his powers to obtain a large area of fertile land, 2,452 hectares, where he established his farm Vergelegen in Hottentots Holland (today Somerset West). Unlike previous governors, he did so at a time when the Lords XVII had decided that the VOC should gradually scale down their own farming operations (Theal 1913). He also favoured his friends and relatives with generous land grants. In this, he followed the already established tradition of nepotism among the colonial authorities that had been practised since the very early years of the colony. As long as land was abundant, these actions were not met with any major criticism from the settlers. It was when van der Stel and his associates began to take a firmer grip on the markets that the wealthier settlers started to react. Major criticism was heard in 1705 after it became clear that van der Stel had favoured a small group of friends and allies when handing out trading licences. This, together with the reintroduction in 1702 of the prohibition on settlers trading cattle with the Khoesan, sparked organized resistance among a group of wealthy settlers in the south-western Cape (Schutte 1989).

The group of protesting settlers was led by Henning Huising, who at that time was the richest man in Cape Town, having made his fortune mainly from the meat trade. The settlers sent a petition to the VOC at the Cape that eventually ended up before the Lords XVII in Amsterdam. In the petition, they claimed that the actions of the governor threatened the establishment of profitable European agriculture at the Cape. Fearing that this might be true, or at least acknowledging that opposition from the wealthiest settlers might threaten the supply of provisions to passing ships, the Lords XVII decided to get rid of van der Stel and in 1707 he was dismissed. As soon as van der Stel was gone, the protests stopped, despite the fact that his trading policies remained intact (Schutte 1989).

As Willem Adriaan van der Stel's trade policies did not differ greatly from those of his predecessors, we might wonder why the settler elites protested against him and not earlier governors. In the colony's early years, the south-western Cape was still largely an open frontier characterized by social fluidity and a great deal of uncertainty. Neither the settler elites nor the VOC had yet managed to get a firm grip on the economy. The clash between the settler elites and van der Stel was the final struggle over the control of the markets in a sub-region that was about to be closed. The removal of van der Stel gave the protesting settlers new opportunities to buy the valuable trading licences. And some of them made huge profits from the restrictive trading practices. Huising himself managed to get contracted as the sole supplier of meat to the VOC. This not only generated substantial income; it also enabled him to take control of vast tracts of land in Groene Kloof, about 40 km outside Cape Town (Penn 1995).

The second major clash between groups of settlers and the VOC took place in the late 1730s. As with the earlier conflict, the chief issue was control over trade. This struggle became known as the Barbier Rebellion, after the protest's spokesman, Estienne Barbier. Originally Barbier was a company servant who got himself into trouble when he publicly attacked his highest superior with complaints about malpractice, particularly the illegal trade in wood. This eventually led the VOC to imprison him in the castle in Cape Town. In 1738, he managed to escape and found refuge in the Drakenstein Valley at the frontier of the south-western Cape. There he joined a group of rebels and became their spokesperson (Schutte 1989).

The group produced a document in which it criticized the VOC on a number of different counts. They blamed it for protecting the Khoesan at the expense of the settler-farmers at the frontier. They were especially critical of the repressive measures taken by the VOC against settlers who had been accused of stealing cattle from the Khoesan. They further criticized the VOC for implementing economic policies that made it difficult to survive as farmers, for example the doubling of the annual rent for loan farms from 12 to 24 rixdollars in 1732. Their main concern, however, was the prohibition on trading with the Khoesan (Penn 1995). Barbier never managed to organize a large opposition group. However, the VOC was aware that many settlers on the frontier sympathized with his actions and they thus proceeded cautiously. The first step was to declare Barbier an outlaw and at the same time grant amnesty to his followers, in the hope that in return they would hand over Barbier to the authorities. This did not happen, so the authorities changed their strategy completely. They decided not to confiscate the cattle that the Khoesan said the rebels had stolen from them. This calmed things down and soon after, on 14 November 1739, the VOC captured Estienne Barbier and executed him (Shutte 1989; Penn 1995). The settlers at the frontier had lost the battle.

This conflict reveals the potential tension between the settlers on the frontier and the VOC officials. The view that VOC officials paid too much attention to the Khoesan and at the same time used both illegal and semi-legal means to enrich themselves and their friends was widely shared among frontier settler-farmers (Schutte 1989). The complaints were not only about the VOC officials but also the settler elites in the south-western Cape, who, two decades earlier, had also opposed the VOC's control over the domestic market. Now these elites were criticized by frontier farmers for the same practice.

The tension between groups of settlers and the VOC peaked at the very end of the era of Dutch rule, leading to the Cape Patriot Movement. Increased economic difficulties in the Cape, together with a general weakening of the VOC, led a new group of settlers to call for a change in the colony's political and economic structures (Ross 1983; Schutte 1989). Up to 1780, the VOC's global operations had always generated profits. This now changed. Over the period 1780 to 1795 the Company registered a net loss of 44 per cent. The increased cost of territorial rule in the east and the intensified competition from English, Danish and Chinese merchants, combined with the shocks of the fourth Anglo-Dutch war (1780–4), had 'driven the VOC to the point of bankruptcy' (Ross 1989: 198). This weakened the position of the VOC in the Netherlands and opened the way for economic and political change at the Cape.

In 1778, a pamphlet circulated in Cape Town inciting settlers to take action to change the form of government if the authorities were no longer 'standing for the people, and defending their lives, property and liberty' (quoted in Schutte 1989: 309). A year later, four hundred settlers signed a petition to the governor asking for permission to send a delegation to lay complaints before the Lords XVII in Amsterdam. The signatories became known as the Cape Patriot Movement. It represented a broad group of wealthier farmers and merchants who sought greater access to the export markets (Ross 1983). They wanted to get rid of the VOC's control over exports and they also complained about the fact that two companies, Cruywagen en Kie and Le Febre en Kie, which both had several officials as their partners, held oligopolistic positions over the import markets. The movement wanted the exports and imports to be in the hands of the Cape Town merchants and the settler-farmers themselves, which they hoped would decrease import prices and increase the prices of agricultural commodities (Ross 1983).

Their petition was written in three parts. The first described the economic circumstances at the Cape in very negative terms. It criticized the regulation of the wheat and wine market but did not mention the cattle market. The second part described how the policies and practice of the VOC aggravated the economic difficulties the settlers were facing. It blamed VOC officials for engaging in trade and investing significantly in land, although the Lords XVII had forbidden it (Ross 1983). The third part included a number of economic and political proposals. In the petition, the Cape Patriots said they wanted to be allowed to trade freely with foreign ships and to be better paid by the VOC. In addition they demanded that half of the members in the Council of Policy should be settlers. The governor refused to meet their demands, but they nevertheless managed to send a group of four to the Netherlands in 1779, carrying a petition that they handed over to the Lords XVII in Amsterdam. According to Ross (1983), the movement posed the first serious threat to VOC rule at the Cape. Despite the fact that the movement seems to have dissolved after 1784, it partly succeeded in its mission, as settlers indeed won the right to sell freely to passing ships if there was surplus after supplying the VOC with what it needed.

The conflicts described above illustrate three important points about the colony: that the relationship between the VOC and the settlers changed over time, that the settlers should not be treated as a homogeneous group, and that to understand the colony's political economy we need to acknowledge that it consisted of coexisting and interdependent social contracts.

To consider the third point, let us look first at the conflict between the settlers and Adriaan van der Stel. Huising and his group portrayed the conflict as arising from the settlers' desire for freedom from oppressive policies at the Cape. This is a slightly biased account. What the conflict represented was a clash between an upcoming settler elite and the VOC over economic rents. These elites did not question the system of regulated markets per se. What they wanted was to be allowed to capture a larger share of the rents created by these regulated markets. As the VOC was financially and administratively weak, the emerging elites managed to get their demands met, which marked the beginning of a more stable elite coalition based on a productive contract between the VOC and the settler elites in the south-western Cape, without altering the basis of the VOC's gate-keeping structure.

The second major clash between the VOC and the settlers, the Barbier Rebellion of the late 1730s, took place in a very different context. It happened when the frontier was expanding, and when the interests of the frontier farmers clashed with those of the economic and political elites in the south-western Cape. The conflict was again about control over the domestic market, but also about the relationship between the frontier farmers and the Khoesan. The farmers demanded increased freedom to trade with the Khoesan, but also to use whatever means they found suitable to control Khoesan labour. In other words, they called for a more permissive social contract between themselves and the VOC. Demanding reforms of the markets was doomed to fail as the frontier farmers were not strong enough to threaten the coalition of the VOC officials and the commercial elites in the south-western Cape. However, they did manage to get the VOC to permit the change in the frontier settlers' relationship with the Khoesan, since this did not threaten the coalition between the VOC and the settler elite as it would have done fifty years earlier. The Khoesan had been politically weakened and although, as seen in Chapter 5, sporadic conflicts with the settlers continued, they were not of a nature that would threaten the commercial interests of the VOC.

By the end of the eighteenth century, the main conflicts between the settlers and the VOC had moved again to the south-western Cape. This was an outcome of a gradual economic change within the closed frontier and the weakening of the VOC globally. A larger group of farmers had managed to accumulate sufficient capital to form a new emerging elite with commercial interests that challenged both the VOC and the old commercial elite, especially as the VOC was facing increasing economic hardships which threatened the very basis of the coalition of elites that had governed the Cape since the early eighteenth century. It may look as though the demands made by this rising group of commercial farmers were the same as those made by the settler elites in the early eighteenth century. Just as then, the settler-farmers wanted to increase their control over the markets. However, the implications of such demands were much greater now than before. The demands could not be met without challenging the VOC and the old commercial elite. To grant the new settler elites, sometimes referred to as the 'Cape gentry', free access to trade on the domestic market would mean that the VOC would have to abandon the *pacht* system and thereby lose their most important source of revenue. It would also threaten the economic position of the wealthiest settlers, who controlled most of the trade. The conflict in the 1780s was thus as much a conflict among the settlers as between the settlers and the VOC (Williams 2013). The economic interests of the gentry clashed with this old elite. As the old coalition was weakened, the VOC decided to meet some of this group's demands. Allowing them to trade to some extent directly with passing ships was something the VOC could agree to, as this trade was then in decline and no longer generated much profit for the VOC.

Conclusion

It is commonly assumed that the European colonial authorities had the capacity to formulate and implement policies that aligned with their immediate economic interests. Further, these interests in most times aligned with the interests of the settlers. The case of the VOC at the Cape calls for a modification of these claims. The Company never regarded the Cape Colony as a prioritized investment. Instead, the authorities at the Cape had to fund their own recurrent expenditures. This caused the VOC's grip on power at the Cape to be fragile. During its nearly 150 years of rule, the VOC authorities there never experienced a single year of budget surpluses. The most important sources of revenue stemmed from imports and exports. To boost export incomes, the VOC had to carefully balance divergent settler interests. The foundation of its rule was an elite coalition that it formed together with the top wealthiest settlers. The economic basis of the coalition was to allow the settler elites to grant monopsony control over the domestic trade of wine, livestock and grains. It was a win–win situation. It reduced the VOC's cost of administrating domestic trade at the same time as the licence fees that the settlers had to pay provided the Company with an important source of revenue. For the settlers, their monopsony control over the trade enabled them to accumulate significant amounts of wealth.

Meanwhile, the system periodically came under attack from upcoming economic elites among the settlers, but also those settlers who were less wealthy and lacked political influence over the VOC. The upcoming elites posed a real threat to the coalition to whose interests the Company had to adjust, either by including them in the elite coalition or by reforming its economic policies.

Opposition from the larger group of settlers, including the gentry, was met by allowing them a great deal of freedom in the way they controlled and treated the Khoesan labourers.

Looking at the relationship between the colonial authorities and the settlers at the Cape, it becomes obvious that it was more complex than usually anticipated in the literature on settler colonialism. It was a system that was based on a productive social contract between the VOC at the Cape and the settler elites. To uphold the system, the VOC maintained a permissive social contract with the larger group of settlers, even when this went against the Company's interests. The recurrent opposition from various settler groups against VOC policies testifies to how weak the VOC's control over the colony was. Once the power balance in Europe changed and thereby also the global economic conditions, the VOC's power over the Cape was easily overthrown.

Concluding remarks

On 6 April 1652, Jan Anthonissen van Riebeeck and a crew of eighty-two men and eight women built a fort in Table Bay on the Cape of Good Hope, thereby changing the direction of the region's history. The fort was meant to serve as a trading post to facilitate commercial exchange with the Khoesan, who had been present in the area for thousands of years. Ensuring that the Khoesan were willing to supply sufficient provisions to passing ships was crucial for VOC operations in Asia. The VOC had given van Riebeeck clear instructions not to *colonize* the Cape – that is, not to allow agricultural settlement. Soon after building the fort, however, the boundaries of VOC control began inexorably to expand. One hundred and fifty years later, when the VOC's rule in the Cape came to an end, the Company was in control over an area comparable in size to Italy. This book has analysed this century and a half of expansion, asking why it came about and what its consequences have been. It is a history of growth and prosperity as well as one of coercion, inequality and exclusion.

A large literature has shown that European settler colonization around the globe distinguished itself from other forms of colonialization in two meaningful ways. First, settler colonies experienced an early and significant degree of political autonomy in relation to the imperial powers. Second, because of continuous expansion of the land frontier and access to imperial markets, the settler colonies achieved sustained high levels of growth, which in turn enabled the settlers to prosper. The expansion was made possible by the marginalization and subjugation of the indigenous peoples, who were brought under Dutch control with relative ease.

The establishment of European settler societies may have the surface appearance of a planned process, driven by the motives and economic interests of the colonizers and their agents. But such a view would be ahistorical and Eurocentric. It would neglect the fact that European settlement was a gradual process with an uncertain outcome. Assuming that intention equals outcomes makes it difficult to explain the many instances in which plans to establish settler colonies failed, for example sixteenth-century Canada and Venezuela and twentieth-century Malawi and Ghana. The failed cases take us to the second problem: the neglect of indigenous agency and its impact on the development trajectory of colonized regions. Nowhere in the world were settler colonies established on empty land. They were all begun in areas already occupied by indigenous groups. Nor were indigenous people often marginalized with ease as often assumed in the literature. The agency and interest of the indigenous people therefore needs to be acknowledged and its effects need to be taken into account. The interaction between indigenous people and colonial intruders is key to understanding how settler societies evolved over time.

If settler colonialization in general, and the expansion of settler-colonial boundaries in particular, cannot be reduced to a matter of settler interests, choices and strategies, then how should we understand the process? The Cape Colony provides an excellent case with which to study this question, for two reasons. First, though the initial plan was never to take territorial control of Africa's southern tip, this is exactly what happened, and that requires an explanation. Second, compared to other former colonies, the historical data for the Cape Colony is remarkably rich and has been explored extensively by scholars, including myself. This allows for a relatively detailed account of the establishment and expansion of the colony and how it affected the settlers, their slaves and the Khoesan.

A theme woven throughout this book is the VOC's limited financial and administrative capacity. In the early years, in particular, the Company lacked the capacity and means to ensure sustained trading relations with the Khoesan. It was this failure that eventually led the VOC commander at the Cape to allow a small number of European settlers to set up farms. This started a process of continuous expansion of settler farms farther into the interior, a process that was not directed by the VOC. The continued expansion was instead an outcome of a bundle of factors, most notably factor endowments, property rights and, paradoxically, Khoesan resistance. Land scarcity in the physical sense of the term – often used to explain the expansion of the land frontier in settler colonies – can only partly explain the geographical expansion of the frontier in this case.

Equally important was the vagueness with which property rights in the colony were structured. This gave settlers the flexibility to move their cattle and sheep across vast areas to adjust for seasonal changes in climate, while at the same time it made land relatively cheap. Meanwhile, it also led to a dispersion of the settler community. Attempts by the VOC to reform the property rights system to make it less vague faced opposition from settler-farmers. A chief reason for settlers' reluctance to allow changes in the system was Khoesan defiance, which presented recurrent obstacles to Dutch settlement throughout the seventeenth and eighteenth centuries. Every now and then, groups of Khoesan were able to chase settlers away. Under these conditions, settler-farmers wanted to keep the cost of acquiring land as low as possible. The history of the Cape is the history of violent conflicts between the intruders and the indigenous populations, and these conflicts had a lasting effect on how the institutions at the Cape evolved.

While Khoesan resistance in part explains the expansion of the colony, Khoesan labour played a key role in the rise of profitable settler agriculture. Several scholars have argued that the use of imported slaves was central to the growth of settler agriculture at the Cape. They have held that slaves provided a solution to the labour shortages settlers faced as Khoesan societies disintegrated. The situation was not helped by the fact that the VOC did not allow the Dutch to enslave the Khoesan.

In this book, I have demonstrated that the Khoesan played a far more important role as farm labourers than most of previous research has acknowledged. Europeans accessed Khoesan labour through a wide range of mechanisms, from voluntary agreements to brutal force. Acknowledging the importance of Khoesan labour implies that we need to revise our estimate of the efficiency of slave labour at the Cape. If slave labour was not necessarily higher in productivity than Khoesan labour, as current data makes clear, this begs the question of why settlers invested in slaves. Slavery was distinct from Khoesan labour, or any other form of coercive labour relations, in that it gave settlers complete rights over a mobile property. This enabled slaveholders not only to use slaves as a labour input, but also to access capital by using slaves as collateral and/or leasing their slaves to other farmers. In that regard, imported slaves complemented indigenous Khoesan labour, rather than replacing it.

The trajectory of economic development at the Cape was affected not only by the relationship between the settlers and the Khoesan, but also by the relationship between the settlers and the VOC. Scholars studying settler colonies have sometimes assumed that the settlers were a homogenous group with shared interests. This was far from true in the case of the Cape. As scholars have come to appreciate about twentieth-century South African history, the white community at the Cape in the VOC period consisted of both very affluent settlers and those who could hardly make ends meet. VOC rule remained fragile and dependent upon a coalition between the colonial authorities and the settler elites. The coalition was maintained by giving a small group of settlers exclusive rights to purchase wine, meat and wheat on behalf of the VOC. Other settler groups recurrently challenged this arrangement, but it proved resilient. It was only at the very end of VOC rule, when the Company was severely weakened financially, that it took certain steps towards opening the market for all settlers.

The non-elite settlers were not completely without influence over colonial policies, but it was limited to district politics. This enabled them to ignore the VOC's instructions to treat the Khoesan fairly and decently because most complaints regarding the treatment of labour were dealt with at the district level.

Looking at the century and a half of VOC rule at the Cape, what really stands out is how fragile it was. Its policies were recurrently questioned by groups of settlers, while the Khoesan also continued to resist the settler presence. Minor changes in the playing field could theoretically have had a major impact on long-term developments in the region. What would have happened if the Khoesan had managed to force the Europeans to leave – as they nearly did in the seventeenth century? Would the presence of the VOC at the Cape have held if the elite coalition between VOC officials and the wealthiest settlers had broken down? The answer to these counterfactuals cannot be known, but the questions are relevant. They suggest that the fragility of the process needs to be taken into account, and this is likely also the case with studies of settler colonialism around the globe. The history of the Cape Colony is the history of various groups driven by multiple and sometimes conflicting interests. None of the actors was strong enough to solely direct the path of development.

The history of the Cape Colony is not purely of academic interest. Debates about the legacy of apartheid are still, for obvious reasons, very lively in South Africa. These debates are important and play a crucial role in the formation of new democratic South Africa, a project that is still in its early phase. A paradox arises from the fact that the early period of dispossession, segregation and coercion is currently not debated to the same extent. Various Khoesan interest groups fight for recognition. This book is not aimed at taking sides or solving this complicated political issue. But it shows that the establishment of the Cape Colony cannot be understood without taking the agency of Khoesan into consideration. Neither is it true that the expansion of the colonial frontier happened without the deprivation of the Khoesan from their land. Independently of our views of Khoesan rights for recognition, we cannot capture the formation of what is today South Africa without recognizing their role and destiny in the process.

References

Acemoglu, D. and J. A. Robinson (2002) 'The Political Economy of the Kuznets Curve', *Review of Development Economics* 6 (2): 183–203.

Acemoglu, D. and J. A. Robinson (2012) *Why Nations Fail: The Origins of Power, Prosperity and Poverty*. New York: Crown Publishers.

Acemoglu, D., S. Johnson and J. A. Robinson (2002) 'Reversal of Fortune: Geography and Institutions in the Making of the Modern World Income Distribution', *Quarterly Journal of Economics* 117 (4): 1231–94.

Acemoglu, D., D. H. Autor and D. Lyle (2004) 'Women, War, and Wages: The Effect of Female Labor Supply on the Wage Structure at Mid-Century', *Journal of Political Economy* 112 (3): 497–551.

Adhikari, M. (2010) 'A Total Extinction Confidently Hoped for: The Destruction of the Cape San Society under Dutch Colonial Rule, 1700–1795', *Journal of Genocide Research* 12 (1–2): 19–44.

Alfani, G. (2021) 'Economic Inequality in Preindustrial Times: Europe and Beyond', *Journal of Economic Literature* 59 (1): 3–44.

Alston, L. J. and M. O. Shapira (1984) 'Inheritance Laws across Colonies: Causes and Consequences', *The Journal of Economic History* 44 (2): 277–87.

Alston, L. J., G. D. Libecap and B. Mueller (1998) 'Property Rights and Land Conflict: A Comparison of Settlement of the US Western and Brazilian Amazon Frontiers', in J. H. Coatsworth and A. M. Taylor (eds), *Latin America and the World Economy Since 1800*, 55–84. Cambridge, MA: Harvard University Press.

Altman, I. and J. Horn (1991) 'Introduction', in I. Altman and J. Horn (eds), '*To make America': European Migration in the Early Modern Period*. Oxford: University of California Press.

Angeles, L. (2007) 'Income Inequality and Colonialism', *European Economic Review* 51 (5): 1155–76.

Armstrong, J. C. (1979) 'The Slaves, 1652–1795', in R. Elphick and H. Giliomee (eds), *The Shaping of South African Society, 1652–1840*, 75–115. London: Longman Group.

Armstrong, J. C and N. Worden (1989) 'The Slaves, 1652–1834', in R. Elphick and H. Giliomee (eds), *The Shaping of South African Society*, 2nd edn, 109–83. Middletown, CT: Wesleyan University Press.

Arrighi, G. (1970) 'Labour Supplies in Historical Perspective: A Study of the Proletarianization of the African Peasantry in Rhodesia', *Journal of Development* 6 (3): 197–234.

Austin, G. (2008) 'The 'Reversal of Fortunes' Thesis and the Compression of History: Perspectives from African and Comparative Economic History', *Journal of International Development* 20 (8): 996–1027.

Austin, G. (2014) 'Capitalism and the Colonies', in L. Neal and J. G. Williamson (eds), *Capitalism*, vol. II: *The Spread of Capitalism; From 1848 to Present*, 301–47. Cambridge: Cambridge University Press.

Baartman, T. (2015) 'Dutch Contexts of Cape Burgher Protests', *New Contree* 73, Special issue: 40–60.

Baker, M. J., C. N. Brunnschweiler and E. H. Bulte (2008) 'Did History Breed Inequality? Endowments and Modern Income Distribution', Working Paper 08/86. Zurich: CER-ETH.

Bates, R. (1983) *Essays on the Political Economy of Rural Africa*. Berkeley, CA: University of California Press.

Bates, R. (2010) 'A Review of Douglass C. North, John Joseph Wallis, and Barry R. Weingast's Violence and Social Orders: A Conceptual Framework for Interpreting Recorded Human History', *Journal of Economic Literature* 48 (3): 752–6.

Beinart, W. (2003) *The Rise of Conservation in South Africa: Settlers, Livestock, and the Environment 1770–1950*. Oxford: Oxford University Press.

Berkhofer Jr., R. F. (1981) 'The North American Frontier as Process and Context', in H. Lamar and L. Thompson (eds), *The Frontier in History: North America and Southern Africa Compared*, 43–75. London: Yale University Press.

Binion, R. (2001) 'Marianne in the Home: Political Revolution and Fertility Transition in France and the United States', *Population: An English Selection* 13 (2): 165–88.

Böesken, A. J. (1977) *Slaves and Free Blacks at the Cape 1658–1700*. Cape Town: Taffelberg Publishers.

Bogart, F. (2015) 'The East Indian Monopoly and the Transition from Limited Access in England, 1600–1813', *NBER Working Paper 21536*. Cambridge, MA: National Bureau of Economic Research.

Boshoff, W. H. and J. Fourie (2010) 'The Significance of the Cape Trade Route to Economic Activity in the Cape Colony: A Medium-Term Business Cycle Analysis', *European Review of Economic History* 14 (3): 469–503.

Bourguignon, F. and C. Morrison (2002) 'Inequality among World Citizens: 1820–1992', *American Economic Review* 92 (4): 727–44.

Bowman, I. (1928) *The New World Problems in Political Geography*, 4th edn. Chicago, IL: World Book Company.

Bruhn, M. and F. A. Gallego (2008) 'Good, Bad, and Ugly Colonial Activities: Studying Development across the Americas', *Policy Research Working Paper 4641*. Washington DC: World Bank.

Carter, S. B. and R. Sutch (2013) 'Why the Settlers Soared: The Dynamics of Immigration and Economic Growth in the "Golden Age" for Settler Societies', in C. Lloyd, J. Metzer and R. Sutch (eds), *Settler Economies in World History*, 37–64. Leiden: Brill.

Cilliers, J. (2012) 'Cape Colony Marriage in Perspective'. MA thesis, Stellenbosch University, Stellenbosch.

Cillers, J. and E. Green (2018) 'The Land-Labour Hypothesis Revised: Wealth, Labour and Household Composition on the South African Frontier', *International Review of Social History* 63 (2): 239–71.

Cilliers, J. and J. Fourie (2013) 'The Marriage Patterns of European Settlers at the Cape, 1652–1910', *New Contree* 69: 45–70.

Cilliers, J. and M. Mariotti (2019) 'The Shaping of a Settler Fertility Transition: Eighteenth and Nineteenth Century South African Demographic History Reconsidered', *European Review of Economic History* 23 (4): 421–45.

Cilliers, J., E. Green and R. Ross (2021) 'Did it Pay to be a Pioneer? Wealth Accumulation in a Newly Settled Frontier Society', unpublished manuscript, Lund University.

Coatsworth, J. H. (2008) 'Inequality, Institutions and Growth in Latin America', *Journal of Latin American Studies* 40 (3): 141–69.

Cooper, F. (2002) *Africa Since 1940: The Past of the Present.* Cambridge: Cambridge University Press.

Crosby, A. W. (1986) *Ecological Imperialism: The Biological Expansion of Europe, 900–1900.* Cambridge: Cambridge University Press.

De Kock, M. H. (1924) *Economic History of South Africa.* Cape Town: Juta.

Denoon, D. (1983) *Settler Capitalism: The Dynamics of Dependent Development in the Southern Hemisphere.* Oxford: Clarendon Press.

De Soto, H. (2000) *The Mystery of Capital: Why Capitalism Triumphs in the West and Fails Everywhere Else.* New York: Basic Books.

Domar, E. D. (1970) 'The Causes of Slavery or Serfdom: A Hypothesis', *The Journal of Economic History* 30 (1): 18–32.

Dooling, W. (2005) 'The Making of a Colonial Elite: Property, Family and Landed Stability in the Cape Colony, c.1750–1834', *Journal of Southern African Studies* 31 (1): 147–62.

Dooling, W. (2006) 'In Search of Profitability: Wheat and Wine Production in the Post-Emancipation Western Cape', *South African Historical Journal* 55: 88–105.

Du Plessis S., S. Jansen and D. von Fintel (2013) 'The Wealth of Cape Colony Widows: Inheritance Laws and Investment Responses Following Male Death in the 17th and 18th Centuries', *Economic History of Developing Regions* 28 (1): 87–108.

Dye, A. and S. La Croix (2020) 'Institutions for the Taking: Property Rights and the Settlement of the Cape Colony, 1652–1750', *Economic History Review* 73 (1): 33–58.

Easterly, W. and R. Levine (2012) 'The European Origins of Economic Development', *NBER Working Paper 18162.* Cambridge, MA: National Bureau of Economic Research.

Elkins, C. and S. Pedersen (2005) *Settler Colonialism in the Twentieth Century: Projects, Practices and Legacies.* London: Routledge.

Elphick, R. (1975) *KhoeKhoe and the Founding of White South Africa.* Johannesburg: Ravan Press.

Elphick, R. (1977) *Kraal and Castle: KhoeKhoe and the Founding of White South Africa.* New Haven, CT: Yale University Press.

Elphick, R. (1979) 'The Khoesan to c. 1770', in R. Elphick and H. Giliomee (eds), *The Shaping of South African Society*, 3–40. Pinetown: Maskew Miller Longman.

Elphick, R. and H. Giliomee, eds (1989a) *The Shaping of South African Society*, 2nd edn. Middletown, CT: Wesleyan University Press.

Elphick, R. and H. Giliomee (1989b) 'The Origins and Entrenchment of the European Dominance at the Cape, 1652–c. 1840', in R. Elphick and H. Giliomee (eds), *The Shaping of South African Society*, 2nd edn, 521–56. Middletown, CT: Wesleyan University Press.

Elphick, R. and V. C. Malherbe (1989) 'The Khoesan to 1828', in R. Elphick and H. Giliomee (eds), *The Shaping of South African Society, 1652–1840*, 2nd edn, 3–65. Middletown, CT: Wesleyan University Press.

Engermann, S. L. and K. L. Sokoloff (2000) 'History Lessons: Institutions, Factor Endowments, and Paths of Development in the New World', *Journal of Economic Perspectives* 14 (3): 217–32.

Engerman, S. L. and K. L. Sokoloff (2002) 'Factor Endowments, Inequality, and Paths of Development among New World Economics', *NBER Working Paper 9259*. Cambridge, MA: National Bureau of Economic Research.

Engerman, S. L. and K. L. Sokoloff (2005) 'Colonialism, Inequality and Long-Run Paths of Development', *NBER Working Paper 11057*. Cambridge, MA: National Bureau of Economic Research.

Engerman, S. L. and K. L. Sokoloff (2013) 'Five Hundred Years of European Colonialization: Inequality and Paths of Development', in C. Lloyd, J. Metzer and R. Sutch (eds), *Settler Economies in World History*, 65–103. Leiden: Brill.

Feder, G. and D. Feeny (1991) 'Land Tenure and Property Rights: Theory and Implications for Development Policy', *The World Bank Economic Review* 5 (1): 135–53.

Feinstein, C. (1988) 'The Rise and Fall of the Williamson Curve', *The Journal of Economic History* 48 (3): 699–729.

Feinstein, C. (2005) *An Economic History of South Africa*. Cambridge: Cambridge University Press.

Fenske, J. (2012) 'Land Abundance and Economic Institutions: Egba Land and Slavery, 1830–1914', *The Economic History Review* 65 (2): 527–55.

Fibaek, M. and E. Green (2019) 'Labour Control and the Establishment of Profitable Settler Agriculture in Colonial Kenya, 1920–45', *Economic History of Developing Regions* 10 (1): 72–110.

Fisher, R. (1984) 'Land Surveyors and Land Tenure at the Cape 1657–1812', in C. G. C. Martin and K. J. Friedlaender (eds), *History of Surveying and Land Tenure in South Africa*, 55–88. Cape Town: Department of Surveying, University of Cape Town.

Forbes, J. D. (1968) 'Frontiers in American History and the Role of the Frontier Historian', *Ethnography* 15 (2): 203–35.

Fouché, L. (1909) *Die Evolutie van die Trekboer: Lesing gehoou voor die Christelike Jongelieden Vereniging*. Pretoria: Volkstem.

Fourie, J. (2013a) 'Slaves as Capital Investment in the Dutch Cape Colony, 1652–1795', in E. Hillbom and P. Svensson (eds), *Agricultural Transformation in a Global History Perspective*, 136–59. London: Routledge.

Fourie, J. (2013b) 'The Remarkable Wealth of the Dutch Cape Colony: Measurements from Eighteenth Probate Inventories', *Economic History Review* 66 (2): 419–48.

Fourie, J. and D. von Fintel (2010a) 'The Dynamics of Inequality in a Newly Settled, Pre-industrial Society: The Case of the Cape Colony', *Cliometrica* 4: 229–67.

Fourie, J. and D. von Fintel (2010b) 'The Fruit of the Vine? An Augmented Endowments Inequality Hypothesis and the Rise of an Elite in the Cape Colony', WIDER Working Paper No. 2010/112, United Nations University (UNU).

Fourie, J. and D. von Fintel (2011) 'A History with Evidence: Income Inequality in the Dutch Cape Colony', *Economic History of Developing Regions* 26 (1): 16–48.

Fourie, J. and D. von Fintel (2012) 'Fruit of the Vine? An Augmented Endowments-Inequality Hypothesis and the Rise of an Elite in the Cape Colony', in A. H. Amsden, A. DiCaprio and J. A. Robinson (eds), *The Role of Elites in Economic Development*, 87–119. Oxford: Oxford University Press.

Fourie, J. and E. Green (2015) 'The Missing People: Accounting for the Productivity of Indigenous Populations in Cape Colonial History', *Journal of African History* 56 (2): 195–215.

Fourie, J. and E. Green (2018) 'Random or Ricardian? What Determined European Settlement Decisions at the Cape of Good Hope', unpublished manuscript, Lund University.

Fourie, J. and J. L. van Zanden (2013) 'GDP in the Dutch Cape Colony: The National Accounts of a Slave-Based Society', *South African Journal of Economics* 81 (4): 467–90.

Fourie, J., A. I. Jansen and F. K. Siebrits (2013) 'Public Finances under Private Company Rule: The Dutch Cape Colony (1652–1795)', *New Contree* 68: 51–71.

Fourie, J. and C. Swanepoel (2018) '"Impending Ruin" or "Remarkable Wealth"? The Role of Private Credit Markets in the 18th-Century Cape Colony', *Journal of Southern African Studies* 44 (1): 7–25.

Frankema, E. (2009) *Has Latin America Always Been Unequal?* Leiden: Brill.

Frankema, E., E. Green and E. Hillbom (2016) 'Endogenous Processes of Colonial Settlement: The Success and Failure of European Settler Farming in Sub-Saharan Africa', *Revista de Historia Economica* [*Journal of Iberian and Latin American Economic History*] 34 (2): 237–65.

Furniss, E. (2006) 'Imagining the Frontier: Comparative Perspectives from Canada and Australia', in D. B. Rose and R. Davis (eds), *Dislocating the Frontier: Essaying the Mystique of the Outback*, 23–46. Canberra: The Australian National University Press.

Garnsey, P. (1996) *Ideas of Slavery from Aristotle to Augustine*. Cambridge: Cambridge University Press.

Genovese, E. D. (1965) *The Political Economy of Slavery: Studies in the Economy and Society of the Slave South*. New York: Patheon Books.

Gibbon, P. (2011) 'Experiences of Plantation and Large-Scale Farming in 20th Century Africa', DIIS Working Paper 2011:20. Copenhagen: Danish Institute of International Studies.

Giliomee. H. (1981) 'Processes in Development of the Southern African Frontier', in H. Giliomee, H. Lamar and H. Thompson (eds), *The Frontier in History: North America and Southern Africa Compared*, 76–122. New Haven, CT: Yale University Press.

Giliomee, H. (1989) 'The Eastern Frontier, 1770–1812', in R. Elphick and H. Giliomee (eds), *The Shaping of South African Society*, 2nd edn, 421–71. Middletown, CT: Wesleyan University Press.

Giliomee, H. (2003) *The Afrikaners: Biography of a People*. Charlottesville, VA: University of Virginia Press.

Gonzalez, R. D. and H. G. Montero (2010) 'Colonial Origins of Inequality in Hispanic America? Some Reflections Based on New Empirical Evidence', *Revista de Historia Economica* [*Journal of Iberian and Latin American Economic History*] 28 (2): 253–77.

Goody, J. (1971) *Technology, Tradition and the State in Africa*. Cambridge: Cambridge University Press.

Green, E. (2013) 'Land Concentration, Institutional Control and African Agency: Growth and Stagnation of European Tobacco Farming in Shire Highlands, c. 1900 – 1940', in E. Hillbom and P. Svensson (eds), *Agricultural Transformations and Global History*, 229–52. London: Routledge.

Green, E. (2014) 'The Economics of Slavery in 18th Century Cape Colony: Revising the Nieboer-Domar Hypothesis', *International Review of Social History* 59 (1): 39–70.

Griffin, K., A. Rahman and A. Ickowitz (2002) 'Poverty and the Distribution of Land', *Journal of Agrarian Change* 2 (3): 279–330.

Groenewald, G. (2007) 'Een Dienstig Inwoonder: Entrepreneurs, Social Capital and Identity in Cape Town, c. 1720–1750', *South African Historical Journal* 59 (1): 126–52.

Groenewald, G. (2011) 'Dynasty Building, Family Networks and Social Capital: Alcohol *Pachters* and the Development of a Colonial Elite at the Cape of Good Hope, c. 1760–1790', *Comtree* 62: 23–53.

Groenewald, G. (2012) '"More Comfort, Better Prosperity, and Greater Advantage": Free Burghers, Alcohol Retail and the VOC Authorities at the Cape of Good Hope, 1652–1689', *Historia* 57 (1): 1–21.

Guelke, L. (1974) 'The Early European Settlement of South Africa', unpublished PhD diss., University of Toronto.

Guelke, L. (1979) 'The White Settlers, 1652–1780', in R. Elphick and H. Giliomee (eds), *The Shaping of South African Society, 1652–1840*, 66–108. Pinetown: Maskew Miller Longman.

Guelke, L. (1984) 'Land Tenure and Settlement at the Cape 1652–1812', in C. G. C. Martin and K. J. Friedlaender (eds), *History of Surveying and Land Tenure in South Africa*, 7–34. Cape Town: Department of Surveying, University of Cape Town.

Guelke, L. (1985) 'The Making of Two Frontier Communities: Cape Colony in the Eighteenth Century', *Historical Reflections/Réflexions Historiques* 12 (3): 419–48.

Guelke, L. (1988) 'The Anatomy of a Colonial Settler Population: Cape Colony 1657–1750', *The International Journal of African Historical Studies* 21 (3): 453–73.

Guelke, L. (1989) 'Freehold Farmers and Frontier Settlers, 1657–1780', in R. Elphick and H. Giliomee (eds), *The Shaping of South African Society*, 2nd edn, 66–108. Middletown, CT: Wesleyan University Press.

Guelke, L. and R. Shell (1983) 'An Early Colonial Landed Gentry: Land and Wealth in the Cape Colony 1682–1731', *Journal of Historical Geography* 9 (3): 265–86.

Guelke, L. and R. Shell (1992) 'Landscape of Conquest: Frontier Water Alienation and KhoeKhoe Strategies of Survival, 1652–1780', *Journal of South African Studies* 18 (4): 803–24.

Guelke, L., D. Bonner and A. Maisoneuve (1987) *The Southwestern Cape Colony, 1657–1750: Freehold Land Grants*. Waterloo, Ontario: Dept. of Geography, University of Waterloo.

Habakkuk, H. J. (1955) 'Family Structure and Economic Change in Nineteenth-Century Europe', *Journal of Economic History* 15 (1): 1–12.

Heap, P. (1993) *The Story of Hottentots Holland*. Goodwood: National Book Printers.

Herbst, J. (2000) *States and Power in Africa: Comparative Lessons in Authority and Control*. Princeton, NJ: Princeton University Press.

Hillbom, E. and E. Green (2019) *An Economic History of Development in Sub-Saharan Africa: Transformation and Governance*. London: Palgrave Macmillan.

Inter-university Consortium for Political and Social Research (2005) *Historical, Demographic, Economic, and Social Data: The United States, 1790–1970* (ICPSR 3). Available online: https://www.icpsr.umich.edu/web/ICPSR/studies/3 (accessed 5 October 2020).

Katzen, M. F. (1969) 'White Settlers and the Origin of a New Society, 1652–1778', in M. Wilson and L. M. Thompson (eds), *Oxford History of South Africa*, 187–232. Oxford: The Clarendon Press.

Kiewiet, de C. W. (1957) *A History of South Africa, Social and Economic*. Oxford: Oxford University Press.

Kilbourne, R. H. (2014) *Debt, Investment, Slaves: Credit Relations in East Feliciana Parish, Louisiana, 1825–1885*. Tuscaloosa, AL: University of Alabama Press.

Kuznets, S. (1955) 'Economic Growth and Income Inequality', *The American Economic Review* 45 (1): 1–28.

La Croix, S. (2018) 'The KhoeKhoe Population: A Review of Evidence and Two New Estimates', African Economic History Network Working Paper Series no. 39. Lund: Lund University.

Lamar, H. and L. Thompson (1981) 'Introduction', in H. Lamar and L. Thompson (eds), *The Frontier in History: North America and Southern Africa Compared*, 3–42. London: Yale University Press.

Legassick, M. (1980) 'The Frontier Tradition in South African History', in S. Marks and A. Atmore (eds), *Economy and Society in Pre-industrial South Africa*, 44–79. London: Longman.

Legassick, M. and R. Ross (2012) 'From Slave Economy to Settler Capitalism: The Cape Colony and its Extensions 1800–1854', in C. Hamilton, B. K. Mbenga and R. Ross (eds), *The Cambridge History of South Africa*, vol. 1: *From Early Times to 1885*, 253–318. Cambridge: Cambridge University Press.

Lenin, V. I. (1917) 'Imperialism, the Highest Stage of Capitalism', in *Selected Works*. Moscow: Progress Publishers.

Lichtenstein, H. ([1812] 1930) *Travels in Southern Africa in the Years 1809, 1804, 1805 and 1806*, vol. 2. Translated by Anne Plumptre. Cape Town: Book on Demand.

Lindert, P. H. (1986) 'Unequal English Wealth since 1670', *Journal of Political Economy* 94 (6): 1127–62.

Lindert, P. and J. Williamson (1985) 'Growth, Equality and History', *Explorations in Economic History* 22 (4): 341–77.

Links, C., E. Green and D. von Fintel (2018) 'Indigenous Wealth Inequality in the District of Swellendam in 1825', paper presented at the World Economic History Congress, Boston, 29 July–3 August.

Links, C., E. Green and J. Fourie (2020) 'The Substitutability of Slaves: Evidence from the Eastern Frontier of the Cape Colony', *Economic History of Developing Regions* 35 (2): 98–122.

Lloyd, C. and J. Metzer (2013) 'Settler Colonization and Societies in World History: Patterns and Concepts', in C. Lloyd, J. Metzer and R. Sutch (eds), *Settler Economies in World History*, 1–34. Leiden: Brill.

Lützelschwab, C. (2013) 'Settler Colonialism in Africa', in C. Lloyd, J. Metzer and R. Sutch (eds), *Settler Economies in World History*, 141–67. Leiden: Brill.

Malherbe, V. C. (1978) 'Diversification and Mobility of KhoiKhoi Labour in the Eastern Districts of the Cape Colony Prior to the Labour Law of 1 November 1809'. PhD diss., University of Cape Town.

Mamdani, M. (2015) 'Settler Colonialism: Then and Now', *Critical Inquiry* 41 (3): 596–614.

Marais, J. S. (1957) *The Cape Coloured People, 1652–1937*. Johannesburg: Witwatersrand University Press.

Marks, S. (1972) 'Khoisan Resistance to the Dutch in the Seventeenth and Eighteenth Centuries', *The Journal of African History* 13 (1): 55–80.

Martins, I. (2020a) 'Collateral Effect: Slavery and Wealth in the Cape Colony'. PhD diss., Lund University.

Martins, I. (2020b) 'Raising Capital to Raise Crops: Slave Emancipation and Agricultural Output in the Cape Colony', African Economic History Network Working paper No. 57. Lund University.

Martins, I. and E. Green (2021) 'Capital and Labor: Theoretical Foundations of the Economics of Slavery', paper presented at the Global Economic History seminar, Faculty of History, Cambridge University, 11 May.

Mentzel, O. F. (1925–44) *A Complete and Authentic Geographical and Topographical Description of the ... African Cape of Hope*. 3 vols. Cape Town: Van Riebeeck Society, VRS.

Milanovic, B., P. Lindert and J. Williamson (2010) 'Pre-Industrial Inequality', *The Economic Journal* 121 (551): 255–72.

Mitchell, L. (2002) 'Traces in the Landscape: Hunters, Herders and Farmers on the Cedarberg Frontier, South Africa, 1725–1955', *The Journal of African History* 43 (3): 431–50.

Mitchell, L. (2007) 'Belonging: Family Formation and Settler Identity in the VOC Cape', *South African Historical Journal* 59 (1): 103–25.

Mosley, P. (1983) *The Settler Economies: Studies in the Economic History of Kenya and Southern Rhodesia 1900–1963*. Cambridge: Cambridge University Press.

Moyle, H. (2017) 'The Fall of Fertility in Tasmania, Australia, in the late 19th and early 20th Centuries', *Historical Life Course Studies* 4: 120–44.

Muldrew, C. (2012) 'Debt, Credit and Poverty in Early Modern England', in R. Brkaber, R. M. Lawless and C. J. Tabb, *A Debtor World: Interdisciplinary Perspectives on Debt*, 9–35. Oxford: Oxford University Press.

Neumark, S. D. (1957) *The South African Frontier: Economic Influences*. Stanford, CA: Stanford University Press.

Newton-King, S. (1981) *The Khoikhoi Rebellion in the Eastern Cape (1799–1803)*. Cape Town: Center of African Studies, University of Cape Town.

Newton-King, S. (1992) 'The Enemy Within: The Struggle for Ascendancy on the Cape Eastern Frontier 1760–1800'. PhD diss., School of Oriental and African Studies, London.

Newton-King, S. (1999) *Master and Servants on the Cape Eastern Frontier 1760–1803*. Cambridge: Cambridge University Press.

Nieboer, H. J. (1900) *Slavery as an Industrial System*, vol. 1: *Ethnological Researches*. Leiden: Martinus Nijhoff.

North, D. C. and R. P. Thomas (1973) *The Rise of the Western World: A New Economic History*. Cambridge: Cambridge University Press.

North, D. C., J. J. Wallis and B. R. Weingast (2009) *Violence and Social Orders: A Conceptual Framework for Interpreting Recorded Human History*. Cambridge: Cambridge University Press.

Nugent, P. (2010) 'States and Social Contracts in Africa', *New Left Review* 63 (May–June): 35–68.

Ogilvie, F., M. Küpker and J. Maegraith (2012) 'Household Debt in Early Modern Germany: Evidence from Personal Inventories', *The Journal of Economic History* 72 (1): 134–67.

Osterhammel, J. (1997) *Colonialism: A Theoretical Overview*. Princeton, NJ: Markus Wiener.

Penn, N. (1989) 'Land, Labour and Livestock in the Western Cape During the Eighteenth Century', in W. G. James and M. Simons (eds), *The Angry Divide: Social and Economic History of the Western Cape*, 2–19. Cape Town: David Phillip.

Penn, N. (1995) 'The Northern Cape Frontier Zone, 1700–c. 1815'. PhD diss., University of Cape Town.

Penn, N. (2005) *The Forgotten Frontier: Colonists and Khoesan on the Cape's Northern Frontier in the 18th Century*. Athens, OH: Ohio University Press.

Price, A. G. (1950) *White Settlers and Native People*. Cambridge: Cambridge University Press.

Putterman, L. and D. N. Weil (2010) 'Post-1500 Population Flows and the Long Run Determinants of Economic Growth and Inequality', *Quarterly Journal of Economics* 125 (4): 1627–82.

Ricardo, D. ([1821] 2004) *On the Principles of Political Economy and Taxation*, ed. P. Sraffa in collaboration with M. H. Dobb. Carmel, IN: Liberty Fund, Inc.

Robertson, H. M. (1984) 'Distance and Diminishing Returns in Relation to Land Tenure Policy at the Cape in the 18th Century', in C. G. C. Martin and K. J. Friedlaender (eds), *History of Surveying and Land Tenure in South Africa*, 101–51. Cape Town: Department of Surveying, University of Cape Town.

Ross, R. (1977) 'Smallpox at the Cape of Good Hope in the Eighteenth Century', in *African Historical Demography*, 416–28. Edinburgh, Centre of African Studies.

Ross, R. (1983) 'The First Two Centuries of Colonial Agriculture in the Cape Colony: A Historiographical Review', *Social Dynamics* 9: 30–49.

Ross, R. (1986) 'The Origins of Capitalist Agriculture in the Cape Colony: A Survey', in W. Beinart, P. Delius and S. Trapido (eds), *Putting a Plough to the Ground: Accumulation and Dispossession in Rural South Africa 1850–1930*, 56–100. Braamfontein: Ravan Press (Pty) Ltd.

Ross, R. (1989) 'The Cape of Good Hope and the World Economy, 1652–1835', in R. Elphick and H. Giliomee (eds), *The Shaping of South African Society*, 2nd edn, 243–82. Middletown, CT: Wesleyan University Press.

Ross, R. (1993) *Beyond the Pale: Essays on the History of Colonial South Africa*. Middletown, CT: Wesleyan University Press.

Ross, R. (1999) *Status and Respectability in the Cape Colony 1750–1870: A Tragedy of Manners*. Cambridge: Cambridge University Press.

Ross, R. and A. Schrikker (2012) 'The VOC Official Elite', in N. Worden (ed.), *Cape Town between East and West: Social Identities in a Dutch Colonial Town*, 26–44. Cape Town and Hilversum: Jacana and Verloren.

Schoeman, K. (2007) *Early Slavery at the Cape of Good Hope 1652–1717*. Pretoria: Protea Book House.

Schoeman, K. (2012) *Portrait of a Slave Society: The Cape of Good Hope, 1717–1795*. Pretoria: Protea Book House.

Schulz, J. (2008) *The Financial Crisis of Abolition*. London: Yale University Press.

Shell, R. (1986) 'Slavery at the Cape of Good Hope, 1680–1731'. Unpublished PhD thesis, Yale University, New Haven, CT.

Shell, R. (1994) *Children of Bondage: A Social History of the Slave Society at the Cape of Good Hope, 1652–1838*. Hanover, CT: Wesleyan University Press.

Shell, R. (2005) 'Immigration', *Safundi: The Journal of South African and American Comparative Studies* 6 (2): 1–38.

Shutte, G. (1989) 'Company and Colonists at the Cape', in R. Elphick and H. Giliomee (eds), *The Shaping of South African Society*, 2nd edn, 283–323. Middletown, CT: Wesleyan University Press.

Slotkin, R. (1992) *Gunfighter Nation: The Myth of the Frontier in Twentieth Century America*. New York: Atheneum.

Smith, A. ([1776] 1982) *An Inquiry Into the Nature and Causes of the Wealth of Nations*, Textual editors: R. H. Campell and A. S. Skinner. Oxford: Oxford University Press.

Smith, K. W. (1974) 'From Frontier to Midlands: A History of the Graaff-Reinet District, 1786–1910'. PhD diss., Rhodes University, Grahamstown.

Swanepoel, C. (2017) 'The Private Credit Market of the Cape Colony, 1673–1834: Wealth, Property Rights and Social Networks'. PhD diss., University of Stellenbosch, Stellenbosch.

Theal, G. M. (1913) *Willem Adriaan van der Stel and Other Historical Sketches*. Cape Town: Thomas Maskew Miller.

Theal, G. M. ([1922] 1964) *History of South Africa before 1795*, vol. 3. London: George Allen and Unwin.

Thoen, E. and T. Soens (2009) 'Credit in Rural Flanders, c.1250–c.1600: Its Variety and Significance', in T. Lambrecht and P. R. P. Schofield (eds), *Credit and the Rural Economy in North-Western Europe, c. 1200–1850*, 19–38. Turnhout: Brepols.

Thom, H. B., ed. (1954) *Journal of Jan van Riebeeck, 1651–1662*. Cape Town: Balkema.

Trapido, S. (1990) 'From Paternalism to Liberalism: The Cape Colony, 1800–1834', *The International History Review* 12 (1): 76–104.

Trotter, A. F. (1903) *Old Cape Colony: A Chronicle of Her Men and Houses from 1652 to 1806*. London: Selwyn & Blount.

Turner, F. J. (1921) *The Significance of the Frontier in American History*. New York: Henry Holt and Company.

Ulrich, N. (2013) 'Rethinking Citizenship and Subjecthood in Southern Africa: Khoesan, Labour Relations, and the Colonial State in the Cape of Good Hope (c.1652–1815)', paper presented at the Department of Political and International Studies, Rhodes University, September.

Ulrich, N. (2016) 'Rethinking Citizenship and Subjecthood in Southern Africa: Khoisan, Labour Relations, and the Colonial State in the Cape of Good Hope', in E. Hunter (ed.), *Citizenship, Belonging, and Political Community in Africa*, 43–73. Cambridge: Cambridge University Press.

Van Duin, P. and R. Ross (1987) *The Economy of the Cape Colony in the 18th Century*. Leiden: Centre for the History of European Expansion Leiden University.

Van der Merwe, P. J. ([1938] 1995) *The Migrant Farmer in the History of the Cape Colony, 1657–1842* [*Die Trekboer in die Geskiedenis van die Kaapkolonie, 1657–1842*], English translation by R. B. Beck. Athens, OH: Ohio University Press.

Van Ryneveld (1797) *Replies to the questions on importation etc. of slaves into the colony: Proposed by His Excellency the Earl of Macartney, Etc., Etc.* Cape Town: University of Cape Town.

Veracini, L. (2011) 'Introducing Settler Colonial Studies', *Settler Colonial Studies* 1 (1): 1–12.

Veracini, L. (2013) '"Settler Colonialism": Career of a Concept', *The Journal of Imperial and Commonwealth History* 41 (2): 313–33.

Viljoen, R. (2001) 'Aboriginal Khoikhoi Servants and their Masters in Colonial Swellendam, South Africa, 1745–1795', *Agricultural History* 75 (1): 28–51.

Walker, E. (1930) *The Frontier Tradition in South Africa.* Oxford: Oxford University Press.

Weaver, J. C. (2003) *The Great Land Rush and the Making of the Modern World, 1650–1900.* Québec: McGill-Queen's University Press.

Willebald, H. and J. Juambeltz (2016) 'Land Frontier Expansion in Settler Economies (1830–1950): Was it a Ricardian Process?', Documentos de Trabajo [Working Papers] 16–08, Instituto de Economia – IECO.

Williams, G. (2013) 'Who, Where, and When Were the Cape Gentry?', *Economic History of Developing Regions* 28 (2): 83–111.

Williamson, J. G. (2015) 'Latin American Inequality: Colonial Origins, Commodity Booms or a Missed Twentieth-Century Leveling?', *Journal of Human Development and Capabilities* 16 (3): 324–34.

Worden, N. (1985) *Slavery in Dutch South Africa.* Cambridge: Cambridge University Press.

Worden, N. (2017) 'Slavery at the Cape', in *Oxford Research Encyclopedia of African History.* Oxford: Oxford University Press.

Worden, N. and G. Groenewald (2005) *Trials of Slavery: Selected documents concerning slaves from the criminal records of the Council of Justice at the Cape of Good Hope, 1705–1794.* Cape Town: Van Riebeck Society for the Publications of South African Historical Documents.

Index

Acemoglu, D. 6, 14
Africa 5, 7, 13, 50, 75, 107, 130
    black population 130
    colonial 120, 130, 132, 135–6
    postcolonial 130, 132
    precolonial 15
    twentieth-century 120, 131, 135–6
    see also Cape Colony/Cape of Good
        Hope; East Africa; Ghana;
        Kenya; South Africa; West
        Africa
African Development Bank 7
agrarian populism 9
agriculture
    agricultural investments 70–2
    Asian 34
    development 84
    intensive 36
    settler agriculture 4, 36, 37, 47, 56, 76,
        79, 101, 115, 139
        profitable 128, 153
    slave-based system 20, 88
    see also farming; land
American exceptionalism 5
American Historical Association, Chicago
        meeting (1893) 8
An Inquiry Into the Nature and Causes of the
        Wealth of Nations (Smith) 136
Armstrong, J. C. 77, 97
artificial scarcity 13, 15, 127
auction rolls (slaves) 84, 85t
Austin, G. 5

Barbier, E. 145, 146
Barbier Rebellion 144, 145, 147
Barrow (nineteenth-century travel writer)
        66, 94
Batavia 27, 29, 44, 79, 80, 116
Beinart, W. 63
Berg, M. A. 67
Blignault, J. 126
Bogart, F. 18

Bokkeveld Mountains 47
Bonner, D. 54
border expansion 20
Boshoff, W. H. 116
British East Indian Company 18, 31
Bushmen (the San) 23–5

Cape Colony/Cape of Good Hope 24
    annexation by Britain 98
    backward economy, perceived as 44
    boundaries of freehold farms at 55
    compared with New World slave
        societies 88
    in the eighteenth century see
        eighteenth-century Cape Colony
    history (1652–1796) 4–5
    map of 26, 42
    in the nineteenth century 3
    patriarchal economy 126
    Portuguese trading posts 27
    in the seventeenth-century see
        seventeenth-century Cape
        Colony
    slave labour see slave labour
    south-western vs. northern and eastern
        regions 54–5
    see also farming; slave labour; South
        Africa
Cape Coloured People (Marais) 30
Cape Patriot Movement 144, 146–7
Cape Peninsula 47, 119
    and indigenous population 25, 28, 31,
        33–5, 37, 38
capital
    formation of 12–13
    human 20
    initial sources 117–19
capital–labour ratios 12
Carter, S. B. 12
cattle/livestock 21, 133, 135, 144
    demand for 109
    exchange of 21, 27, 108

herding 78
and indigenous population 24, 25, 29,
    31–8
and inequality 108, 109, 116, 118, 119,
    121, 122
loss of 25, 31, 121–2
ownership among Khoesan workers
    122
and population growth 51, 52, 54,
    57–9
property rights 62, 64, 66, 67
and slavery 78, 86, 91, 97
theft of 4–5, 25, 30, 67, 68, 140, 145–6
transporting 57, 58, 63
Chainouqua (Khoesan group) 25, 121
Cilliers, J. 2, 51, 52, 62, 116
Cloppenburg, J. W. 49
closing of frontiers 9–12, 16–17
    defining a closed frontier 3, 11–12, 18
    distinction between an opening of and
        closing of frontier 10
    impetus for opening new frontiers 12
    institutional order 16
    literature 10
    south-western 53–9
    uncertain outcome 10
coalitions
    elites 18, 19, 129–30
    forms 131
Coatsworth, J. H. 6
Cochoqua (Khoesan group) 25, 36, 121
coercion 10, 12, 30, 34, 75, 104, 151, 154
    coercive social contracts 18–19, 130
    of Khoesan population 79, 127, 139
colonialism/settler colonialism 4, 16, 17,
    38, 131
    in Africa *see* Africa
    'diehard' 5
    and inequality 103, 106
    legacies 2, 6, 104
    literature 3, 106
    studies 21, 107, 154
    twentieth-century 7, 8
    typologies 131–3
conflicts 12, 63, 64–8
Cooper, F. 132
co-ordination costs 28
Council of India 27
Council of Policy 100, 140
Craa, J. 99

credit market 99
crop farming 78

de Chavonnes, D. P. 84
de Grevenbock, W. 89
de Kiewiet, C. W. 29
de Kock, M. H. 135
de Mist, J. A. 44
Denoon, D. 5, 10
'diehard' colonialism 5
Dooling, W. 2, 115, 124–5
Drakenstein district 47, 54, 57, 76, 82, 88,
    92, 145
Dutch East Indian Company *see* VOC
    (Dutch East Indian Company)
Dye, A. 64, 65, 66

East Africa 27, 30, 80
economics
    colonialism 38
    economic growth in Dutch Cape
        Colony 44–7, 153–4
    GDP-per-capita growth 45–6
    plantation economies 76, 77
    of settler economics 38
    of slave labour 76, 83–8
    socio-economic institutions 10, 43
economies of scale 78, 87, 97, 115
eighteenth-century Cape Colony 3
    expansion of frontiers/settler colonies
        12, 13, 48, 49
    inequality 108–14
Ekma, K. 2
Eksteen, H. O. 118
elites 129–50
    coalitions 18, 19,129–30
    divergent interests 17–18
    fiscal capacity of the VOC 133, 134t,
        135–6
    Khoesan 29
    local 18
    see also VOC (Dutch East Indian
        Company)
Elkins, C. 16, 131–3
Elphick, R. 12, 24, 25, 29, 30, 31, 36, 89,
    119, 122, 141–2
Engerman, S. L. 7, 14, 114
European institutions *see* institutions
European settler colonies *see* settler
    colonies, European

exceptionalism, American 5
expansion of frontiers/settler colonies
    41–73
  artificial scarcity 13
  complexity 16
  economic growth in Dutch Cape
    Colony 44–7
  eighteenth century 12, 13, 48, 49
  factor endowments *see* factor
    endowments
  first steps 35–7
  forces of expansion 12–16
  geographical expansion, resistance to
    from Khoesan 4–5
  immigration 12, 13, 41, 52
  and inheritance 68–70
  inheritance systems 14–15
  landed property rights 41, 43
  from mid- to-late seventeenth century
    47
  population growth 13, 41, 43, 49–59
  property rights 13–14, 59–64
  see also frontiers

factor endowments 39, 43, 53, 75, 102,
    114, 152
  and forces of expansion 12, 15, 16, 19,
    20
farming
  arable farms in south-western Cape 61
  boundaries of freehold farms at Cape
    Colony 55
  crop farming 78
  Europeans permitted to establish farms
    4
  family farms 8
  farm workers 79, 86, 88, 119, 120
  freehold farms 53, 54, 55, 60, 63,
    69–71, 118
  gentry farmers 21, 115–19, 123, 149,
    150
    limited political influence of 142–3
  grazing land 58–9
  inequality among settler farming
    population 114–17
  intensive, failure of 33–5
  loan farms (leaseholds) 43, 52
  mixed farms 97
  ownership 123
  role of Khoesan as farm labourers 153

  settler-farmers 34, 43
  stock farming 56
  stratification levels among settler
    community 108
  wealth generation 107
  wealth of farmers 116–17, 118–19
  see also agriculture; pastoralism/
    pastoral farming
Feinstein, C. 44
Fisher, R. 65
Forbes, J. D. 9
Fouché, L. 8–9
Fourie, J. 2, 25, 44–5, 46, 54, 77, 86, 89–94,
    108, 109–10, 114–15, 116, 123
Franschhoek district 54
freeholds 58, 73, 116
  farms 53, 54, 60, 63, 69–71, 118
    boundaries 55
  land grants 53
  private property rights 68
  purchase of land 60–1
  tenure 54, 118
  see also land; leaseholds; loan farms;
    property rights
frontiers
  concept of the frontier 3
  critique of early literature 9, 10–11
  distinction between an opening of and
    closing of frontier 10
  early literature 7, 8–9
  expansion, first steps towards 35–7
  inter-group situation 9
  as 'inter-group situations' 9
  opening and closing of *see* closing of
    frontiers; opening of frontiers
  south-western, closing of 53–9
  Turner's thesis 8, 9
  see also expansion of frontiers/settler
    colonies
Furniss, E. 9

Garnsey, P. 76
gender 108
Genovese, E. D. 97
gentry farmers 21, 115–19, 123, 149, 150
  limited political influence of 142–3
Ghana 130
Gideon, J. 125
Giliomee, H. 2, 10, 11–12, 116, 139, 141
Gini coefficient 110, 111, 112t

Gonnema (Khoesan group) 36–7
Gonzales, R. D. 5, 106
Graaff-Reinet (frontier district) 52, 62, 63,
        82, 92, 93, 112, 113, 141
Great Trek 9
Green, E. 25, 46, 52, 54, 62, 75, 89, 91–4,
        116
Groenewald, G. 135
Guelke, L. 2, 25, 44, 47, 50, 52, 53, 54,
        59–60, 61–2, 63, 64, 108,
        109–10, 122, 124, 138

Habakkuk, H. J. 15
Heap, P. 36
heemraden (district officials) 65
history of Cape Colony (1652–1796) 4–5
*A History of South Africa, Social and
        Economic* (de Kiewiet) 29
Hop, M. 126
Hottentots (the Khoe) 23, 24, 30, 66
Huguenots 116
Huising, Henning 145
human capital 3, 6, 20, 104, 116
hunter-gatherers 24–5

indigenous (Khoesan) agency
        combined effect with settler agency 2
        importance 133
        and increased cost of trade 28–33
        intensive farming, failure 33–5
        neglect of 151–2
        and unintended consequences 37–9
        see also Khoesan (indigenous)
                population
inequality 20–1, 103–28
        and cattle/livestock 108, 109, 116, 118,
                119, 121, 122
        evolution over time 107
        gender, inheritance and wealth
                accumulation 123–6
        Gini coefficient 110, 111, 112t
        within-group 111
        and initial sources of capital 117–19
        Kuznets inverted U-shaped curve 105
        labour and accumulation in
                the seventeenth-century
                Cape 119–23
        negative correlation with numbers of
                settlers 107
        in pre-industrial colonial societies 105–8
        in settler economies 106

trends among the settler farming
        population 114–17
trends in the eighteenth-century Cape
        Colony 108–14
inheritance systems 14–15
        demographic effect 15
        and expansion of the frontier 68–70
        and inequality 123–6
        multigeniture system 14, 15
        primogeniture system 14, 15
institutional order 5–6, 8, 17
        coercive and segregationist 7
institutions 3–7, 11, 19, 20, 39, 41, 107
        and credit market 99
        developmental 103
        European 6, 8, 128
        evolution 10, 43, 153
        extractive 103
        forces of expansion 13, 14
        governing an open vs. closed frontier
                107
        growth-enhancing and growth-
                facilitating 6, 7
        inclusive 103, 106
        socio-economic 10, 43
        socio-political 9
        see also institutional order

Jamaica, 'median sugar estate' 4, 77
Janszen, L. 28
Johnson, S. 6, 14
Journal of Cape Governors 31, 35

Kenya 7, 132
Khoe, the *see* Hottentots (the Khoe)
Khoesan (indigenous) population 62
        agency *see* indigenous (Khoesan)
                agency
        'Bushmen' (the San) 23–5
        at the Cape 23–7
        and cattle/livestock 24, 25, 29, 31–8
        expanding of relations with the VOC
                31, 35
        Hottentots (the Khoe) 23, 24, 30, 66
        hunter-gatherers 24–5
        incorporation into colonial economy 46
        kinship groups 25
        labour 4, 12, 20, 30, 79, 88–93, 104,
                143, 153
        lack of data 104
        logic of elimination 16

neglect of 9, 88, 101
nomadic pastoral people 24
numbers of Khoesan 34, 91, 93, 108,
119, 120
perceived by some as passive victims
9, 30, 66
political centralization 15–16
relationship with the VOC 27
resistance to settler expansion 4–5, 16,
20, 66–8, 107, 141, 152, 153
role and destiny 17
size 15, 16–17, 27, 50–1
sporadic conflicts with European
settlers 12
transhumance practised by 51
see also Chainouqua (Khoesan group);
Cochoqua (Khoesan group);
indigenous population
Khoesan–Dutch wars 36
Kirsten, J. F. 98
Kloof, G. 145
Kogmans Kloof 47
Kuznets, S./Kuznets curve 105

La Croix, S. 25, 27, 64, 65, 66
labour
annual volatility 97
farm workers 79, 86, 88, 119, 120
of Khoesan population 4, 12, 20, 30,
79, 88–93, 104, 143, 153
and landlords 139–42
reluctance of Europeans to perform
hard work of slaves 83
in the seventeenth-century Cape
Colony 119–23
slave *see* slave labour
vineyards 96–7
VOC labourers 79
Lamar, H. 10–11
land 8, 15, 21, 124, 153
access to 13, 20, 52, 118, 121, 140
arable 53, 54, 59
claims 37, 47
common 58
concentration 14, 15, 119, 122
conflicts/disputes over 63, 64–8
control over 12, 13, 14, 21, 54, 123, 145
distribution 3, 108, 127, 128
empty 152
and expansion of the frontier 5, 72,
106, 151, 152

fertile 13, 61, 127, 144
fragmentation 125
freehold 54, 60–1
grants 144
grazing 35, 43, 54, 58–9, 64
investment in 13, 66, 118, 119, 147
land-labour ratios 75, 78, 102
ownership 6, 119
registration of 43
regulation of rights 53
scarcity 13, 49, 53, 54, 59, 63, 120–1
see also agriculture; farming; freeholds;
landlords; leaseholds; loan
farms; property rights
Land van Waveren (later Tulbagh) 54, 67,
113, 144
landlords 75, 118, 120
and labour 139–42
landrost 67, 143
Latin America
compared with North America 6, 8, 107
hacienda plantations 107
institutional order 6, 7
slavery in, compared with the Cape 4
leaseholds 52, 63, 73
contracts 43, 60, 64
see also freeholds; land; loan farms;
property rights
Legassick, M. 9, 12
Lichtenstein, H. 62
Liesbeek River 4, 33
limited-access social order 17, 18
Links, C. 2
livestock *see* cattle/livestock
loan farms 99, 108, 118, 123, 146
and expansion of the frontier 43, 52,
59–66, 68–72
see also leaseholds
Lords XVII (executive council) 79, 132,
145, 147
and indigenous population 27, 28, 30,
31, 33, 36
see also VOC (Dutch East Indian
Company)

Maisoneuve, A. 54
Malherbe, V. C. 24, 25, 30, 89
maps
Cape Colony 42
settler expansion through 1750 48
Marais, J. S. 30

Mariotti, M. 51
Marks, S. 2, 23, 30, 36, 66
marriage 125
Martins, I. 2, 75, 101
Melck, M. 126
Mentzel, O. F. 77, 96, 115
Mississippi, slaves in 77
Mitchell, L. 125
Montero, H. G. 5, 106
Mosley, P. 131
multigeniture inheritance system 15

natural state 17, 18, 136
   inherently fragile 129, 130
Neumark, S. D. 52
New World 53, 78, 88, 94, 97, 101, 114
Newton-King, S. 2, 12, 52, 67
Nieboer, H. J. 76, 77, 78, 101
Nieboer-Domar hypothesis 13, 75, 78, 79,
   82, 102
Nieuwe Haarlem (VOC ship) 28
nineteenth-century Cape Colony 3
North, D. C. 17
North America
   compared with Latin America 6, 8, 107
   Europeans settled in 5
   slavery in, compared with the Cape 4
Nugent, P. 18, 19, 130–1

Olifants River valley 67
open-access order state 17
opening of frontiers 9–12
   conflict and coercion 12
   as a consequence of closing previous
      frontiers 12
   defining an open frontier 3, 11–12
   distinction between an opening of and
      closing of frontier 10
   old frontier literature 9
   see also closing of frontiers
Osterhammel, J. 131

pacht (licence) 118, 137, 149
pachters (licensed private traders) 111,
   137–8
pastoralism/pastoral farming
   expansion in the south-western
      Cape 59
   fragility of pastoral economies 25
   frontier settlers as pastoral farmers 54

indigenous population 24, 25, 38
   Khoesan used for pastoral farming 91
   and slavery 77–8
   transhumance 51
   wandering pastoral farmers 8
Pedersen, S. 16, 131–3
Penn, N. 10, 30, 89
permissive social contracts 18, 19, 130
   vs. productive 139–42
plantation economies in the Americas
      76, 77
population growth 13, 41, 43, 49–59
pre-industrial colonial societies, inequality
      in 105–8
primitive accumulation 13, 16, 89
primogeniture inheritance system 15
privilege, settler 131, 132f
productive social contracts 18, 19, 130
   vs. permissive 139–42
property rights 5, 13–14, 15
   and agricultural investments 70–2
   cattle/livestock 62, 64, 66, 67
   conflicts 64–8
   de jure landed property rights 99
   and expansion of the frontier
      59–64
   'inside' vs. 'outside' risks 65
   land control 54
   landed property 13–14, 41, 43, 99
   relative access to land 13
   secure 14
   of slaveholders 76
   structure of 152
   weak 20

rational choice political economy (RPE)
   and inequality 103
   literature 3, 6–7, 10
   and settler economies 5–7
refreshment station, establishment 27–8
resistance 8, 15, 143
   forms 14
   and the Hottentots (the Khoe) 30, 66
   indigenous 4–5, 16, 20, 66–8, 107, 141,
      152, 153
   organized 67, 144
   recurrent 39
Ricardian rents 106
Ricardo, D. 106
Rink, A. 65

Robertson, H. M. 118
Robinson, J. A. 6, 14
Ross, R. 2, 12, 13, 44, 47, 52, 89, 98, 115,
    116, 117, 123, 124, 136–7, 138,
    147
Rossouw, A. 126
Rossouw, P. 65, 66
RPE *see* rational choice political economy
    (RPE)
rule of law 5

San, the *see* 'Bushmen' (the San)
scarcity
    artificial 13, 15, 127
    and settler movements 53
Schoeman, K. 84, 100
settler agriculture *see* agriculture
settler colonies, European
    agriculture 4
    comparison with tropical Asia, Africa
        and Latin America 5
    doubling of European population 4
    establishment of 1–21
    and history of Cape Colony
        (1652–1796) 4–5
    non-farming settlers 111–12
    and non-settler colonies 7
    vs. other forms of colonialism 131
    and RPE 5–7
    'spiritual fathers' 8–9
    sporadic conflicts between settlers and
        Khoesan people 12
    typologies of settler colonialism 131–3
    see also expansion of frontiers/settler
        colonies
seventeenth-century Cape Colony 3
    building of fort 28, 29, 30
    establishment of trading post at Cape
        of Good Hope (1652) *see*
        trading post, established at the
        Cape (1652)
    expansion of frontiers/settler colonies
        47
    expansion of relations between VOC
        and Khoesan communities 31
    labour and accumulation 119–23
sex ratios 51, 52, 97, 125
Shell, R. 25, 51–2, 79, 100, 108, 109–10,
    122, 124, 138
Shutte, G. 28, 30, 64, 65

slave labour
    Cape Colony as a slave economy 44,
        76–8, 101
    and cattle/livestock 78, 86, 91, 97
    comparison of the Cape with Latin and
        North America 4
    cost of slaves compared with European
        labour 84, 86
    economics of 76, 83–8
    imported slaves 4, 75, 79, 80, 107, 153
    Khoesan labour (indigenous) *see* labour
    leasing out by slaveholders 100
    mean holding of slaves 81t, 82
    non-economic factors in respect of 97
    numbers of slaves 4, 76, 77, 79, 82, 93,
        95t, 97, 98t, 116, 117
    and pastoral farming 77–8
    percentage distribution of holdings
        82, 83t
    productivity of 93–8, 95t
    property rights of slaveholders 76
    rationale for investment in 86, 101–2
    reluctance of Europeans to perform
        hard work of slaves 83
    rise of slavery at the Cape 78–83
    slave ownership in the Cape 76, 115
    slavery in general vs. as an industrial
        system 76
    slaves as capital at the Cape 98–101
    slaves at rural auctions (1682–1795)
        84, 85t
    used as collateral 100
    used to acquire capital 100–1
Slotkin, R. 9
Slotsboo, K. J. 83
smallpox epidemic 89
Smith, A. 136
social contracts 18–19, 129, 130, 131
Sokoloff, K. L. 7, 14, 114
South Africa 3, 7, 9, 10, 24, 64, 152–4
    apartheid 130, 154
    see also Africa; Cape Colony/Cape of
        Good Hope; East Africa; West
        Africa
South Carolina, slaves in 77
Southern Rhodesia 132
south-western Cape 4, 21, 141, 143
    clashes between the VOC and settler
        144, 145, 146, 148
    closing of frontiers 53–4, 56–9

expansion of frontiers/settler colonies
41, 51, 53–61, 63, 64, 70
indigenous population 23, 25, 27
and inequality 109, 115, 116, 120–3,
127
and slave labour 77, 82, 89, 92, 93
Stellenbosch district 47, 54, 57, 58, 67,
76, 82, 88, 92, 93, 112, 113, 126,
135t, 140, 141
Sutch, R. 12
Swanepoel, C. 99
Swartland 54
Swellendam district 63, 76, 82, 92, 113,
135t, 141

Table Mountain 4, 34, 38
Theal, G. M. 119–20
theft 25, 30–1, 84, 88, 119, 121
of cattle/livestock 4, 25, 30, 67, 68, 140,
145–6
Thom, H. B. 34
Thompson, L. 10–11
Tijgerberg region 36
trade regulations 7, 139, 144
trading and profits 136–9
trading post, established at the Cape
(1652) 2, 75
increased cost of trade 28–9
and Khoesan communities 29–30
transhumance 51
Trapido, S. 44
Trekboers (wandering pastoral farmers) 8
Tulbagh (formerly Land van Waveren) 54,
67, 113, 144
Turner, F. J. 8, 9

Ulrich, N. 96
United Provinces of the Netherlands 27

van Aarden, J. 125
van Aarden, S. F. 125
van Beaumont, F. C. 83
van der Merwe, P. J. 59, 66
van der Stel, Simon 58, 89, 121, 144
van der Stel, Willem Adriaan 47, 58, 60,
144, 145, 147
van der Werwe, P. J. 49
van Duin, P. 44, 47, 117, 136–7, 138
van Riebeeck, J. 25, 28, 31, 32, 34, 36, 80,
151

van Rijneveld, F. W. W. 84
van Zanden, J. L. 44–5, 90
Veracini, L. 17
Vereenigde Oostindische Compagnie
see VOC (Dutch East Indian
Company)
Verwey, D. 125
Verwey, D. G. 125
Verwey, M. A. 125
Viljoen, R. 140
viticulture 116
VOC (Dutch East Indian Company)
19–20, 46
administrative capacity 45
building of fort 28, 29, 30
clashes with settlers 144–9
establishment of trading post at Cape
of Good Hope (1652) *see*
trading post, established at the
Cape (1652)
executive council *see* Lords XVII
(executive council)
expanding of trade relations with the
Khoesan communities 31, 35
and expansion of the frontier 47
financially weak 135–6
fiscal capacity at 133, 134t, 135–6
fixed pricing policies 44
fragility of presence at the Cape 21, 30,
33, 35, 140, 153, 154
and indigenous agency 29
labourers 79
loss of control 19
mercantilist trade policies 86
monopsony power 136
power 140
pragmatism of 28
territorial control 4
theft 30–1
trading activities 2, 27
von Fintel, D. 2, 86, 108, 114–15, 116,
123
von Imhoff, G. W. 84
Vrye Burghers ('free burghers') 33–4, 52

Walker, E. 9
Wallis, J. J. 17
wealth
of certain Khoesan 25
of farmers 116–17, 118–19

gender and inheritance 123–6
generation of 107
persistence of 20
in the seventeenth-century Cape
    Colony 119–23
Weingast, B. R. 17, 18, 129

West Africa 27, 30
Williams, G. 115–16, 117, 118
Worden, N. 2, 77–8, 82, 87, 88, 89, 93, 94,
    97, 116, 117, 137–8

Xhosa (indigenous group) 62, 66, 141

CPSIA information can be obtained
at www.ICGtesting.com
Printed in the USA
LVHW080234280722
724622LV00003B/56

9 781350 258235